THE
WAY
YOU
MAKE
ME
FEEL

PENGUIN PRESS • *New York* • 2024

THE
WAY
YOU
MAKE
ME
FEEL

Love in Black and Brown

Nina Sharma

PENGUIN PRESS
An imprint of Penguin Random House LLC
penguinrandomhouse.com

"Shithole Country Clubs" by Nina Sharma, copyright © 2019
by Nina Sharma, as first published by *The Margins*, the digital
magazine of the Asian American Writers' Workshop.

"Not Dead" by Nina Sharma, copyright © 2017 by Nina Sharma, as first published
by *The Margins*, the digital magazine of the Asian American Writers' Workshop.

LIBRARY OF CONGRESS CATALOGING-IN-PUBLICATION DATA
Names: Sharma, Nina (Writer), author.
Title: The way you make me feel : love in black and brown / Nina Sharma.
Description: New York : Penguin Press, 2024. |
Includes bibliographical references.
Identifiers: LCCN 2023026570 (print) | LCCN 2023026571 (ebook) |
ISBN 9780593492826 (hardcover) | ISBN 9780593492833 (ebook)
Subjects: LCSH: Interracial marriage. | Love.
Classification: LCC HQ1031.S462 2024 (print) |
LCC HQ1031 (ebook) | DDC 306.84/5—dc23/eng/20230830
LC record available at https://lccn.loc.gov/2023026570
LC ebook record available at https://lccn.loc.gov/2023026571

Printed in the United States of America
1st Printing

Designed by Nicole LaRoche

To my husband

To my parents

To Afro-Asian solidarity

And anyone at the edge of a feeling

CONTENTS

THE
WAY
YOU
MAKE
ME
FEEL

BIRTHMARK

My eldest sister, ten years older than me, is, as the saying goes, the fairest of them all. What I mean to say is that she's lighter skinned than both my middle sister, eight years older than me, and myself, "Baby." Ten shares my mother's milky coloring while Eight and I veer more toward my father's almond brown. But this is not the explanation my mother provides. "It's probably because she was born in England," she says and leaves it at that.

How could this be? I always think. My mother and my father are both doctors, and when it comes to the body, they tend to talk with precision. My sick notes for school were embarrassingly scientific— not just "Nina has a cold" but "Please excuse Nina from soccer. She has been suffering a rhinovirus infection."

But when it comes to melanin, or lack thereof, the language of science is drained of its color. We are, simply, dark or light, kali or gauri, born in the U.S. or born in England.

England, this suspension of science, this mythical, sunless country.

My parents' reminiscences of London and their bohemian Chelsea neighborhood are more often positive, if not star-studded—my mother seeing the Beatles play on a roof, my father encountering Mick Jagger and Tom Jones on his way to work at the hospital, and this child that seemed to carry an entire country on the dermis.

"Why did you leave?" I once asked.

"Because it was racist," my mother said—so quickly I almost missed it.

There is another set of stories that run a parallel track: the England where my mother had one child who passed away from birth complications before Ten was born, where the Swinging Sixties passed them by as they climbed up the ranks of medicine, where my father got his fondness for both biting British humor and heavy midday drinking, where my mother interrupted her residency to be a first-time mom. These are the shadow stories. They come out quick, if at all.

Their stories of America are more raw, glaring and open wounds even now. My mother can still picture the "bright yellow wallet" she could not find when she disembarked at JFK in 1972. She can still feel how tired she was all the time, "like I had been beaten." Sometimes the exposure is quite literal—the roof peeling off their moving truck, all their possessions open to the elements.

From the shores of Coney Island, they slowly crept inward, first to the Bronx, where Eight was born, a shade browner than the first kid, and then to central New Jersey, to the suburbs. There, in what would become an enduring Indian community, I was born, only to up the brown quotient just a bit more. Atop my ruddy newborn skin lay a big black birthmark. The mark was just above my butt, at the small of my back, the size of a potato or the palm of a hand.

I don't remember thinking much of the birthmark as I grew up. I could not even see it unless I looked in some kind of double mirror, which I never made an effort to do. I wasn't a fan of looking in mirrors.

But when I was ten years old my mother took me to a plastic surgeon, and before I could say "general anesthesia" the birthmark was lopped off.

All I remember is what came after—the big pad of gauze stuck on my back for weeks like some bulky diaper, and my mom forcing me on the bed, ass up. I cried and writhed as she yanked stitches out.

The surgery never healed properly, leaving a thick keloid in the shape of the number five. It is purple sometimes, red others. A rupture more than erasure. A color releasing more colors.

Twenty years later, my mom quips with a sneer and a grin both, "Maybe we can cut that off, too."

When I think of the Hindi words for black and white, kali and gauri, I can't help but think of the accompanying Hindu goddesses. Images of fair-skinned Mahagauri are scattered about the house and family home temple—a statue here, a picture there. Kali does not hold such a place. My first exposure to her was not through my devout parents but through *Indiana Jones and the Temple of Doom*, the horn-headed evil cult leader chanting: "Kali-ma, Kali-ma!"

And yet, whiteness always seemed more like the big baddie to me. "She is so gauri," the auntie would praise. But I always heard *gory*, heard it like a curse, a brutal thing. The two words have different etymologies—gory coming from the Germanic "gor" meaning dirt, gauri coming from Sanskrit: shining, bright.

It was the paradox of my life—to be told constantly to stay out of the sun to stay shining, light, and brilliant. To know that under the surface of their comments was not a fear of the sun but a fear of Blackness.

It was the paradox of my life—to know the racism my parents experienced at the hands of white America and yet to be saddened by how they desired to be white themselves.

It was the paradox of my life—to watch with family Black performers on stage and screen, to cheer for Black athletes, to benefit from the gains of the civil rights movement, Black Power, yet to meet their rejection of Black people in real life. Too long in the sun and I'd hear "you have become black!" which even then I understood was something to fear.

I didn't spend much time heeding this advice. Skin to me was an afterthought, a container for the body that I just wanted to take outside to play. I like to think I grew up to be someone who is not very preoccupied with coloring or appearance overall. I don't have a vanity table and my makeup bag consists of a blush brush but nothing to dip it in.

But maybe this isn't true. Maybe I gaze more than I know or want to acknowledge. For even now I can see it, more than I can see any other section of my body—that birthmark—and I must have looked at it more than I thought. I can see its deep black hue, a constant, nearly a perfect circle, a still and deep place, a place where all the light goes.

In my twenties, I gave the scar a story. A man I was dating asked about it. "I got it at Five Points. That's why it's in the shape of a five. That's how I joined the Five Points Gang!" My intention was never to tell a convincing lie; I didn't want to prove any sort of toughness. I was just sick and tired of being asked "What's that?" I kept the lie up for a few days, even bringing him to a brunch spot called Five Points. After fifteen minutes of looking worriedly into his pancakes he finally asked, "Are you okay to eat here?" He had believed what I thought was a very far-fetched tale. I dumped him soon after that.

A year later, I was in New York, lying in bed next to the man I would go on to marry, the man who, based on the color of his skin, my parents were hoping I would not marry, the man who was Black, whose skin was the same color as mine.

As the morning light poured in, I pried myself out of our tangle of brown limbs and bedding. I got up to go to the bathroom naked—the kind of naked that stretches out all over you like a ball gown. The bathroom door opened to a full-length mirror and I couldn't help but linger there a bit.

"You never asked about my scar." I did a big stretch and arched my back.

"I just assumed it was a tail," he joked.

"It was nothing big. A surgery." I set my hands to my hips and fanned my fingers, sliding them across keloid and skin.

"I'm sticking to cat tail," he said.

"You know, you are the first person who hasn't asked." My fingertips met the top of my butt.

"Because," he said, "whatever it was, you survived."

THE WAY YOU
MAKE ME FEEL

When people ask if it was love at first sight, I tend to lie and say yes. The truth is, it was more dread.

Justine turned up the radio, her bedroom thick with the July heat and Michael Jackson's voice. It was the sultry murmur-turned-moan intro of "Don't Stop 'Til You Get Enough." He had died not more than ten days before. Ever since, it was impossible to go too long without hearing his voice. I couldn't help but feel like I had come down to Philly from New York not to celebrate the Fourth but really just to celebrate him.

Justine carried lateness with aplomb. "Can you text him that we'll be down in five?" She nodded to her phone and kept applying her mascara to the rhythm of Michael's mamase mamasa mamakusas in "Wanna Be Startin' Somethin'." I fretted over things like lateness, worrying even now if I was letting down this stranger I was about to text—Justine's friend who was our ride to a Fourth of July barbecue.

"Sorry, what's his name again?" I asked.

"Quincy."

"We'll be right down, Quincy"—I paused my typing. "This is Nina," I added.

As we came down, I spotted a man sitting on her apartment complex stoop, a handsome man who I looked up and down.

"Hi, Quincy!" I said.

"No, Nina," Justine corrected.

She pointed to a man who was tall and gangly and hurriedly moving around a car, hoisting stacks of papers into the trunk. He opened doors for both of us but then rushed past so quickly, I barely got to see him.

As I settled in, I looked at a sticker pasted on the rear window next to me. "Brown," I said. The school I lasted at for a year before I was shuttled out for a nervous breakdown. I never knew how much to reveal about that story, or even how to acknowledge that period in my life. But Justine, who knew me well and was a good, loving friend, did know.

"Quincy went there. You guys have a lot in common," she said.

I was somewhere in Taos, New Mexico, when I began to crack. My boyfriend and I got stranded on a road trip. Our car had broken down again and we had been hitching. This wasn't unusual for us. We were always on the road. I would come from Providence to where he went to school in St. Louis, WashU, and we'd go from there. Our adventures more often came from our car breaking down than from getting anywhere we intended to. These were the stories I carried back to friends at Brown.

The breakfast line we'd stumbled upon was supposed to be for people experiencing homelessness, but all I could see were hippies, well-kept white hippies. I saw one heavyset young Black boy who was talking about how he was "tripping face" the night before. A group of people milled around him, other hippie kids. He didn't seem to be talking to any one person in particular and no one in particular seemed to be listening to him. I knew "tripping face" meant it was a good night, but I just felt sad. I wasn't sure why. I thought he might have been sad. I had nothing to go on but a feeling.

I wanted to hear more of what this guy was saying, but I didn't draw myself further into the fold of the conversation. I always let Waspy Lion be our "in" to this world—that was the nickname my boyfriend gave himself for his blue eyes and shaggy blond hair. On the road in Colorado, we passed a restaurant named Red Lion and kept calling it Waspy Lion. The name stuck. He devised an accompanying impression; he would smooth out and pop the collar to the flannel shirt he always wore, making it look more polished than grungy-prep, and then emit a dull, monotone "rawr."

Sure enough, some of the people Waspy befriended at the breakfast invited us to the nearby "hippie house."

"The guy who lives there is a hundred-year-old hippie!" a young man told us while waving us in the direction everyone would be heading.

I wasn't excited. I didn't want to meet the hundred-year-old hippie. A thought kept cropping up in my head: would I ever have gotten an invite if I was on my own? I was bothered by this new thought. I couldn't name why. I wanted to swat the thought away.

We lost the pack of hippies but kept walking in the direction that the young man had pointed in. Once we found the hippie house—a modest white wood-shuttered home—I wasn't in a better mood. Just a few yards away from it, I stopped walking. I plopped down in the field near the house, covered my face with my hands, and began to cry. Waspy sat down next to me and pulled me close.

"I don't fit in anywhere," I said.

"Me either," he whispered.

He gripped me tighter, my body bound up in his flannel.

"Do you have enough room back there?" Quincy asked as he pulled out.

I was surrounded by stacks of photocopies, student papers, and books. A teacher's car, I thought.

"Yes," I said.

I spied one of my favorite books amid the stacks, Maxine Hong Kingston's *The Woman Warrior*. I had been introduced to the book a year ago, while teaching a class on fairy tale writing at the nonprofit where I worked, the Asian American Writers' Workshop. It was in a youth workshop for Asian American girls called UnFairy Tales. A friend recommended we read Kingston's Fa Mu Lan chapter. I felt hesitant to admit to her I didn't know the book and really only knew the story from Disney.

I remember being overwhelmed by the book when first I opened it. I couldn't follow what was going on exactly and was panicked to teach that chapter. But I instantly loved the poetry, the mixing of fantasy and reality. Even when I found it inscrutable, I loved how familiar the story was, more familiar to me than anything I had read in a long time. And I loved how the Asian American kids in UnFairy felt the same way. What was Quincy doing with it? I thought. Who is this rushing-around, up-on-his-Asian-American-literature man?

I wanted answers. But Quincy and Justine were in the throes of a discussion, Justine's "what's new" turning into a catch-up about the master's program where they had met. So-and-So had a new book, a kid, a new job.

"I haven't seen them since we were at the wedding and that guy's hand caught on fire from the table candles," I heard at one point.

I wanted to know what happened then but was reluctant to ask. Instead, I tried to think of ways of entering their conversation by bringing up *The Woman Warrior*.

But before I could mention any book, I heard a "congrats" from the front. Justine was congratulating Quincy on the recent publication of his own book of poetry.

"Congrats!" I chimed in quickly, too.

Justine passed the book back to me. *The T-Bone Series*. I flipped to the first poem, "T-Bone and Zeus."

"Zeus will go 'cross the world for a good martini," it began, going on to tell a story of nights the narrator, T-Bone, spends clubbing with the Greek god. "Zeus and I at this Goth club / What's a Black man suppose to do at a Goth club?"

I found myself laughing. Against all odds, it felt like. Even as I felt the gnaw of my anxieties, a little laugh escaped.

That laugh was enough to make me look up, to lean a bit forward out of the comfort of the backseat and try to get a better look at Quincy. The most I could see of him was his hair. His dreadlocks were so long and thick, it seemed as if a helmet of hair was driving us. I could see that he'd had them for a while. Each dread seemed to have earned its position, like the one at the peak of his forehead, which insisted on sticking up even when Quincy tried to flick it down. There was fray, too, especially at the top of his head, a tangle of frizz where most of the locks seemed to have lost their hold.

This man is a little bit sad, too, I thought. Dread meeting dread it felt like. I began to think about his poem and wondered if Quincy was more like Zeus or the friend, T-Bone. The one who feels invincible or the one who needs convincing.

My relationship was in trouble, so I did the only thing I could: slept with a second boy behind Waspy's back. When that didn't work, I sought out a third boy for advice.

"Jerry Garcia saw a bunch of women at the same time, why should it be any different for you?" Louis said. Lou was my closest friend at Brown. We had gone to both grade and high school together. There, we helped each other get through, sharing notes and homework and the like. But his group of too-cool record-store boys seemed to keep a wide berth from my pack of hippie-cheerleader queen bees. We got closer our first semester in college and ended up doing a campus radio show together where we played, among many things, a lot of Grateful Dead.

His aligning my infidelities with Jerry's worked for a few weeks. I managed to get myself to classes, most times without breaking down in tears halfway through. I saw friends but didn't stress myself with going out and socializing. When I stayed in, I painted with my roommate's finger paints. I tried to be cute and normal, but I felt anything but cute and normal. I could barely concentrate. Every thought, every decision, even if just to dip my finger in the paint, was a flame.

One day, I called my older sister Diksha, crying. After talking to me for a few minutes, she had to go back to her job. "Don't do anything rash, okay?" she said. A few minutes later, I took a bunch of pills and downed a handle of vodka. My father called me, probably tipped off by my sister, and when he realized I wasn't making proper words, he dialed 911.

I vaguely remember being carried out on a stretcher. I remember more of waking up in the school infirmary with my mother sitting at my right, a hairbrush in her hand; Lou, sitting at my left, his head in his hands.

For most of our ride to the barbecue, we were turning around. It felt less like movement forward and more like an undoing of a knot. Traffic cops waved us in one direction and then another.

What would usually be a fifteen-minute ride out to the suburbs was turning into an hour and change.

Philly, because of the big annual Fourth of July concert, was a mess of detour signs and orange traffic cones, a maze designed to make Ben Franklin Parkway into a public square and the Museum of Art's "Rocky Steps" a concert stage.

The detours didn't seem to get Quincy down. He seemed happy to be stuck in the car with us, listening to the R&B coming from the stations Justine had charged herself with navigating or to the beats from old-school boom boxes wafting in along with charcoal and meat smoke from grill-fests outside.

It's live, live, all the way live.

Justine and Quincy knew these songs more than I did. As we made our way, they swapped childhood stories over these songs and traded lyrics.

Come along and ride on a fantastic voyage.

I wouldn't know what it would mean to have listened to these songs as a kid. The soundtrack of my childhood consisted of mostly Hindi film songs or classical ghazals and bhajans. The only American music I can remember is Lipps Inc.'s "Funkytown"—I remember it always played at the New Year's parties we'd attend at Indian banquet halls. I'd watch my aunties and uncles gyrate to the song and feel embarrassed on their behalf.

Justine and Quincy kept going. All of a sudden I felt like I would be found out. For what, I did not know, but if I didn't participate in some way, I believed I would be.

"I used to think it was 'your *blood* is mine' as a kid, not 'your *butt*.' I thought that was the scariest taunt ever," I heard Quincy say. "How are you going to take someone's blood?"

I thought to myself then, Quick, propose a car game.

"What Michael Jackson video would you be in?" I asked them.

They jumped in as if we had been deliberating on this the whole ride.

"No-brainer. 'Smooth Criminal,' the greatest video of all time," Quincy said.

"'Remember the Time'—just like 'Smooth Criminal,' greatest video of all time but not as much work," Justine said. "What about you, Nina?" she asked.

I realized I did not have an answer in mind. "The Way You Make Me Feel," I blurted and immediately felt self-conscious. I remembered that this was the one where Michael essentially chases a sexy girl around the car while she is all like *no, no!*

I could have picked "Thriller" and shared what I always thought of as my central Michael anecdote: I was a toddler when "Thriller" came out. My mother once told me that she would put the video on at my mealtimes. Apparently, it was the only thing that got me to sit down and properly eat. I don't know why I didn't share this. It is not only one of my favorite Michael stories but also one of the few family anecdotes I felt I could comfortably deliver.

But Justine and Quincy were either very supportive or just relishing any memory of Michael through and through. We only talked about how exciting it would be to be chased around a car by him.

The suicide attempt happened at the end of the school year. I was sent home for a week to recoup and then I finished up the term in what felt like an adrenaline push. I locked myself up in my dorm room and wrote a few papers. Then, in what felt like a comedown, I completely fell apart.

I withdrew from the New York City apartment where I was supposed to live with friends from Brown.

I went back home to my parents. I barely got out of bed, though I barely slept.

When I did get out of bed, I fought with my parents. I wrote "my moment" on the beam in between my two bedroom windows. I wrote this in black marker on a piece of medical tape. I thought that every other moment in my life had been a performance for someone else. I spent June and July mostly sitting there alone, quietly staring out this window and fuming.

One sunny August day, I stopped looking out the "my moment" window, went to my closet, and pulled out a very beautiful dress, a dress my sister had once let me borrow and had not yet asked for back. It was long sleeved and made of soft cotton-mesh fabric with a ruffled V-neck and colored a beautifully irreverent fuchsia. I slipped it on, hopped in my car, and started to drive. I drove and drove for three days straight. I thought if I traveled far enough away from my family, I'd be free to live life however I wanted, with whomever I wanted, and I'd be happy.

Every street in Philly seemed to be filled up with people. People carrying coolers to parties. People playing music out of their cars. People walking on the sidewalks and on the street itself. Grills set up on patios and lawns and public greens. No one seemed to be too much in a hurry.

The pace of this city was so different from New York. In New York I found myself walking like I was weaving through a race, upset at the person walking slowly in front of me, passing them, only to say in my head, "Finally, I can enjoy a nice slow walk." But perhaps it was being in the backseat that made me feel this way. Neither driving nor sitting shotgun, I was forced to kick back and take in the scene, whether it was my nature to do so or not.

A girl walked by who seemed to carry the July heat as nothing but one more pleat in a summer dress. Justine checked her out and Quincy made a show of not checking her out.

"Can't even look, could be one of my students," he said.

I wasn't sure if he was eyeing the young woman along with Justine and just joking or if he was reserved or if he just didn't care for her either way. None of that came through to the backseat.

I watched the girl. I thought about how even she seemed less shy than me, and I felt frustrated by that feeling. I felt competitive without knowing what I was competing for exactly.

All of a sudden I had the feeling that I should be making a party, a fun and lively backseat party, one that everyone wants to go to. It was a dead zone back there. Quick, how do you make a party with a Maxine Hong Kingston book?

I made it as far as Chicago. There, I decided I would find the next flight from O'Hare to Paris. I called my parents from a hotel room to tell them so. We didn't fight. I hung up feeling if not peaceful, just a little bit more settled and excited about what lay ahead.

In the airport the next day, I thought I looked great in my elegant but playful fuchsia dress. Perfect for the start of my Parisian life. The red in the dress hid how my period had bled through. I was lost in these thoughts when I felt a tap on my shoulder and saw my father standing next to me. He must have driven through the night. Twelve hours. He promised me he'd get me a plane ticket if I just got in the car with him.

In the car, he pressed the CD player and I recognized the voice of Jagjit Singh. Usually my dad loved to sing right alongside him, but he wasn't singing now. Instead, he just tried to translate the ghazal, losing its beauty as it slipped into English, and he broke down into tears. I grew quiet then and remained so for the rest of the ride. It still took me some time to register that we were going home. Twelve hours and I don't remember one minute of the trip. I opened my eyes in New Jersey.

The next day I got some kind of escape. I was checked into New York's Payne Whitney Clinic at Weill Cornell Hospital. In the waiting room hung pictures of famous depressed people—mostly distinguished white men and Virginia Woolf. My father tried to cut the tension by doing impressions of their serious faces, tilting down his head and furrowing his brow like Beethoven and then doing another and another.

I don't remember laughing or not laughing. I don't remember much. But I always think of the story my sister Diksha tells. As the admitting nurse waved us in, Diksha and my mother came upon a man, maybe in his thirties, dressed neatly and having a conversation with a wall. At the sight of this man, Diksha felt like crying. But in that moment, my mom turned to her and said, "I like him."

As soon as they left, I met my new roommates: there was the woman who said if she was a psychiatrist, she'd just play "Eleanor Rigby" on repeat in her waiting room, an older man who walked around wearing headphones and holding a carton of Newports his kids had dropped off, and another man who rode a stationary bike and didn't do much else.

I mostly just looked out the window, into New York City summer: a delivery truck's ample double-park, taxi drivers honking with such ire, people walking, jostling one and another, everyone going somewhere even if it was nowhere, out of the office or back, to the FedEx on the corner, the ice cream truck—all that life moving along without missing a beat, more than anything else, more than bed checks or stool softeners or outbursts or nurses rushing, that was the most humiliating and scary thing to me.

The sun seemed brighter and less cruel once we got out of the knot of the city and drove into the sleepy suburban landscape—an apartment complex of identical beige units with matching mini-porches. We got to the barbecue very late. The grill was shut, and the party had moved inside. The sun was dipping and with it any signs of the Fourth of July.

In the distance stood several tall steel poles with blinking red lights—radio antenna towers. Something about them there, looming, read spooky to me. I felt as if there lay the third level beyond the city, when the curtain of everything drops.

As we got out of the car and all did a stretch, I took Quincy in for the first time. He seemed to me an impossibly tall and thin blade of a man, with a narrow face on which delicate, sharp features had an almost exaggerated quality to them, all framed by his long, past-the-shoulder locks. They seemed like the largest part of him, as if they were what buoyed him here, prevented him and all his silly from floating up past those tall towers and into outer space. Maybe it made sense that I got to know them first.

My attention shifted as we neared the apartment door. I was nervous about the barbecue from the beginning. While the car offered distractions and excuses to not have to socialize, there was no avoiding it at the party.

The people were laid-back. I found myself unfettered of my New York defenses, and soon enough that unfetteredness became a rabbit hole for me—I delved into all manner of things I usually don't pull out until the waters have been tested. Namely, I talked about my crush on Norm, the big fat white man on *Cheers*. Quincy and I discussed Norm for a good long while. It seemed as if it was only the two of us in the room, he seemed as committed to the conversation as I was. The anxieties that usually crept about me at the edges, the worry that anything I said was manic, depressed, or irrational, were not gone but less on the watch.

We kept up our patter even as we were walking out.

"You have funny taste," Quincy said.

"I just know what I like," I said. As I said this, I found myself looking him dead straight in the eyes. My directness took even me by surprise. It was as if I said it in spite of myself.

We continued walking for a quiet moment and then Quincy spoke up.

"You know, I think I could have a kid and do that whole sort of thing." He said it like we had been talking about this all day, not debating the best Michael Jackson videos. His saying this seemed so far away from how he had been. There was no Zeus or T-Bone or poet at all now. The words tumbled out of him as if they were tripping over themselves.

He didn't plan to say this, I could sense, just as much as I didn't plan my hard eye contact. It was as if another part of him was speaking to another part of me, some daring part, picking up some signal only God and those radio antennae could know.

KISSABLE

The club is called Fluid. It won't be there in a few years, but we don't know that yet. Tonight is just a deeply Philly night. Justine, me, and Quincy walk into the club, going through a small hallway that opens up into a circular dance floor, balcony, and bar off to the side. We look up into the DJ booth. "That's Questlove," Justine says or I say or Quincy says or we all say together at the same time. The Roots aren't yet the 11:30 house band on *The Tonight Show Starring Jimmy Fallon*, but they aren't that far off.

No one is in there besides us and Questlove. The chill of the blasting AC goes right up my American Apparel tube dress. I try not to rub my shoulders. The whole point of this night is the tube dress. It's still early on a summer Saturday—Philly's two a.m. liquor sale cutoff not yet looming. Did I rush us out too soon? Justine was still in the bed while I was wrestling the dress on. Our roles had reversed. I was at the mirror, applying makeup in my nonexpert just-rub-things-all-over-your-face technique. "Wow, okay, you really want to go out," Justine said as I lined my eyes.

"You should talk to him," I say to Justine now or she decides on her own. Either way, before I know it, she is at the DJ booth, Questlove leaning toward her, and I am alone with Quincy, just the two of us for the first time since Justine called me, saying, "I have good news, he was asking about you, too."

My polyblend-wrapped body aches with all the stupid things you have to say when all you want to do is touch. "Drinks?" I say. But Quincy doesn't drink and orders a cranberry juice for himself and a vodka something for me and Justine's signature "Captain and Diet." The club is quiet enough that I can hear Justine's request to Questlove, "Biggie."

We all reconvene. "What happened?" I say to Justine, but before I can get an answer "Juicy" comes on. "It was all a dream . . ." Maybe all night we will have this club and the drummer of the Roots to ourselves.

"This is cool," I say.

"This is Fluid," Justine says. "I can't believe we haven't been here together before."

But I only started coming to Philly a few weeks ago, once out of guilt for not having visited Justine sooner and all the other times hoping it would lead to this moment.

Fluid. This is Fluid, yes. And I take him in, sneaking sips. Those eyes that should be covered up with a white line like my mother's God posters. "Because they can blind you with their glory," she'd say. I imagined lasers. Quincy's eyes pierce like that. His torso, slender and long, the type to wrap limbs around and keep climbing. The blazer and jeans with panels and pockets fit for a secret slip of hands.

The saddest song plays. Pete Rock and C. L. Smooth's "They Reminisce Over You (T.R.O.Y.)" echoes through the empty club, that guitar opening always feeling more like a middle than an opening, a sample of another opening, the Beginning of the End's "When She

Made Me Promise," followed by Tom Scott's saxophone, another sample, from Scott's cover of Jefferson Airplane's "Today," all seeming to emerge from out of a time tunnel and into the song's present, "I reminisce, I reminisce . . ." a soulful mourning. But I love this song and I am not cool and jump up without thinking, I am only my body, my hands, which seem to be pulling Quincy to dance on the chilly dance floor. The song goes on, with its reclamations—"Mama's getting married in the house"—and with its sorrows—"I can hear his head banging on the wall in the next room"—and I know it is totally inappropriate to make a sexy dance out of this, but I am sick of making excuses to come down to Philly. So I draw him closer and closer, tube dress grazing tall torso, breasts against shirt buttons, the sax returns, and I wonder, Isn't that sexy in its own way. And I think about any other efforts this body could do, my tube dress could do. But then I feel his hand, his hand against the small of my back, a support, a way of saying *Don't do all the work, please*. And then he is hovering, coming down to my eye level. I am not just dancing with a torso anymore. We settle into our crouch-reach mambo.

Stevie Wonder's "Isn't She Lovely" comes on and he whoos loudly. A Stevie fan. Fits his old-school blazer-and-button-down-even-in-hundred-degree-thick-Philly-July-heat look. It's the only time he breaks away from our dance, just to whoo with the rest of the crowd, and I look up, too—the club has more people, many more people. I realize I haven't looked up in a couple of songs. Bodies upon bodies are fitting into each other's grooves, a stream of rhythm, not between two but many. I look over and Justine is lost in the music, dancing with someone.

I wish I hadn't looked up. I feel nervous now. This crouch-reach dance, how long can we do it? But the thing is, he never stops looking at me, with those eyes that should be covered with a white line. His hand on my back steady, unwavering. His mouth more sincere and serious than I've seen it, no joke in its corners, no witty repartee forming. A new seriousness, an unlikely seriousness, a seriousness I'd like to soften.

My uncle took one look at the newborn in front of him and said, "Kissable." Papa. Kissable. Pappi is Hindi slang for kiss. My mother said I looked like I was in a meditative state, in the process of transitioning from my past life, a swami's samadhi. But my uncle Champak, who also goes by Champ, who is a charming flirt of a man, who goes to Carnival in Rio and comes back with a Lambada record that he blasts at family parties, who hires belly dancers and throws money at them at these same parties, said the word—Papa—and it stuck.

Champ no longer shared a room with one of my sisters in a crib. He had his own middle-class suburban home, just like my parents. They were all making it in America, their private physician practices steadily growing, making it enough for my parents to have a moment of pleasure, that pleasure becoming a love child. I was clearly an accident, born eight years after the last. My birth marked a new phase for my family, a steady momentum into upper-middle-class life— larger home, housekeeper, babysitters to pick me up from school or swim practice while my parents kept grinding, a credit card on which I'd buy meals for white friends, clothes for white friends, buying my own kissable white American dream in their absence.

"Where is Papa?" my cousin would say, and my little toddler body would waddle over to play with her. "Papa, come," my mother or father would say, and I'd obey. "Papa?"—my father would see me first and then my friend, a white girl from school, and correct himself—"Oh, hi, Nina."

"Dekho, Papa"—my grandmother wide-eyed—"Look, Kissable"—the very last time we saw each other. I don't think I ever heard either of my grandparents call me by another name. And Uncle Champ still says, "Oh, hello, Papa, how are you?" if I answer the phone. The name resides in every stitch in my kissable body, not on a birth certificate but within me, a meditation, my samadhi.

Maybe my uncle is right. Maybe my mother is right. Maybe Audre Lorde is right. Lorde says, "There are many kinds of power, used and unused, acknowledged or otherwise. The erotic is a resource within each of us that lies in a deeply female and spiritual plane, firmly rooted in the power of our unexpressed or unrecognized feeling."

Of course, born a month early, still sorting out my past life, I hadn't gotten to Audre Lorde yet.

But I did get to Bollywood, the almost-kissing era of Bollywood. There was no lip contact, but there was rolling around in fields and choreography that left pairs panting and slick with sweat, there was lip biting and chest heaving, there was unfolding the wrap of a sari, and rainstorms that left lovers wet from the outside in, songs full of innuendo and sung by Lata Mangeshkar at a climactic crescendo. It's 1986, I'm six and sitting with my cousin Pooja on her parents' bed, letting the hot summer day pass us by as we hole up in a stuffy room and watch *Saagar*, transfixed as Rishi Kapoor and Dimple Kapadia serenade each other on rocky shores, a touch of hand becoming a warm embrace, becoming face-to-face, and just when you think they might kiss, Dimple bites his earlobe before pulling away and belting her own solo.

I grew up in this earlobe-biting era of Bollywood, where the leading lady was no demure beauty, could be as bold and playful as the two men vying for her attention. There were always two. And the two were often fighting over the actress known by one name. Rekha. The boldest and my favorite. I watched our VHS of *Umrao Jaan* countless times, so many that I knew how long to forward the tape to get up to my favorite scene, the one where Rekha, acting the part of a famed but sorrow-struck nineteenth-century courtesan, sings "Dil Cheez Kya Hai." The scene is a master class in eye sex even within the confines of a period piece. Then there is Rekha and Amitabh Bachchan in *Silsila*, their lust extending far past the screen. Even as a child I knew they were rumored to have had an affair and that transgression always mingled a cut deeper into the love triangle plot.

"Oh! Me so horny! Oh! Me so horny!" I was nine and dancing around the kitchen table like a Bollywood heroine, but instead of "Saagar Kinare," I was singing this lyric from 2 Live Crew's 1989 hit, "Me So Horny," and wearing one of my favorite shirts—my Cheetos Chester Cheetah T-shirt, him in his sunglasses and high-tops prancing with me against my budding boobs.

"Stop singing that," my two teenage sisters said to me. "Do you know what that means?"

I shook my head. I did and I didn't. I didn't until they asked me and then I did.

The 2 Live Crew sampled Kubrick's *Full Metal Jacket*, Papillon Soo Soo's voice in her role as a Vietnamese sex worker. I'm not sure if my sisters knew that history. I'm not sure if they had seen the movie. I believe they objected to the phrase's raciness but not its anti-Asian racism and misogyny. We were nearing the 1990s, after all; the culture wars and its white crusaders like Tipper Gore and Jesse Helms had their priorities. The 2 Live Crew's *As Nasty As They Wanna Be* was the first album ever to be deemed obscene under the rule of law, the era of parental advisory labels ushered in with it.

The song seems comically pornographic now—getting a girl's number and calling her to ask her for sex. I think of the Cheetos T-shirt–wearing girl prancing around to "Me So Horny" unawares, much like Tipper Gore's daughter, who, at eleven, was caught singing along to "Darling Nikki," Prince's ode to female masturbation. I think of how much fun I was having, I think of how much fun Tipper Gore's daughter was probably having, I think of how much fun Darling Nikki was definitely having. "Do you know what that means?" Behind Chester the Cheetah, behind my training bra, into the most "unused" and kissable part of me, I knew.

Long before she cofounded the Parents Music Resource Center, Tipper Gore was a young girl obsessed with music, an obsession that led her to form a girl group in which she was the drummer. "I wanted to play drums," she said, "and I got a set when I was fourteen and just started to play in the house, to the stereo."

The group called themselves the Wildcats. They played early Beatles and Bob Dylan, radio hits they all mutually adored. They would play around town—at local festivals, schools, and even once at a local event for Barry Goldwater, their run ending with high school graduation.

The Parents Music Resource Center was another incarnation of Gore's girl group. Nicknamed the "Washington Wives," this band of white women's greatest and most enduring hit was the "Parental Advisory: Explicit Lyrics" label.

....

In 1990, as rap entered suburbs like mine, Gore published an op-ed entitled "Hate, Rape, and Rap" in *The Washington Post*:

> In New York City, rape arrests of 13-year-old boys have increased 200 percent in the past two years. Children 18 and younger now are responsible for 70 percent of the hate crime committed in the United States. No one is saying this happens solely because of rap or rock music, but certainly kids are influenced by the glorification of violence.

Just a year before, sixteen-year-old Korey Wise, sixteen-year-old Yusef Salaam, fifteen-year-old Antron McCray, fourteen-year-old Raymond Santana, and fourteen-year-old Kevin Richardson had been falsely accused, arrested, and indicted for the rape and assault of a white woman jogger in Central Park. There was no DNA evidence or fingerprints that could connect the boys to the crime scene. Instead law enforcement, speaking to them without parents or lawyers present, used coercive interrogation tactics to break them.

The footage is chilling: Assistant DA Elizabeth Lederer says to Korey Wise at the start of his interrogation, "I see you have a soda in front of you." He quickly takes the soda off the table. "No, no, that's all right"—she asserts her power—"you asked for a soda a while ago, and a detective brought you a soda. Are you feeling okay." She isn't asking, she's demanding. The aggression grows with each passing minute, minutes turning into an hour, into over an hour, and she puts a photo of the victim's bloody shirt to his face. Shock and fear at the image visibly shows on his face. She does not acknowledge his emotion the way she did the soda; instead she asks him leading questions, questions leading to the conclusions she had already made.

After at least seven hours of highly confrontational and manipulative questioning from cops, detectives, and prosecution, the teens plead guilty to a crime they did not commit. The "Central Park Five," a group of Latino and Black teenagers now referred to as the "Exonerated Five," were around the same age as Gore's Wildcats.

In "Rape, Racism and the Myth of the Black Rapist," Angela Davis writes, "In the history of the United States, the fraudulent rape charge stands out as one of the most formidable artifices invented by racism. The myth of the Black rapist has been methodically conjured up whenever recurrent waves of violence and terror against the Black community have required convincing justifications."* "Hate, Rape, and Rap"—Gore's op-ed title alone stokes that myth. "In New York City, rape arrests of 13-year-old boys have increased 200 percent in the past two years . . . No one is saying this happens solely because of rap or rock music . . ." Gore writes. A concession perhaps. Yet what is that concession without a real and sustained conversation? Conversations beyond the '90s culture wars and the ways in which crime was attributed to personal failure; conversations about how the 1994 crime bill offered billions in incentive grants to build and expand prisons, so much so that for a period in the 1990s, a new prison was built every fifteen days; conversations that resist the urge to label children as "superpredators" with "no conscience" and "no empathy."

....

*"Rape, Racism and the Myth of the Black Rapist" is an essay in the collection *Women, Race and Class* by Angela Davis.

....

"You just need to put earphones on and you can walk through the halls and no one will bother you," Marc said. My sister Diksha had put her college boyfriend on the phone. Diksha and I talked and traded letters regularly once she went away to college. She even sometimes sent care packages that included Marc's mixtapes, Music 101.

On one of those cassettes, I heard for the first time the voice of someone who shared my name. It was 1992, twenty-six years since Nina Simone had released "Four Women," but the song was a whole new sound to me. Its slow pace, its piano kissing drums kissing flute, its pacing holding space for a cast of characters. Nina's announcement of "my," over and over again, as each woman described her body, body as something significant as a lyric, the lyric becoming a stanza, each stanza becoming a woman. I always looked forward to the last one, the one that seemed most like mine: "My skin is brown." I listened to the elegant restraint of Simone's voice then unleash into the name "Peaches"; I thought of Kissable.

Nina Simone would lie alongside Gang Starr and Dylan and Beastie Boys. And I'd get lost in their individual songs and the story they told together. What story was Marc trying to help me understand?

Upon its release, "Four Women" was banned by radio stations across the nation, due to, according to *The Pittsburgh Courier*, "its misunderstood lyrics."

Nina Simone, according to *The Virgin Islands Daily News*, was hurt, reportedly saying she was "denied the privilege as an artist to communicate with the public."

In prep school, twelve-year-old me would listen to "Four Women" on Marc's mixtape, forwarding the cassette to the part where she would scream, "Peeeaches!"

James Baldwin used to tell Nina Simone, "This is the world you have made for yourself, now you have to live in it."

Marc offered me one way to live in it. "You just need to put earphones on and you can walk through the halls."

But I didn't do that.

The questions would start up from the boys in my school as soon as the ski trip bus got going. "Let's ask Nina if she knows what that sample is."

"Curtis Mayfield."

"Hey, Nina, what's that you are listening to?"

"You can listen till we get to the rest stop," I'd say and pass it over heads on the bus.

"Nina, hey, Nina, do you know this one?"

I took all the questions from the too-cool white record-store boys of my prep school to be a form of flirting. And when the question and answer portion of the program was over, when they went back to chasing after one or the other blond white prep school girl, I'd put my headphones back on.

I haven't looked up in a couple of songs. When I do, I feel out of my depth. When "Isn't She Lovely" comes on and the dance floor lets out a collective "whoo"—that whoo to me is less "I like this song" and more "I remember this feeling." Strangers seem less strange, sharing a feeling. I feel like a fraud. What right do I have to dance to this song? I am not a Black person. I am not Julia Stiles in *Save the Last Dance*, but I don't fit in either. Then I look back, into Quincy's eyes—they haven't left me. I haven't lost his attention. And I respond in kind. I dare to stare back. I stare back into those eyes. I find my place in them. I find a new place as I reach up on my tiptoes and he crouches down.

At the 2000 Democratic National Convention, the stiff presidential nominee and prospective FLOTUS melt back into high school sweethearts. Gliding onto the stage to accept the nomination, Al goes straight for Tipper's lips. One second and she thinks it's done, looks like she's about to break away even, but he holds close, a close mouth opening, closer, wrapping an arm around her back and she wraps as well, arms around the neck, a kiss so famous it was timed—three whole seconds, it made headlines, a prom-worthy make-out for the world to see.

Ten years later, they split.

We grind but Stevie Wonder's "Isn't She Lovely" is a song more heartwarming birth announcement than dance floor bump and grind. A song that begins with a baby's cry. A song that exclaims: "Isn't she precious / Less than one minute old." A song so wholesome it played at Gore's rallies. It's featured on *Songs in the Key of Life*, one of Prince's all-time inspirations.

I forget it all, that hyperawareness of space I'm used to, until I am nothing but the forces of our bodies playing out, tube dress cinching up impossibly high, over my thigh and across his jeans.

....

With their hands over mouths to muffle laughter, sleepover party laughter—not my house but at the home of a white prep school classmate—the white girls passed around the VHS cassette, giggling over the name, *Spanking the Monkey*. It was 1995; I was a sophomore and did not laugh at the VHS cover, palms splayed together, *Spanking the Monkey* written across them, the white boy's face in the background, an eyebrow raised. Watching this movie was a plan that had been in the works for a while. I didn't know about it until the sleepover. The giggles were about the possibility of watching this white boy jerk off. Someone popped in the video. The lights went out. And then I was out. I jumped downstairs, to the basement, the place where we'd be sleeping. I did it without saying anything, without thinking really, my body making decisions.

In the basement, I watched PBS. A Jimi Hendrix interview. I thought of my punk rocker cousin Arun, who would wear a T-shirt with Jimi's *Axis: Bold As Love* album cover on it, the one with all the Hindu gods, avatars of Jimi. Years later, I'd learn that Jimi didn't like that cover, that he would have preferred a cover that highlighted his Indigenous heritage. I thought of the white boys taking one of my mixes, to listen to "Crosstown Traffic." I thought of *Wayne's World*, a movie that came out a few years before, Jimi's "Foxy Lady" becoming a comic ode to awkward white boy horniness and Midwestern blondes.

I watched Dick Cavett trying to engage Jimi in conversation, but Jimi was replying from some faraway place, not taking any of the white man's bait, and I wanted to be far away with him. I loved his kimono top, which Dick Cavett tried unsuccessfully to make fun of. I loved his speaking voice, a riddle of a voice, a strange contrast to his extraordinary singing.

I didn't want to discover my sexuality with these girls nor did I want to witness white girls discovering their sexuality. These girls knew me as funny, as popular, as crucial to their invitation-only sleepover party. But there, in the basement, with Jimi, I wasn't this funny-popular-assimilated Nina. I was someone Jimi might have introduced at some psychedelic party, "Oh, yeah, that's Kissable, she's the inspiration behind 'Little Wing.'"

As Jimi Hendrix told Dick Cavett that sitcoms would be a passing fad, Sammy, the sleepover host, came down to check on me.

"I'm okay, I'll come up soon."

Sammy nodded, her blond ponytail bouncing with her as she climbed the stairs. She went back to *Spanking the Monkey* and I watched Jimi writhe on the ground with a burning guitar between his legs.

"I'm reading the Upanishads right now," Chris said.

"Oh, cool."

I vaguely knew this was part of the Vedas. I didn't know much more to say. This was the first time a white teen had shown interest in something South Asian besides the impersonation of my mother that made the white girls at the lunch table laugh. I thought of Jimi and his *Bold As Love* cover.

By the end of junior year, our college counselor recommended me for a summer creative writing program. I didn't know how she knew I liked to write. Writing to me was an urge, a kiss deep inside. What would it be like to share this pleasure with the world?

Instead of the writing workshop, I ended up going to a precollege program like my sisters went to. It was about civics. I didn't care about civics.

I saw Chris on the first day at the orientation gathering. I took him in: tall white boy, not slinky like the music-loving white boys I flirted with in school, heavy but in a muscular way. He stood a bit separated from others. His look seemed less neatly pressed than everyone else's, his hair kind of stuck out, he remained on the perimeters of the mingling. I went up to him and introduced myself, began to talk about music and books that I sensed we had in common.

We would lag back from class, walking up tree-lined walkways back to our "house"—the coed dorm where we all stayed, boys on the ground floor, girls on the second. We were both social and part of a group, the coolest of the nerds settling in with each other, but I would find my way to his side whenever we all hung out.

We talked a lot. My talk-flirting. Flirting with him as I did with the white boys in high school, wrapped in songs, books, concerts until I was wrapped around him in the boarding-school twin where we'd kiss and kiss and maybe get some pants action. Did I get off? He had the smallest room in a suite of three; I don't remember a door or it never got loud enough to shut it.

He also talked a lot about a girl in his hometown and showed me the letters she wrote him. "Look, she calls her brother 'the boy'—isn't that awesome?" It was. Once, glancing into a notebook lying in his room, I saw a faint scribble of her name in the margins. Cindy? Candy? A name like some girl who discovered her sexuality while watching *Spanking the Monkey*.

One day we were rolling around in his bed and smoking weed and I was making him laugh. "I think you are an artist, but I don't know what kind," he said.

He told me that he planned to hike the Adirondacks, which he called "the 'dacks."

I imagined him there with Candy.

Senior year and I was in the hallway of a jam band concert with my friend Sammy, the one who had the *Spanking the Monkey* slumber party way back when. I smiled at a guy. He seemed older. Shaggy hair, Carhartt, a '90s hippie finest. He offered us candy—M&M's, not LSD. I began to trade Joni Mitchell lyrics with him, like a rap battle but with lines from *Blue*. I was aware of my prep school girlfriends watching. He was thirty and gave me his name and number on a slip of paper, putting a random apostrophe in his very white last name: Jack Wil'em, the punctuation to make it exotic. I was eighteen. "My name is Jenna," I said.

Jenna and Jack went on one date. It was a Tuesday and I told my parents I was sleeping over at a friend's. We went to a Black Crowes concert. It was January 1999, and we were on Irving Plaza's second level, taking in the whole guts of the stage. The lead Crowe came out. He seemed to sing with his whole skinny white man body, like Mick Jagger, but less pretty.

I looked over from my dancing and saw that Jack had a pen and paper out. He was a music reviewer. I thought I'd like to do that instead of dancing.

We went to a Chinese restaurant. The hot and sour soup was comforting in the January cold. He passed me a cassette—not a mixtape but two albums—Joni Mitchell's *Don Juan's Reckless Daughter* on one side and her *Hejira* on another. I talked about Miles Davis's *Sketches of Spain.* "*Sketches of Spain?* Man, I never met a girl who knew *Sketches of Spain.*"

We went back to his house after the show. We smoked up. It was the weed he got in Amsterdam. "My Cannabis Cup winnings." We were kissing in bed. He kept getting up to run to the bathroom to do lines. I had my period. I remember the maxipad clinging to my pubic hair and maybe his fingers down there for a brief lucid moment before he passed out entirely. In the early morning, I left without waking him up. It was snowing a little. One patch of snow to another, I drove straight from his house to another Wednesday at prep school. As I walked into the senior lounge, a slim corridor of a room each class couldn't wait to inherit, one of the cool white boys, the slinkiest and quietest, gave me a knowing nod and smile. I nodded back.

Jack called the house once asking for Jenna. Diksha answered, "Who?"

A dance floor is a liminal space. A transgressive space. A dance floor is a place to assume a different version of you. Yet not so different. A you with heightened spatial awareness or a newfound orientation to inhabiting and occupying space. And a dance floor is not a dance floor really until there are more than three people on it while a living legend deejays just above in near anonymity. A dance floor is what happens when you look up and there are many, many more. Bodies upon bodies are fitting into each other's grooves, a stream of rhythm, not between two but many. You becomes a we. We is too much for me. Out of step, out of the rhythm, out of that collective whoo, into a far less expansive and imaginative land, I go in for the kiss.

....

I was eighteen and reading for pleasure. I pulled a book out from the library for the title—*The Unbearable Lightness of Being*. I loved that phrase "Unbearable Lightness of Being," the way it rolled around the tongue. I loved the bowler hat on the cover, suspended in space. I don't know what the book named, but it named something for me, a feeling. I flipped through it in our high school courtyard, trying to catch this feeling.

A few pages in, I looked up and saw a guy.

The guy was like all the others—a cool white boy. Waspy Lion— or Erik, as I called him then—was a year ahead of me. I guess he was coming back from college for a visit. A trumpet player in the jazz band, the music-loving boys of my grade idolized him and his jazz cool.

Once, when he was a senior, I saw him catching a glimpse of a middle schooler acting up. He knocked on the senior lounge glass window. "Stop it," he mouthed to her.

Now he waved and I waved back. I thought he'd keep on walking, like the way we'd pass each other a million times at school, but he came up to me. What does he have to say to me? What do I have to say to him?

I shut *The Unbearable Lightness of Being* and craned up from my perch to his face, a kind smile, as if we had already been sharing a laugh, light in his eyes. He stood right there.

"How are you?" he said.

"Just enjoying some sun," I said.

I didn't mention the book, as I would with the boys. I didn't talk much at all. None of that talk-flirting. But it felt like something private had occurred between us, I wasn't sure what.

When I returned to the senior lounge the plan was already made. "We're going to the diner with Erik." A flock of the boys and my girls went, ten people squeezing uncomfortably into a diner booth.

"Nina and Erik should go to prom together," Lou said as we sat there. I was happily going alone until then.

"Why did you scold that girl that one time?" I asked.

"She was on scholarship," he said. "I didn't want her to lose it."

I didn't realize we had students on scholarship. No one had talked about it openly, at least not with me. It seemed like the thing you'd only know if you were on scholarship, too.

"I don't have a tux," he said when I called him a few days later, Sammy pressing the phone she had dialed up to my face. He borrowed one from my father, much too small for him.

She and the rest of my girlfriends took me to Macy's and picked out a "proper gown" for me.

On the dance floor, Erik did a sexy dance with me that felt more like a dance making fun of sexy dancing. He crouched farther and farther down the length of my gown though my gown felt too fussy for this type of dance. And while his tight tux seemed funny, too, I tried to follow suit. Our prom song was Marvin Gaye's "Sexual Healing"—more a white kid's joke than earnest embrace—all the taboo of sex and none of the soul. I started laughing and he started laughing and we laughed and talked through the evening.

He headed to the after-party with me, which was at a Days Inn on the Jersey shore owned by the parents of a classmate who would soon regret the decision to invite us all there. The motel was our playground. Someone set off a fire extinguisher. We called it the CO_2 room and kept on partying. As the sun rose, we all went down to the beach. I felt a tongue in my ear. I don't think I'd even had a tongue in my mouth yet. Not with Chris. Not with Jack. Erik really went for it—really went for my ear—and it felt more surreal than sexy, like that bowler hat without a face or head. I had landed on some surreal planet where people kiss lip-to-ear. Then we kissed for real, not a pretend ironic dance floor white kids listening to "Sexual Healing" kiss, not tongue in ear, but tongues in mouths, exploring, relishing. My first french.

Erik and I slipped into the only free bed—the one in the CO_2 room—and didn't care what we were breathing in. I imagine there was a prom king and queen, but I didn't care. I knew we were.

After that, after the after-prom, after a month or so, he crawled down the sheets of my bed, and after my body soared and I moaned, he returned with some news to share. "You have a mole on your labia." I didn't know.

While his parents were away for a while in the summer, I'd sleep over at his place. But I didn't quite avoid them. "Here, my mom did laundry," he would sometimes say, a pair of underwear I hadn't been able to find now neatly folded.

He'd stay at my place, too. I rolled over in bed, put *Kind of Blue* on the stereo, and found him humming along. Not only the beat but pauses reverberating across our bodies. My bedroom was far away from the rest of my family. He rushed up to my room, tore my dress to pieces before we collapsed onto the bed. It wasn't a dress really, more a slip.

We found our way to the condom section of Stop & Shop and he joked, "I'll get studded for his pleasure."

I asked my mother to take me to get birth control.

"Did you like it?" she said while driving.

I have a mole on my labia.

....

I slide my leg between Quincy's legs. Crouch-reach. My tube dress cinches up over my thigh and across his jeans. Crouch-reach. We close the final gap, our eyes meeting, our bodies committing to the alignment. Crouch. All that effort. Reach. Peck.

A peck?

Erik and I did what we thought was unthinkable in the summer— began to date through college. I'd put the airfare on my parents' credit card and sometimes pay for Erik to come to me. But more often I'd go there, once a month at least. We'd have sex in the airport. We'd have sex in his roommate's car, which he drove to pick me up. We'd have sex in his dorm, which looked out on the baseball field, smoke a joint afterward or Erik's Parliaments, listening to the crack of a baseball or talking to his roommate, the one who had the car.

Erik sometimes went to class. And sometimes we'd go on trips, throughout the Midwest, again in that car that we nearly drove to the ground, having sex in there even as we waited for AAA. We didn't tell Erik's roommate about what was happening in his backseat. I'm still amazed he let us drive his car so much.

I'd come back to Brown like a gust of wind, a gust of stories. I'd go straight to where I knew I'd find my two closest friends, the wind tunnel room, which had perfect ventilation to smoke as much weed as we wanted while letting the air cycle out.

"You won't guess where we ended up . . ."

"And then we hitched and this guy picked us up that we simply called God . . ."

"Annie, meet Nina"—I made even the new friend in our group smile and laugh.

They were envious, they were entertained, they were stuck in the opposing forces of the wind tunnel while I rode the wind.

Another new friend came into the mix. I met him by the cafeteria cereal dispenser. He was complaining about the lack of vegan options, a word I had only just learned—a word that signaled possibly good weed. He saw me behind him and said I could go ahead. He helped me with the dispenser. I invited him to our table, me and my friends. He complained about Brown's meal plan the whole way.

Taller than me by a foot, blond hair that seemed to glow on too-white skin, a scraggle sticking out of a train conductor's hat, which from that day on I rarely saw him without.

Conductor Hat liked to talk weed, or not weed but marijuana, and not just who had it or how good it was but as a plant, like any other. He made connections to his biology classes. He carried around a well-worn copy of *Marijuana Law*. His rants had a slight Southern tinge, Nashville stuffed up by New England.

I thought of that Grateful Dead song "Casey Jones."

> *Driving that train*
> *High on cocaine*
> *Casey Jones, you better watch your speed*

He had made the storage closet in his dorm into his personal smoke-up shack.

We did it in that storage closet. He did a cigarette trick afterward, making the box choo-choo.

We did it in an elevator, him holding the stop button.

We did it everywhere except our rooms.

Pep rallies in the Midwest were the opposite of any place I'd ever think to find myself. They were the opposite of the kind of stories I'd want to bring back to Brown. They were joyful in a way that I was not. They were all-American in a way that I was not. They were a regimented formation, while I wanted to get lost and have wild highway sex.

I was to attend a pep rally at WashU with Erik and a whole crew of his friends that I hadn't yet met. I rarely hung out with any of them when I came to visit. I was okay with that.

"I have a headache," I said. I had started to get them more and more. Sex in the car, sex first thing in his dorm, and then he reached for me again and I'd turn away, my head a storm cloud. "I'll just stay in."

"You know, my friend Tim has a girlfriend, he says she has anxiety, she stays in bed sometimes and he just takes care of her. I think that's a beautiful thing."

"Just go with your friends."

He wasn't going. So I told him.

"I cheated on you."

There was silence. He told me he wanted to break up. I raged. He bawled. I blacked out. The next day I woke up.

"You threw a chair, did you know that?"

Oh, yeah. I had thrown a heavy dorm chair.

I guess I really didn't want to go to that pep rally.

....

After the vodka, after the pills, after the charcoal they pumped in me to wash it all through, I didn't feel entirely sad. And perhaps, more than I'd ever admit then, the violence of my suicide attempt filled me with a kind of pleasure. And then there was the sympathy and the love.

Conductor Hat and I met up right after I checked out of the hospital. I asked him for a cigarette. "You sure you should have that?"

"I'm okay." I just had charcoal in my throat.

After throwing a chair, after a suicide attempt, after running away only to end up in a mental hospital, after heading back to school only to land in another mental hospital, after heading home only to get my stomach pumped again from another suicide attempt, my parents and I thought maybe I should talk to someone.

I began to see a psychiatrist, a family friend who I had seen off and on during childhood.

"Go to him, but don't tell him anything," my parents said.

There was a picture of him in our house, as a young man, at my parents' wedding, part of my father's cool-boy groom's crew.

I told Uncle-Doctor I was fine. And in the space where I didn't tell him anything, he would talk about this one patient of his. One of his most outstandingly happy ones.

"She has so many boyfriends all at the same time, she says she makes them do this and this." He touched his nipples, pretending they were breasts; he rocked his head back and forth, pretending it was a mane of hair. "She says, I don't care, it makes me happy."

There was something that was making me happy—I'd get up in the middle of the night, go down into the pantry, open a cake mix box.

"She says she likes it when they suck on her lip," he said.

I'd take a spoon from the drawer and open the box.

"Suck," he said again, holding the *k* like it was the lip itself.

I'd scoop in the raw mix, untouched by egg or water. One scoop, then another.

Her sexual appetite astonished him. "Can you imagine? She's so happy."

I didn't tell my shrink about my snack.

I tried other forms of therapy.

I began to run up a phone sex line bill.

When I called, I put on a breathy voice. Once, I heard the person in the billing center laugh. I gave my credit card number and they would ask who you'd want to chat with, a man or woman. I said woman.

I tried taking classes at Rutgers, but more so I studied the goods of dingy sex stores on the way. "I'm just an ordinary guy," the white man who ran the place would say. He'd say it every time I came in.

I tried heading to New York, past midnight and waiting in a darkened waiting room in Midtown. Men waiting there in a lightless room with me. Windows taped shut. I was waved in and onto a massage table. "Undress"—her voice Eastern European and stiff. She went to the side of the room. The smack of latex gloves pulled on. In the corner, I saw a leather swing. Then above me, her gloved hand hovering. I shot up.

"Go, honey," she said.

One day, the credit card bill came, racked up with phone sex charges.

I tried to deny it.

"We didn't believe it," my mom said. My parents had sat me down. "They made us listen to the tapes."

Worst of all, I tried normal. I was ready to give it up, to follow the heaviness—my body and the sixty pounds I had gained over the year and a half I had been home, a cocktail of medication and cake mix. It was fall 2001. My friends were in their sophomore year. The country was in 9/11. I was ready to drift back into sleep. Sleep was always hard to fight off. It was a sunny day and I hated being awake on those the most.

Then I heard in the distance, beyond the walls of my bedroom, a guitar line, sped up and looped, an odd keyboard overlaying, a strange alien beat in time with the lyrics:

> Break me off
> Show me what you got
> 'Cause I don't want
> No one minute man

I heard Missy Elliot, loud, like the radiating sun. It made me get up out of my childhood bed willingly. It made me look out the window. It made me look down at the cable guy. I felt like a princess in a tower. He was blasting the song out of his truck, even if it was parked, even if he wasn't at his own home or at the club, even if he was just at work in the middle of the afternoon, he had made it a party.

Who blasts a song that loud? He clearly wanted me to know.

I saw some twinkle lights in my mother's office. It wasn't my birthday, but I wondered if this was for a surprise party for me.

I went to the basement, looked at all the junk me and my sisters had dumped there. I found the stuff that felt like a party. CDs and posters. I brought them back up to the bedroom with me. The ones that clearly announced: *We're here, trying to help you party. All you have to do is pay attention.*

At night, I'd sneak out in my Jeep Cherokee and go on drives, trying to figure out more about the party. Once, I landed at a QuickChek in Fords, New Jersey, where our first home was. I saw my friend Axel hiding by our front door. Shhh. I'll let him hide. I went to the Quick-Chek around the corner and walked around. In the newspaper section, I read the headlines—phony headlines, I saw my friend Kylie's face photoshopped in. My friend Dahlia, who lived in the wind tunnel room, loved to take pictures. How kind, I thought, I must be hot on the trail.

And then I saw him. The younger of the two QuickChek clerks. I batted my eyelashes a million times. The princess had left the tower.

"She's looking for you," the older clerk said to him.

He came around from the register. We went to my car. I drove for a while and then we parked. Memory slim as a lightpole. Folding the backseat. Popping the trunk. Cold weather seeping in. My parka on. Why was it still on? Pants wrestling. Jeans. Hard to come off. Did they come off? Memory like a puff of cold. I mostly remember what he did after, him spitting out the window, over and over again, as I drove him back to the QuickChek.

Afterward, I went to a diner. One of the diners me and Erik used to hang out at. Every table had clues. I sat at every single one. Everyone wanted to talk to me, everyone saw that I wanted to get to the party and that I was close to the party. The last thing I remember is sitting with a young boy, a white boy about my age, with a journal, who sat quietly and kept me company.

....

And then darkness. I lifted my head and I was in some sort of examination room. Police around me. I lifted my head again, minutes later it felt like, but I was in a hospital bed. Carrier Clinic.

Diksha and my parents were there with me.

"We found a condom. Did anything happen?" Diksha said.

"No," I said.

Nothing happened, only because I couldn't remember.

They checked me out of the hospital quickly; my parents knew too many people at Carrier Clinic, too many colleagues. My mother now kept the car keys locked in a drawer.

In a year, I would start at Barnard, where I was three or four years older than my classmates.

I went back to seeing Uncle-Doctor, who prescribed a new medication. This time, it took fifty pounds off.

When people asked me about the years before I transferred, I just said, "I traveled."

One day, when I couldn't bear things being so locked up, I told Diksha about visiting the prostitute.

She set me up on a date. A young Indian investment banker met me at Diksha's place, making polite conversation with me and my sisters over a cheese platter. The banker and I left for dinner, ate Brazilian meat, and said goodbye. He never called.

"He was weird . . . he didn't eat the cheese."

I kept going on dates where nothing happened. I ate Tasti D-Lite like they did on *Sex and the City* and talked about the dates with my Barnard friends like they did on *Sex and the City*. But unlike Carrie, I never sat at my laptop pondering the date afterward. The dates weren't memorable. They didn't feel good or bad. They didn't have any feeling.

One day, one of my closest friends at Barnard invited me to a talk with a feminist and sexpert she admired. We could ask her anonymous questions. She unfolded an index card, to my question.

"Are you ashamed to masturbate?"

"No," she simply said.

Scientists and anthropologists debate if kissing is an innate or learned behavior. Theories abound—before lightbulbs, people sniffed one another out to recognize family; before baby food, parents fed children from their mouths; before Salt Bae, cavemen licked each other's cheeks for salt.

Audre Lorde says, "The need for sharing deep feeling is a human need."

A 3,500-year-old Vedic text says kissing is "inhaling each other's soul."

Prince says, "I just want your extra time and your . . ."

It's just as Stevie whips out his harmonica, the song rounding the bend, it's then that I go in for the kiss, only to be met by the fence of Quincy's lips. A peck—that's all I get.

A peck is not a period, a peck is not a kiss. A peck is its own region, its own unbearable lightness.

Yes, this is Fluid and this is different from private school proms, more Black and brown people than I've seen in a long time, and no ironic sexual healing. When Stevie Wonder comes on, everyone cheers together, bodies in flow, not only in pairs or groups but all together, a shared knowing. Our peck but a comma in this dance. It's no Al and Tipper Gore mushy headline-maker, it's no tongue really going for the ear, it's no Conductor Hat choo-chooing.

I climb back up the length of him. This time, I make sure to stay, to hang on his lower lip, holding it between my lips, slow and serious and steady, releasing only with the momentum of that suck. And I can feel my heart dip right in between my legs and back up, rising with me as I look Quincy straight in the eye, my whole body right in the eye.

AFTER HOURS,
A POSTSCRIPT

Every time I think back to that night, I remember myself wearing stockings, but it was July, too hot for stockings.

"Last call!" A crowd once united by Stevie Wonder disperses. We break our dance, wander back to the bar to wait for Justine. Quincy leans his back against a stool and turns to me.

"What do we do now?"

I lean my legs into his.

After two a.m. Philly goes dry, the post-Prohibition-era state liquor law to "prohibit forever the open saloon" still in play. Bars crammed with people become ghostlands minutes later. No one hanging over its edges lunging toward the bartender, no effort of shoulders to nudge in or out or race toward a stool before someone else does: just a bone-dry, stained, about-to-be-Cloroxed counter. Soon after, the club empties entirely.

We go back to Justine's place, where the walls are paper-thin and this "artist loft" building is filled with all kinds of unartful noises—hipster rock, white kids listening to MGMT's "Time to Pretend." Justine puts a mix on over it: Total crooning to Biggie, the heat like a glaze over us.

We three are four now; Aisha has joined us. I've known her as long as I have known Justine. I met them both at a month-long writing conference in a part of upstate New York that feels more deep South, in a town where Solomon Northup was drugged to be later sold into slavery, at a conference where a white woman once came up to Justine and said, "Hello, Jamaica Kincaid." We found refuge in each other. And one of us, or maybe all three of us, found a local bar that, one night a week, played hip-hop, good '90s-, early-2000s hip-hop, where we stole away after the Big Important Book Reading and became better friends.

What luck, I think. Not because I want to see my friend but because I'm not through with Quincy and I hope he's not through with me: after hours, after the kiss, this is my one focus. This man, who as I stretch out on Justine's couch, has taken my feet in his hands. I try to steal a glance to see what Aisha thinks. She doesn't seem to notice anything. But then again Aisha is a poet, a great poet, the kind who knows how to leave out all the right things.

Quincy suggests David's, an after-hours Chinese restaurant that has good wings. "That's the spot."

I'm not hungry. I'm ravenous. Horniness might seem like a wild, incoherent thing. But I feel it sharp and piercing, nothing but concentration, the mind and body joined at a single point—the mole on my labia maybe. That's the spot.

It's decided that Quincy and I will just go to David's together: an artifice of a decision.

"It's worth the wait."

I was used to the backseat of Maxine, as Q referred to his car—*Maxine, oh, Miss Maxine*—me and grade stacks and good books. But now I'm approaching the front.

Quincy opens the door, a habit of his I'm noticing. For a moment, it's just me and Maxine, all her gunmetal gray sharpness, the automatic shift, the tape deck knobs, the steering wheel locked by the Club, heat making it hard to touch any one of these things for too long. Any contact would inevitably singe.

Q climbs into the driver's seat. The door closes.

"We really should get the food," Quincy says.

The drive itself is short, Chinatown not so far from Justine's place on Spring Garden. Quincy parks a couple blocks away: another habit I'm noticing. We make up for the short drive by staying in the car for thirty minutes. We see other people climbing in and out of cars in party dresses and night looks. We see other cars fogged up with weed or love or some mix. We see people milling in and out of shops, Chinatown active at two a.m. like no other part of Philly. But that's the outside world. Inside, Maxine is all steam, the faintest curtain of privacy, our heat pressing against Philly summer.

"We really should get the food," Quincy says.

David's is the spot, the bustle beginning even before stepping foot inside. Cars double-park with abandon out front of a simple brick building that looks just like the one next to it and the one next to that save for the decorative green ceramic tiles that fan out into an awning. There is a large neon rectangle that sits atop the door, proudly announcing David's Mai Lai Wah in both English and Chinese characters in distinct primary colors, neon that continues to burst through the three octagonal windows each meant to tantalize in its own way, neon signage that overwhelms any other light source on the block: "OPEN," "COCKTAILS," "BEST FOOD IN TOWN."

There is not much room left to move once inside. Everything feels alive and lively with drunk hunger. We can barely hear ourselves, postclub chatter wafts and mixes with the place's sugar-and-smoke smell, the steam of rice and countless orders of their famous salt-and-pepper chicken wings. The owner himself, David, approaches us. His appearance completes the fever dream that is this evening. We order too much. "Forty minutes." David shakes Quincy's hand vigorously. "Okay!" we say.

We make our way back to Maxine. Too many blocks away. Too many cars to pass. Streets getting darker with each block, but I can still spot which car is his—the one with the Club locked on to the steering wheel. I want to fasten myself upon him like that.

I hurdle the gearshift, a perfect 10 of a landing, straddled atop him. His hands are not at ten and two but on my hips. His feet not braking but slipping as we send the seat farther back as I rise and rise, my back arching against the steering wheel, grinding, the hot metal buckle making my knees jerk, my body flinch, and then everything clicks into a groove.

My thighs get slick. I go faster, but he doesn't: the rhythm more and more off between the two of us until he pulls away entirely, which is not so far away, as I'm still on top. So it's more like a very awkward distance in name.

I see him move his lips first, before he says anything, trying to talk himself through, it seems.

Fuck the food, I'm prepared to say.

"I'm fresh out of a relationship," he says, breath still steadying. "I'm a little broken."

Every time I think back to that night, I remember myself wearing stockings, but it was July, it was too hot for stockings.

At some point after Fluid, Aisha is there. I don't know why she wasn't with us at the club. It was too hot for stockings. It was too late for Aisha to join us at the club. And I don't recall her in the after-hours planning either. I don't recall her being part of the moment when, between debating plans, while Q slipped out of the car, Justine whispered: "He and his ex might be still figuring it out . . . watch out for him."

The next evening Justine, Aisha, and I decide to go to the Irish pub down the road, on the other side, closer to city hall, farther down from the gun shop and club.

Quincy joins us there. Blasting old-school R&B like only an Irish pub in Philly can, in this crowded narrow bar with a floor that slightly tilts, Quincy and I find a way to wiggle-dance.

Justine, Aisha, and I want to drink some more, drink in a state with no liquor stores open on Sunday. Quincy and I drive across Ben Franklin Bridge to Camden, New Jersey, to the first liquor store we see: a huge and harsh-white fluorescent brick block, the type of place that says you need it more than it needs you. I spy a soccer-mom-style minivan a few feet away from us with a dent, like a kid's ball went through it. I see a young Asian boy come out, a bandanna over most of his face, followed by two more teens with same-colored bandannas over their faces followed then by the van's hip-hop: loud but indiscernible, incoherent, mostly just a vibration through the dented exterior. I guess it's not that kind of minivan.

Quincy parks Maxine and before he can even take the key out, I'm leaning toward him. "How about we get the liquor first?" he says.

Inside, the space is vast and overwhelming with choices. We are charged with getting Justine's Captain Morgan and Aisha's Don Julio. Quincy suggests something, too: "Bahama Mama, my cousin likes that." Quincy is not a drinker and I know this isn't the type of mix my friends prefer, but we pick up the mixer anyway. I just want to go back to the car.

There is no forty-minute wait. I climb over him and fasten myself upon him. He doesn't pull away this time under a sputtering parking lot light, in front of this van of dented incoherent hip-hop, in the part of town that is but a strip of liquor stores screaming competitive deals to those that have crossed over from Philly, but something doesn't feel right. "We should get back," I say even as my body wants to go further. It takes all my energy to put myself back together and on the passenger side. Are there other hesitations underneath that one? And do I have my own?

I'm fresh out of a relationship.

I try not to worry.

I'm a little broken.

I try not to imagine or hope or anything too much.

How about we get the liquor first? How is Prohibition still ruining everything?

Back home, Justine is going through the free movies on cable. We all decide to watch *Vampire on Bikini Beach*—the softest of soft porn, except free, so sans sex scenes. I have my legs up on the couch and Quincy takes hold of my feet. I feel equal parts self-conscious and proud that our friends can see. The porn only makes us sleepy.

Justine gets up to go to bed. Aisha nods off on the couch and I nudge her. She smiles a "love you, girl," smile and dozes again. I nudge her once more. She gets the hint.

I flip off *Vampire on Bikini Beach*. Quincy helps me convert the couch to a bed. I get up to walk him to the door, which becomes us falling atop the bed. I climb on top of him, enjoying my new perch without a hot steering wheel singe. I ask him to spank my ass, quietly, "a guest slap," I say, as we whisper and giggle.

There, now, on Justine's pull-out couch, I grind on Quincy so hard that when I eventually pull my tampon out, it is wet not with blood. I climax with a moan into his ear. And I discover something new—that he likes a kiss there, his body giving way the more I linger there. I feel like I found my own vampire region.

I don't tell Aisha and Justine what they have missed. I don't tell them about the guest slap or about the ear. I don't tell them about *I'm fresh out of a relationship, I'm a little broken.*

Instead, Aisha tells me what I have missed: Opening the bedroom door to find Justine asleep with a book on her head. Justine's voice fighting through *The Bell Jar*: "Is Nina okay?"

Every time I think back to that night, I remember myself wearing stockings, but it was July, it was too hot for stockings.

But let's put myself in stockings. Let's find a world in which they exist. Let's make this world the kind of world where Quincy and I don't have a past. In this world there is no after. In this world we are forever in firsts—first kiss, first lover, first time.

But then Quincy still says it, there is no avoiding it. No amount of my ass up against the steering wheel. He still says it—"I'm fresh out of a relationship, I'm a little broken."

This is the truth. Unvarnished. I know my legs are bare without stockings. I know we have less than forty minutes to go. I don't know what to do with this truth yet.

ANIMAL STRIP CLUB

ookah bars seem like good places to talk. There is a pipe in the center of the table, the type of pipe that screams YES! You ARE at a hookah bar! A broad base, a soaring tower out of which the smoking pipe extends, leading up to a tin gold dome higher than the tops of our heads. It's more of a conversation starter than we—Justine, Aisha, Quincy, and me—need, already cracking each other up. It's Justine's birthday party. It's early August, when those who can flee New York City's hot garbage heat. It's Sunday at eleven p.m. in the East Village. Still the crowd is surprisingly decent at Karma.

"Karma" originated from Sanskrit before it was adopted into a variety of South Asian languages. In Sanskrit and in your local yoga class it means "action." More often, especially at yoga, we hear it as "good karma" or "bad karma," as in the idea that the right- or wrongness of present actions will have consequences on your life, come back around to you at an undetermined future date, John Lennon providing the addendum, "Instant karma's gonna get you." But here it just means a place you can smoke indoors. I don't know where going to a hookah bar called Karma late on a Sunday night falls on the spectrum of right or wrong action and I don't care. All I know is that my short nylon Urban Outfitters sheath of a dress is rising up as I cross my thighs and laugh. All I know is that Quincy is sitting next to me. All I know is that my bare thigh rests on his pant leg.

From our table we watch young white women dance and flail in a sad way.

"There should be a stripper pole that is portable," I say as I watch, "you know, for strippers on the go."

"I can see the commercial for it now," Quincy chimes in right on time, "the Portable Pole."

I never really liked dating. I'm not a wine-and-dine type of person; but this, trading jokes like jazz musicians trading eights, this I like better than almost anything else. Comedy has never left my side. And this laughter, our laughter—Justine's, Aisha's, Quincy's, and mine—it feels like the best and realest of my whole entire life.

Justine's college friend Ruby has joined us. Our party complete, the waiter comes by to fill our hookah pipe. Someone requests a fruity flavor and I immediately regret not speaking up, the smell of the fruit smoke not unlike an old lady's perfume. The waiter opens the ornate golden dome, gaudy in a way that is Trumpy, but we are not there yet. These are just the start of the Obama years, and amid fruit-flavored smoke, amid the debates and anxieties over a "postracial" America, there is still a feeling of celebration in the air—or at least the feeling we can test new waters.

Ruby finishes her first drink. "Obviously *Sex and the City* is a great show because now you can see all these young white women moving here and new white restaurants serving them. Like, when was there ever sushi in my neighborhood?"

Aisha leans back in her chair. "Do you know they haven't even paid me for my last semester?"

Justine sips her drink. "Like Basquiat says, samo, samo."

As for me and Quincy, cozied in the corner, in this Obama-era, postracial America, we draft our own new world.

FADE IN:

INT. BAR—NIGHT

> V.O.
> Tired of sexy dancing in a
> semicrowded bar on a Sunday night
> without anything to cling on to?

WHOO GIRLS fall on the ground willy-nilly.

> V.O.
> Sick of having to step on a
> sticky bar to get people's
> attention?

WHOO GIRL struggles to wipe off random gunk on her heel, stepping on someone's foot as she does, knocking over drinks.

> V.O.
> Why not try the Portable Pole?
> Made out of the same tungsten
> metal military warheads are made
> out of, these poles can take your
> sexy dance to the next level in
> no time flat.

MAN getting a dance from woman on PORTABLE POLE tries to get her attention.

> MAN
> Are you sure I'm not going to be
> charged for this?

WOMAN shrugs.

FADE OUT.

....

Ruby continues to talk about *Sex and the City*, but really she's talking about gentrification. Aisha continues to talk about adjuncting, but really about gentrification. Justine turns to me and Quincy. "What are you talking about?" she asks.

We bring her up to speed.

"The pole can hold up to four hundred pounds," Quincy explains.

"Oh, so the big girls can get on it," Justine says.

At some point, I move to sit on Quincy's lap. I remember Aisha's look as I did this, a smile and nod. It made me register what I was doing. I was not flail-dancing but making a choice. A choice to directly plant myself on this man. She seems happy for me.

I am happy, too, and maybe a little bit shocked, but not for my boldness at sitting on Quincy's lap. I realize I am the only South Asian woman in a group of Black people. I don't feel only-ness. I feel exclusive. I feel Quincy's knee on my thigh. I feel his hand reach around my hip as I settle into his lap. I feel a warmth on my neck as he chuckles.

Ruby talks about a new lover, a man she met in Italy. "He bought me shoes as a present." We analyze this gift and debate the pros and cons of Ruby possibly moving to Italy. All the conversations start to blend as they would at a family dinner. A quiet settles over us at some point. Ruby begins again, and I'm anticipating the shoes or the Italian lover or moving to Italy like her own *Sex and the City* finale, but instead it's: "Let's talk about Skip Gates."

|

On July 16, 2009, Henry Louis Gates Jr. was arrested at his Cambridge, Massachusetts, home by Sgt. James Crowley, who was responding to a 911 caller's report of a suspected breaking and entering into Gates's home.

The image of Gates trying to break into his own house feels like a joke, but the arrest is not. The image of this genealogy-tracing scholar unable to unlock his own front door feels like a joke, but the officer's approach is not.

The arrest occurred just after Gates returned home from China, where he was researching Yo-Yo Ma's ancestry for *Faces of America*. His front door was jammed and, with the help of his driver, he tried to force it open. Sometime around then a passerby placed a 911 call.

By the time Officer Crowley arrived, Gates was already in his home. When Crowley asked Gates to step outside, he did not. When Crowley asked Gates for ID, Gates produced his Harvard faculty ID card. Still, Crowley did not leave. Instead, he called the campus police.

Gates was held for four hours, charged with disorderly conduct, charges dropped four days later. But we weren't talking just about Gates. We were talking about the specter of possible violence in that moment Officer Crowley confronted Gates. We were talking about how it could have been worse given the inherent violence of the police, given their ability to act with impunity especially toward Black people, and given their long history of doing so.

Policing Black communities can be traced all the way back to slave patrols in the antebellum South, white men who used terror tactics including excessive force to capture those escaping slavery and to discourage revolt and uprising. Post-Emancipation, Southern states empowered vigilante groups to take up the work of slave patrols. The Ku Klux Klan was founded just weeks after Reconstruction. It is this history that has shaped and continued to shape policing. It is this history that met us at the start of 2009.

On January first, twenty-two-year-old Oscar Juliuss Grant III, unarmed and restrained while facedown, was shot in the back by Bay Area Rapid Transit police officer Johannes Mehserle.

It was one of the first murders via police to be captured on cell phones, by multiple witnesses, and spread without media intervention. As the video went viral, Mehserle's initial excuse—"I thought he had a gun"—turned into silence and an eventual resignation rather than a full statement.

Grant's death brought about national fury and protest, with new coalitions of people calling for greater police transparency. Black Lives Matter cofounder Alicia Garza has said, "When people tell the story of Black Lives Matter, they either start it in 2014 with Mike Brown, or they start it in [2012] with Trayvon Martin. But for us, right, for those of us who created Black Lives Matter, it really does kind of start with Oscar Grant."

But in 2009, we aren't there yet. We are not even at Mehserle's involuntary manslaughter conviction the following year, nor his eventual release from prison eleven months into his two-year sentence. We are not at the officer who restrained Grant, Anthony Pirone, who was only fired in early 2010.

We are just midway through a year that started with the death of a young Black man who, as he struggled for his life, tried to reason with the officers by saying his four-year-old daughter respected the police. A year that would soon be marked with many other law enforcement murders of unarmed Black people, people whose names we know, like

Domonick Washington, Roy Glenn Jr., Steven Eugene Washington, and Michael Patrick Jacobs Jr.—and those we don't.

But am I allowed to talk about this? What is the right or wrong action? My thoughts were a flurry of worry as if there was a right or wrong, as if speech wasn't a personal choice, as if there was some authority allocating power and designating who gets to speak. It was hard to get past these worries and fears. It was hard to see them for what they were: distractions.

And while I'm in my head, the conversation over Gates is already long underway, has been going on for some time. Now I feel off time, out of sync. Now I feel Quincy's pant leg pull away from my bare thigh, as he leans forward to participate and I recede, ever so casually, into a very unlively silence.

II

Obama's press conference on health care reform, six days after Gates's arrest, is a joke that almost tells itself. In fact, it is a joke already told. In Richard Pryor's 1977 sketch "The 40th President," Pryor plays the first Black president of the United States. Pryor could be mistaken for a time traveler with how he seems to be doing an impersonation of Obama: playing it straight, erudite and intentional in the way Obama always seems to.

Pryor's president takes questions from reporters from a mix of backgrounds. The first few, from two white men and an Indigenous Hawaiian reporter, reveal the president's command on a range of subjects from international relations to economics to the Cold War. He then takes questions from a series of Black reporters, the questions growing more personal in nature. Each time a reporter heightens the stakes, Pryor's president escalates in kind.

The sketch ends with a white reporter insulting President Pryor's mother. Pryor lunges at the white man and is carried off by his security detail as the reporters brawl among themselves.

A brawl between reporters ensues and "Hail to the Chief" plays. The studio audience laughs at the only way America could conceive of a Black president, a president who, in giving voice to frustration, loses his own, and is hauled off from the podium amid the chaos, punching at the air. But Obama isn't Pryor. Pryor's working in tandem with the comedic heightening, escalating things, laying his frustration more and more bare. Obama works to keep things on track and focused—with the singular aim of getting health care passed.

It's minute fifty-one of a fifty-five-minute conference, my brain drilled with more health care information than I ever wanted.

FADE IN:

INT. WHITE HOUSE PRESS CONFERENCE—PRIME TIME

> OBAMA
> Okay? All right. I tried to
> make that short so that Lynn
> Sweet would get her—the last
> question in.

> SWEET
> Thank you, Mr. President.
> Recently, Professor Henry Louis
> Gates, Jr. was arrested at his
> home in Cambridge. What does that
> incident say to you? And what

does it say about race relations
in America?

Obama gives a preface: "I should say at the outset that Skip Gates is a friend," and "I don't know all the facts." This might have been the most extemporaneous part of the press conference, a detour from health care. But even here Obama offers a thoughtful answer, even throwing in a joke of his own.

> OBAMA
>
> I mean, if I was trying to jigger
> into—well, I guess this is my
> house now, so it probably
> wouldn't happen. But let's say my
> old house in Chicago.
>
> [beat]
> Here I'd get shot.

He resumes his Obama smooth and thoughtful, his distinctive cool, "The police are doing what they should," and "My understanding is that Gates then shows his ID."

> OBAMA
>
> Now, I've—I don't know, not
> having been there and not seeing
> all the facts, what role race
> played in that. But I think it's
> fair to say, number one, any of
> us would be pretty angry; number
> two, that the Cambridge police
> acted stupidly in arresting
> somebody when there was already
> proof that they were in their own
> home. And number three, what I
> think we know separate and apart

```
from this incident is that there
is a long history in this country
of African Americans and Latinos
being stopped by law enforcement
disproportionately. That's just a
fact.
```

FADE OUT.

And that's what happened, Sweet gets her eleventh-hour question answered, the whole Gates matter gets buttoned up, and everyone goes back to talking health care.

I'm kidding.

OBAMA: CAMBRIDGE POLICE ACTED "STUPIDLY"
—Politico

OBAMA: POLICE WHO ARRESTED PROFESSOR "ACTED STUPIDLY"
—CNN

OBAMA: POLICE ACTED "STUPIDLY" ARRESTING BLACK SCHOLAR
—Reuters

TOP COP: OFFICERS "PAINED" BY OBAMA REMARK
—NBC News

OBAMA CRITICIZES ARREST OF HARVARD PROFESSOR
—The New York Times

All the headlines only hours later. Obama writes in his 2020 memoir, *A Promised Land*, "You would have thought I donned a dashiki and cussed out the police myself." You would have thought he was Pryor, punching at the air, hauled off kicking and screaming.

Obama continues in *A Promised Land*, "The Gates affair caused a huge drop in my support among white voters, bigger than would come from any single event during the eight years of my presidency. It was support that I'd never completely get back."

There are things I could mention. Things that come to mind as the conversation continues. I think of Gates's *African American Lives*, one of PBS's most watched programs. As he traced the ancestral lines of Black celebrities from Oprah Winfrey to Ben Carson, he brought a public conversation on enslavement to the televised stage and tapped into a national fascination with genealogy in the process. Soon his programs and specials featured non-Black celebrities, many of them white people shocked at their family trees (slave owners) and their "karmic" inheritances (slavery). I then think about how I'd be a poor candidate for these shows with how little familial recordkeeping we have—I don't even know my mother's real birth date. I think about how so many of my South Asian friends know that their parents' "birthday" is likely an arbitrarily picked day—"because our parents weren't born in hospitals," my friend once said. I think about other faulty records, gaps in time and information—the ways we do and do not talk about Partition in my family or what they really experienced in their first years here. I think about the way when I told my father I was thinking about taking Hindi in college, he said, "How about

German?" I think about what it means to talk about race and identity, after a lifetime of rarely talking about it; what it means to be a living erasure of memory both public and private, willful and not; what it means to forget oneself if only to remember and reproduce the myths of superiority as encoded in caste.

What is caste? It's race but it's not. It's class but it's not. It's a silence.

Nine years from now, Equality Labs will release their survey "Caste in the United States," in which they define caste as "a system of religiously codified exclusion that was established in Hindu scripture," one in which people are "ranked hierarchically according to ritual status, purity, and occupation" and one that, most crucially, is both "inherited" at birth and "unalterable" through life. While not limited to India or Hinduism, caste emerges from Hinduism and divides society into four groups of people, highest to lowest caste, with its accompanying jobs, privileges, and powers or lack thereof. Those of the lowest-ranking castes and those outside caste structures, Dalits, are marginalized and brutalized, robbed of social, economic, and political rights, and suffer discrimination and violence from those of upper castes. Karma is used to justify caste segregation, making caste not only a familial but a spiritual birthright. Don't like the caste you're in? Tough. Take it up with your past life.

Eleven years from now, in her book *Caste: The Origins of Our Discontents*, Isabel Wilkerson will describe caste as the "wordless usher" guiding our lives in the U.S. Finding a through line between Nazi Germany, India, and the "shape-shifting, unspoken, race-based caste pyramid in the United States," she writes, "Race does the heavy lifting for a caste system that demands a means of human division. If we have been trained to see humans in the language of race, then caste is the underlying grammar that we encode as children, as when learning our mother tongues."

"Right or wrong" then is neither a spiritual nor a moral code. It's not humility that's got my tongue. Karma is artifice. Karma's gonna get you.

Caste is my inheritance. It is with me now at Karma Bar, my silence hovering ever-present like hookah smoke.

But this is not sexy—this pit in my stomach part existential despair, part old-lady's-perfume-fruity smoke. Instead of talking, I take more puffs, slow and steady, as if my own silence (hookah smoke—more carcinogenic than we give it credit for) isn't killing me, as if it doesn't matter that Quincy's leg is against mine, as if it doesn't matter that I can feel his leg quake when he laughs as people crack wise and dig into the absurdities of the arrest, as if I am not dying for the chance to make his whole body quake against mine.

And yet, as they talk, I don't want to just make jokes about Gates's arrest, I don't want to make zingers just to get Quincy going. What I really want to do is what they are doing, bonding, which is what's always underneath a joke anyway.

|||

Weeks before our Karma hang, the weekend just after Quincy and I met, I went down to Philly. I had some formal reason for visiting—a reading or event Quincy and Justine were doing together—but it was a cover story for wanting to see this guy again.

At Justine's, she talked about her heartache, a run-in with an old lover, someone neither Quincy nor I liked anyway. Quincy quipped, "You should go to a strip club."

He didn't seem like the strip club type or at least not the one who would start the plan; it seemed more like sarcasm, exaggeration, a sharp critique of how much or little we cared about this ex-lover.

"Yea!" Perhaps to his sarcasm I was trying to genuinely hash out a plan, another reason to come down to Philly for a third consecutive weekend.

"We could all go to the strip club!"

Justine wasn't into it. "Animal strip club," she said, her own method of using the absurd to deflect.

But my mind couldn't let go. A strip club for and by animals. Animals who I guess in this universe were at some point clothed and so needed a place to get unclothed and return to the wild. Animals who instead of being in a menagerie for others, made one unto themselves.

Finally, a polar bear club for polar bears.

I must have said that part out loud.

"No fish in the polar bear room." Quincy cupped his hands together, making an overhead announcer voice.

"Bats turn left to exit," he continued.

I felt heat rising across my cheeks.

Quincy and Justine went back and forth constructing this world: a Disney movie after dark. I was quiet. A silence weighed down even as I expelled a belly laugh. I told myself I didn't know what to add, as if I hadn't kicked things off in the first place. I told myself, Say anything, do anything. That's when I knew I was falling for this guy. A joke caught in my throat.

I began to extend my arms out straight, clapping my hands together, rushing before I could fully form the words: "Giraffe." I kept clapping. "On the pole." What a weirdo.

But they laughed. And I laughed. It felt good, this laughter, this bonding.

....

. . . You are no better than a white person talking right now, so don't you dare.

I let the old-lady's-perfume-fruity smoke stop up my mouth. *Don't say the wrong thing to a group of Black people. Don't say the wrong thing to Quincy.*

Even deeper, past this inner monologue wafting in my head, I know what I really want: I want to get past the smoke and mirrors of "right" or "wrong." I want to ask myself deeper questions about what I have to say. I want to talk about my identity, my own relationship to Blackness. I want to talk about looks-based hierarchies in my family: I might have inherited the "wrong" skin color, "dark" like my dad, but I had the "right," "Roman" nose (as my sisters called it), with casteist notions of preserving purity of race. I want this conversation mixed in with our running bits and gags. I want Quincy to take note of what I say. I want Quincy to belly laugh at what I joke. I want Quincy.

"It is a dangerous question to ask what does a minority want," Anne Cheng writes in *The Melancholy of Race*. "When it comes to political critique, it seems as if desire itself may be what the minority has been enjoined to forget."

We leave Karma to grab pizza. I feel better out here on the city street. Less like there are eyes on me, waiting to see me get talking about race right or wrong. The Dalit reformer and political leader and author of India's constitution B. R. Ambedkar once said, "If Hindus migrate to other regions on earth, Caste would become a world problem." We leave Karma but we remain in this world.

The New York City night is my friend, as full of neon want as I am.

So much to take in, even as Sunday party energy starts to blend into workweek. I'm taking it in and then it hits me, rising out of me unplanned, from the part that does not care about right or wrong.

"Other poles take five to seven minutes to set up . . ."

Quincy's face lights up into a smile and a big laugh. I feel relieved, I feel pleasured, I feel all the want rushing back, right through my thin sheath.

A few weeks later, Quincy and I have a proper wine-and-dine. I go down to Philly. He picks me up from Justine's and takes me to a local café, Naked Chocolate, a hip spot that centers on hot chocolate rather than coffee and is open late, crowded in the evenings with loyal customers who simply call it "Naked." Except this Naked is closed. So we go to its second location. This one is more like an outpost, near the museum and other touristy spots. It feels strange to be in here, but I'm not sure why. We put in our order and we sit down. A quiet settles over us. I don't know what to say, I feel like I am groping for a joke out of thin air. I don't like that feeling.

"Look at them, looking at us," Quincy begins.

I'm not sure what to say, is this the start of a joke?

"We are the only people of color in here and they know and we know it," he says.

Except I don't know it—or I do but I don't register it the same way he does. All of a sudden I feel embarrassed about that. I don't feel right or wrong anymore. I just feel something like a gong going off within me. And I try to speak, ignoring the alarm feeling.

"This is good hot chocolate," I say.

THIN LOVE

Love is or it ain't. Thin love ain't love at all.

—TONI MORRISON

The early days, that thin lusty sliver of time—it's always bigger on the inside. Even as you accumulate years, they have an outsized presence. So much is on the line. So much is or ain't. Mid-August 2009, a month and change since we met, Quincy and I went on our first movie date. He loves sci-fi and chose a movie that seemed like it could appeal to even someone like me who isn't big into the genre: *District 9*, set in South Africa and billed as a sci-fi movie with social awareness. A white male director thinking through apartheid, filmed on location in a town where forced relocations are still occurring. It would at least be a conversation starter.

But I didn't want to talk. I just wanted to do all the rom-com movie theater things. I leaned my head on his blazer shoulder as the aliens were abused by the white men in power and the Black gangsters who made up the second tier of the power structure. I squeezed his hand cutely as the aliens rose up with the help of a white guy who was turned into an alien. I grazed his pants with my fingers as the movie further devolved from social consciousness to unconscionable violence. And when the Black Nigerian gangster was the first person killed, when the whole, all-white, packed Upper West Side theater cheered his death, I am embarrassed to say, I still tried for something.

As we walked out of the theater, I tried to impress Quincy with my enthusiasm for sci-fi. I was ready to be the life of the party of this conversation. "It was great!"

"Really? I mean, until that part where everyone clapped for the death of the Black man?"

Oh, yeah, that. "That was awful," I said, but more out of embarrassment. How come I didn't register that? Why was I so busy trying to play with his balls?

"Ice cream?" I said. We stopped at a gelato place and he asked for Ferrero Rocker. I wanted to correct him and say Ferrero Roch-ay, but I stopped myself. Now, for some reason, I wanted to cry. *Don't cry in front of him.* I just heard it. Somewhere deep inside of me.

"Want to walk all the way back home?" I said.

He agreed and we came up with a game. I called it "long walk facts."

We traded flirty facts about ourselves while passing by the sights of the Upper West Side. The area was in the midst of change—old mom-and-pop shops wedged out by new gelato places and chain stores I was surprised to see outside a Jersey mall. Quincy fit in more with the remaining mom-and-pops. His manner was undeniably old-school: he rushed past me to open a door; he sidestepped around me so he was between me and the street, I assumed to protect me from the Sharks and Jets; he put his blazer on me when I rubbed my arms in a slight breeze. His teaching bag, a classic brown leather messenger bag, was still hitched on his shoulder as we walked home from the movie, even though he could have left it at my place. It was stuffed with the oldest of old-school writing implements—his trusty No. 2

pencils and marbled notebooks. Writing seemed to be an itch he always needed to scratch, rounding out his sexy disheveled professor vibe. I could have asked him about it—his love of writing, why those marbled notebooks, why the pencils, why was he my age but so old.

Instead I asked, "Who was your first hard-on?"

"Nina," he said, without missing a beat.

We kept talking. I barely registered about what. My mind was preoccupied with a question I had been asking myself, wrestling with for some time: should I have a cigarette?

I felt like having a cigarette. I did and I didn't feel like it. I fumbled with the pack. I decided, *I'll make a choice when we pass the church on Seventy-Ninth.*

"Excuse me!"

I turned around. A Black man in jeans and no shirt or shoes waved at us from the other side of the street. "You happen to have an extra cigarette?"

Quincy was trying to do his gentlemanly walk-the-street-side thing.

"Here, take a bunch, take the pack." I passed the pack across Quincy.

"What? Oh, no." He seemed genuinely put off by my generosity.

"No, seriously, please." I thought this was where we would part ways, but he kept walking and talking.

"Well, I have to give you something in return. What's your name, sir?"

"Quincy," Quincy said, still holding street-side.

"Quinny," the man began, just as we passed by the church.

"It's Quincy," Quincy said.

"Quinny, take your wife-to-be's hand . . ."

"Now, hold on a minute," Quincy said. Now I thought someone should walk street-side to protect Quincy.

Before we could react, the man put Quincy's hand in mine. "Quinny, do you love her?"

I had always thought smoking was part of my allure. I felt it as early as my teens. My first boyfriend mockingly called me a "Marlboro Lights girl" like I was some blonde who wore headbands and drank Miller Lite. I felt it in my twenties, sharing cigarettes outside of bars like I was another carefree college kid. I felt it now, a month after *District 9*, as Quincy lifted a purple lighter to my ready lips. "I bought it just for you, so I could light your cigarettes."

The thing is, I was quitting.

Or trying to.

I didn't tell him this. Not yet.

It was a perfect night. Quincy and I were finally getting a moment alone. It was early September. I had just moved to the East Village and my place was a bit of a party pad. Complete with a deck for smoking.

Justine had returned to smoking recently. One night, I followed a series of extension cords to the deck, sliding open the door to Justine's makeshift office—she had a lamp and her laptop, on which she typed out what would become an award-winning story between puffs of American Spirits. Another night, after a birthday party for Aisha turned into a four-day hang, I came back from work, slid open the deck door to hear Michael Jackson whispering "keep it in the closet" into the open air, glowing ends of Aisha's and Justine's cigarettes like summer fireflies illuminating our swath of East Village night.

Now, with the cupcakes stale from the party, with unopened champagne warming on counters, it was just me and Quincy here on the terrace. And now, with the purple lighter in front of me, pulling myself close to Quincy's face, a flame between us, I reckoned with what I could not bring myself to confront in the party atmosphere— my hesitations over smoking.

I had tried so many things—inhalers, gums, and patches—nothing worked. Inhalers felt like prop cigarettes, the gums weren't very chewy, and I ended up liking the smell of the patches themselves. Sometimes I'd just toss fresh packs into the trash. Paying for cigarettes had become more and more expensive since high school and it felt like $10 down the drain every time.

I tried hypnosis, twice. The first time, I sat in a French woman's holistic practice, the whole office space soft and white as a cloud, a tiny gong in the corner. She put me in a recliner chair and led me through guided meditation, the tiny gong going off from time to time, until I felt lulled into a nice nap, after which I wanted a cigarette.

The next time, I went to the office of a white man whose framed hypnotherapy diploma hung alongside framed photographs of him and '90s-era celebrities. Even though it was only him, a receptionist took me from the brown leather couch in the waiting room to the black leather couch in the hypnotherapy room, where I was told to watch a screen during which messages about smoking cropped up through squiggly lines. Afterward, the man kept talking about "cod liver oil," which sounded not unlike snake oil the way he said it. He followed up the next day, a phone call. I was in a noisy bar bathroom and said I'm not sure if it worked or wasn't sure if I wanted to come back. He yelled at me. I picked up a cigarette.

I had gone back to therapy at this point, to an Upper East Side psychiatrist with a pretty ground-floor office in a gorgeous and well-kept prewar building, just steps away from Central Park. The psychiatrist was a woman with short black hair and a penchant for blazers and pensive gazing who reminded me of Dr. Melfi, Tony's shrink on *The Sopranos.*

I often spent sessions saying some version of "I'm doing really well" or "I'm feeling really good" on repeat. I'd tell her stories of bad dates and memorable nights out and about in New York City. We were together for forty-five minutes, why not entertain?

"Your life is like a *Sex and the City* episode," the therapist said one day.

"You know, you remind me of the doctor from *The Sopranos,*" I said.

"I get that a lot," she said, looking tired and annoyed.

No one wants to be typecast.

One day, I told her my smoking was starting to bother me. By that point, I was on a cocktail of medication and the sheen of "I'm doing really well" had started to wear off. I started to squeak out new things—"can't sleep," "angry," "can't stop thinking"—and medicines were added accordingly, medicines to quiet the mind. When I complained about my smoking, she suggested this new drug, Chantix.

Chantix was released on the market in 2006 for smoking cessation; by November 2007, the FDA was conducting a safety review of the drug after reports of its users experiencing "suicidal thoughts and aggressive and erratic behavior." By February 2008, the FDA issued a public health advisory stating, "As FDA's review of the data has progressed it has become increasingly likely that the severe changes in mood and behavior may be related to Chantix," including that "Chantix may cause worsening of a current psychiatric illness even if it is currently under control and may cause an old psychiatric illness to reoccur."*

"I hear good things," my Dr. Melfi said.

In March 2007, on a cocktail of Chantix and other medications, my brain felt both hazy and speedy, self-criticism whipping around a foggy racetrack. The only way I could pull the thoughts over was to check myself into a mental hospital. My fourth.

I wasn't aware of the growing concern over Chantix, but I'm not sure it was really the culprit. Alongside smoking, I was partaking in another habit-forming activity. Like many in their twenties, I kept a journal, my own private *Carrie Diaries*, but my journal had started to become a place of critique. I'd come home every night to burn myself. "You shouldn't have smiled then, you should have laughed there." After a while, it felt like an addiction, I couldn't wait to write in it. Then one day the thoughts turned violent, sharp, and incessant as physical pain and I knew nowhere else to go when I felt like that except to the hospital—the kind for those not-quite-physical pains.

"Stop writing in that journal," the counselor said on my last day of a one-week stay.

All to say, Chantix got me to successfully quit journaling.

Instead, I stuffed my inner world into grad school academic papers, and in 2009, in my last year of grad school, the last year of my twenties, the third year of a two-year program, I finally took advantage of the rich resources of academia: I got a physical. On the way out of health services, I saw a set of freebies—stress balls, lubes, condoms. I

....

*By 2009, the FDA placed a boxed warning on Chantix's label, and while in 2016 the warning was removed, the FDA noted the risks were still present, but were "lower than previously suspected."

just went for the plain business card next to them: "Neil Moretti, smoking cessation counselor." "Cessation"—a different word than quitting, a bit more clinical, a bit more elegant. Its root is French and luxurious—"to delay, to be idle." I idled in front of that card. "How much does this cost?" I asked the front desk person. "It's free."

Neil and I sat across from his plain wooden desk in an office the same as any other in that place. A white man, ruffled hair and harried-university-worker look not unlike Q's. Wire glasses, eyes that crinkled in the corners as if they had just held a laugh or a good cry, and a sincere, kind smile. "So, tell me about yourself." I told him how I went back to undergrad late in life, going to Barnard after leaving Brown. He told me how he came to public health after a career change, music. When was the cessation program going to start, I wondered. But I didn't mind talking to him, at least not as much as I usually minded talking about myself and what felt like a checkered, shameful history. I didn't tell him about the Chantix or the mental hospital that followed, but it didn't seem like I was holding it back. At no point did I try to assure him that I was doing well. At no point did he compare my life to *Sex and the City*.

On-screen, cigarettes tell stories about women. They speak of a woman's strength, her power, her transgression, and they speak of her vulnerability, her status as an outlier. They're part of Carrie Bradshaw's character and her story.

"I'm having an affair with Big." She riffles through her bag.

"And also, I'm also smoking again"—she waves up her box of cigarettes—she is a Marlboro Lights girl.

"I'm smoking and I'm sleeping with Big. Feel free to delete me out of your Palm Pilot," she confesses to her most judgmental friend, Miranda.

"Give me one," Miranda says.

"Really?"

"I think I need it."

"Oh, you are such a good friend."

Of course the heroines we see with cigarettes most often are white women, just like Carrie and her avatars, just like all the "Marlboro Lights girls" I knew growing up.

And yet, in all my efforts to assimilate to whiteness, smoking felt like the least white girl part of me. My father was a smoker. I felt more like him each time I smoked. Smoking felt like part of his zest for life, or as my mother would put it, his "all he cares about is drinking and friends" mentality. He quit actual cigarettes when I was young but technically didn't leave tobacco. He'd come home and have paan. His heeled dress shoes clacking against the tile, humming a ghazal and clearing his throat at the same time, it seemed, he'd stop at the paan station on the kitchen counter, kissing me sometimes on the forehead, still humming, still chewing, still spice and smoke and whiskey. It's that smell, at the end of a night of revelry, that always stuck with me, the party lingering there.

Neil laid out a plan in just the last moments of the session—give yourself a set amount and really enjoy them. The imperative to enjoy. It sounds corny to say that I was exploring quitting smoking as my life turned a happy corner. That feels in lineage with all those white women's resilience rom-com stories—*Sex and the City* or some *Bridget Jones* way of quitting or, worse, the white woman finding herself in *Eat, Pray, Love*—you are loved, you go to exotic India, so you will stop putting your body through this thing that unloved single white women do. But my quitting, or attempt to at least, felt different from these single white female heteronormative morality plays.

Long before I quit, when I finally returned to school at Barnard, I always passed by this man just outside the Urban Outfitters I liked to go to on Seventy-Second Street. He'd say the same thing to me every time: "Can I have a cigarette . . . please . . . please!!!" He was a white man, nervous and wiry. He'd come out at the same time, at the same spot, whenever I crossed through that area. It scared me every time because it was the exact same thing, no change in tone, no different greeting. I started to think he wasn't real.

There was a plexiglass cage in one of the mental hospitals that I had to step into if I wanted to smoke. A button not unlike a car lighter was built into the wall, I guess because we weren't trusted with regular lighters. To smoke, I had to step in the cage, I had to press that button, wait, and then hold my cigarette, perched in my lips, up to its faint glow. Sometimes I had no cigarette but found someone's stub there and lit that. The cage was in the dayroom so everyone saw the whole ritual play out, like they were watching a caged beast.

Smoking had more moments like these than sexy ones. Moments where smoking was not escaping into *Sex and the City* glamour and transgression but where I sincerely questioned my own grip on reality: Did I see that man? Am I a beast?

Quincy, in the flame of the purple lighter, in the dark of the terrace, wearing a full suit in the summer heat, didn't seem real. We were the best kind of old-school film noir, me and him in some *Casablanca* except with more Black and brown people than just the piano player.

"I bought it just for you, so I could light your cigarettes." Seriously, is this guy for real? I never had a relationship like this before. Such gallantry. Such romancing. Such pain: lighters held up too long can start to burn your thumb where the metal hits skin. So I leaned in, breasts first. Sexy on the outside, mentally tallying for my next session with Neil on the inside. I took a puff, breathing in slowly, breathing out just as slow, making sure a sultry trail of smoke went upwind and not in his face.

Quincy tucked the lighter back into his suit jacket, where I knew it would stay until our next *Casablanca* moment. The tug of wanting to flirt over a flame pulled against my desire to quit. *Maybe he'll misplace the lighter.* But he never was without that jacket. His suit jacket wasn't an act of costuming, some put-upon old-school affectation, at least not in the way it was sometimes interpreted to be.

My first week in the East Village, Quincy and I went to a faux surf shack run by a white man. It was too hot for Q's suit jacket, but he had it on as usual. "Love your jacket," the guy said to Quincy after he took our order. It struck me as an odd compliment because this wasn't some find at the vintage shop down the block. It was the blazer he taught in, the blazer he hoped he wouldn't get pulled over in as he drove to the train station to come up to see me, the blazer he pulled a lighter out of. And I wondered what else white people missed about him or me or us.

A few weeks later, I met an old childhood friend for drinks in the neighborhood, a white woman who taught me that the cool (white) girls proudly chain-smoked Parliaments rather than sneaking Marlboro Lights.

At the bar counter, I caught her up on my weekends with Quincy. She caught me up on her new guy.

"Look at us, both dating Black men, but they're so light, do they count?" she said.

"What?" I said in a way I never spoke to my badass chain-smoking friend.

"Nothing! Let's have a smoke."

....

Back in Neil's office, I was prepared to talk about my progress. I was prepared to give him my "everything is great" or "I'm doing okay." But instead we talked about feelings. What it felt like to have the cigarettes. Which cigs did I enjoy, were there ones that I didn't? Did I want to raise the cap or lower it?

I thought about Quincy's lighter. I thought about the feelings it elicited in me. Mixed feelings. I thought about Neil's imperative to enjoy. I thought about my chain-smoking friend's comment.

"I'm ready to go lower." I was.

We moved on. There was a push to ban smoking on campus. Neil told me he was against it. I wondered why. Wouldn't a smoking cessation counselor want that? But I feigned understanding.

I nodded along, making more small talk until it was almost time to go, and then I blurted it out—"There's just this one thing, though. Quincy bought a lighter and I'm not sure how to tell him I don't need it. It's really nice. It's purple. Like the movie *Purple Rain*—"

In an uncharacteristic moment, he cut me off. "Uh-uh, tell him to get rid of it."

Outside, I tried to imagine what a campuswide ban might look like. I tried to imagine what dating without cigarettes looks like. I found that both were hard for me to see.

On our first New York date, I had invited Quincy over to make gazpacho, but when he came over, he saw only a mud mask in the fridge, one pot and pan in the pantry, and pretty much nothing else. He took the lead, shopping for the ingredients, chopping with a butter knife, stirring with a fork.

I hadn't seen him this way before. I'd seen him steering Maxine, blowing a kiss from his fingers, and tapping the roof of the car as he made a light. I'd seen him cracking wise on the couch, adding to one of our now-recurring comedic bits. I'd seen him in his element in these contexts but not here, not now. Now his professor shirtsleeves were rolled up as he diced and cut and strained, the tomatoes yielding slowly, not to the butter knife but to his entire person, the entire blade of him, his long, angular body, the narrow of his eyes, the razor of thought, of wit, of flirt, of charm held behind them, until they completely gave way and then I gave way, his hand slipping inside of me as I pressed up against the fridge where the gazpacho should have been cooling, then lifting me up on the counter. His rolled-up shirtsleeve went higher as his hand went deep inside of me, until my body gripped just as hard, back arching, legs once wrapped around his hips now dangling, and then we kept going, long after I orgasmed. I was someplace beyond wet and did not want him to stop, I did not want us to stop relishing in this thing we had made. I was on the counter so long the flies found the gazpacho before we did. We let them have at it.

"Pizza?" I said.

Soon, there was no more mud mask in the fridge. It was replaced with leftover seafood and pasta. Now we ate his "stoplight shrimp" and watched *Lost*. He told me stories through food, about his great-grandparents who ran a seafood restaurant. About how he cooked one night a week growing up. We fell into rhythms, our rituals, our idleness, our ease. Leaning into flames, into shared plates and over countertops, into new corners of the East Village streets I was exploring.

We called our dating "short-long distance." Quincy would come up from Philly on a Friday. He'd drop his bag, I'd tear off my clothes, not waiting for him to do the same, we'd make a mess of his one of only two teaching suits, after which he'd realize he'd done a two-hour commute at the end of his five-class adjunct teaching week and promptly fall asleep, sometimes still in that blazer of his. I'd watch TV. We'd wake up, have more sex, and then I'd say I'm hungry. "Yeah you are," he'd gotten in the habit of saying, satisfied by his handiwork.

I introduced Quincy to foods he hadn't tried before. How had he never had sushi?

Neither of us had been to Katz's Deli, the home of the famed orgasm sandwich, so we went one evening. The picture was on the wall—the famous scene from *When Harry Met Sally* where Meg Ryan's Sally, single white unlucky-in-love archetype à la Sarah Jessica Parker's Carrie, revealed how easy it was to fake an orgasm. The scene brilliantly parallels what always is happening with the food in the movie, Sally's particular way of eating. She takes apart her sandwich, perhaps something sacrosanct at a place like Katz's, putting it back together just in the way she likes. She just as easily dismantles Harry's fantasy of pleasing all his women. Heaving herself, throwing back her hair, wild and curly like Carrie's, like mine, moaning into her deli meat. "I'll have what she's having" is the iconic line of the woman seated next to her. The sandwiches were even taller than I thought, turkey breast going up to my breasts. We ate, went home, and a few hours later: "I'm hungry."

"Yeah you are."

We had a few favorite places—there was the spot with the good Southern food and banana cream pie around the corner, another down the block with the mediocre Cuban sandwich but friendly owner. I introduced Quincy to chai. Not homemade chai, not even the chai places the Indian taxis lined up around on Houston, but white American coffee shop chai. This was the reverse of *Eat, Pray, Love*, a South Asian woman finding herself in the exotic cafés of the increasingly gentrified East Village.

I liked Quincy knowing this me. Not a Marlboro Lights girl, not a party girl, not a clever paper-writing intellectual haloed in smoke rings. I liked him knowing this version of me, all hunger and want and going for it.

I didn't think about cigarettes, or not as much. I thought about the things I wanted to talk to Quincy about. I thought about the way food seemed to be talking to me, talking to us, building a shared story, bridging the gaps, the silences between our individual ones.

Sometime in mid-September, I told Quincy about seeing Neil. "He's against the movement to ban smoking on campus." I said it with authority even though I still didn't quite get it. "I've been tapering off my cigarettes." I said it with pride even though I didn't quite believe it yet. "I would rather you not offer that lighter up anymore." I said it with apology, not for rejecting the lighter but for asking for his support.

Quincy just shrugged. "I can light candles with it."

M. F. K. Fisher once said of cravings, "Gastronomy serves as a kind of surrogate, to ease our longings." Food and sex and however else Quincy and I were filling up on each other certainly was making quitting easier than it had been in the past. I don't think it ever was a cigarette I was longing for.

Longing, that tug of memory, our own personal noir nostalgia, the reason why Katz's had a day where people could reenact the orgasm scene—the best orgasm won a free sandwich. The reason why one would put their hand in the trash to fish out a pack. The reason why even the gazpacho with the flies buzzing around it still creates a hungry feeling in me. The reason why "yeah you are." Longing doesn't need to make sense, it needs to live in the senses. And in this way it is not exactly remembering, it's a slippage of memory, letting the mind idle, be easy. Maybe Neil knew that it would be hard to place a ban on longings.

....

I can't point to one moment when I quit, when I was completely ces-sated, when idle became stop. As close as I can get is the biggest party I had that year—not in my East Village party pad, though. In the midst of all that was going on—the falling in love, the moving, the quitting, the overdue finishing of grad school—I was planning the first all–Asian American literary festival in NYC, the Asian American Writers' Work-shop's Page Turner.

The planning stages occurred during the thick of fall semester. There were days I just stopped going to class. My Asian American film studies professor was not impressed. "Nice to see you again!" I had not done the reading because I was booking the authors or, worse, following up on tote bag orders, raffle prizes, all the parts of a literary festival that are less than literary.

I picked out my attire for the first day of the festival. I got a beauti-ful white top that fit more snugly than when I had purchased it earlier in the year. I was a bit embarrassed to put so much effort into my clothes; shouldn't all that effort have gone into the gift bags? But then, as I stepped in, I saw revered writer Alexander Chee, one of the first to arrive, stop and scan my outfit, giving a thumbs-up and an approv-ing nod as he did. Then there was no idling. It seemed like I was on a perpetual swivel. To stand still meant to be spun around by a question or request, one of my trusty team of interns, who in a 2.5-person staff played a more critical part in the organization than their unpaid status might imply. "Nina, the projector isn't working." "Nina, there is some mix-up with the tickets." "Nina, Jhumpa Lahiri just arrived."

At one point during the festival, the projector still broken, I was stressed out and said so to the intern sweating over the projector with me. "Here," he said, pulling out a cigarette. This was mid-November.

I had been two months smoke-free. "No, thanks," I said. Not "I quit"—"I quit" felt like a declaration, but "no, thanks" felt different, like smoking had idled its way out of me.

Months later, after I had well and truly stopped smoking, it wasn't being without cigarettes but being without my bipolar meds that laid me out with withdrawal. At the time, Aisha and my childhood friend Axel became roommates. Aisha's place had been robbed and Axel had rolled in from California, one or the other or the both of them crashing in my East Village pad while I went out of town to visit Quincy. A weekend became a few weeks and an unlikely friendship burgeoned between the two of them: macho Jersey boy and queer working-class poet—as she called herself. How they got along was astonishing to me and yet it made sense. They loved the same music, they loved the same mischief; they loved and that's enough for friendship. I'd open the door to the air-conditioning on full blast, music blasting, no one in the apartment, the two of them out on the terrace with a joint, cracking each other up. At the time, he was dating a burlesque performer who lived in the Village and who literally had a portable pole in her apartment, but he passed on staying with her, enjoying his new roomie. At one point, I mentioned to Aisha that he was the high school bad-boy heartthrob. "I can tell, and you know, if he ever wanted to try 'the Cadillac of women,' tell him to come take a ride," she said. She was queer. He was straight. But it made sense.

I was meant to love this little party, this peak East Village eclecticism. But instead, I would leave the two of them to my place and retreat to the quiet, very uncool nondescript apartment in the suburban outskirts of Philly where Quincy lived. One weekend I realized I had forgotten my pills. The few times I was without one of them, the antipsychotic, I had bad reactions—diarrhea and insomnia. We were getting close, but I didn't want Quincy to see me like that. There was no noir or rom-com equivalent to that kind of longing.

In bed that evening, restless, I wanted to cry. *Don't cry in front of him.* I heard it. Again. Somewhere deep inside of me. But this time I couldn't obey. Tears streamed where I had laid my head on his bare chest. "What's wrong?" I had to tell him. My head still resting on his chest, he told me to count and breathe.

"In. One, two, three, four."

I realized it wasn't cigarettes but the pills that I was scared I'd never be free of. "Out. One, two, three, four."

It had been three years since the Chantix hospitalization. I had been mental hospital–free for the longest stretch since I was eighteen.

Lying with my head on his chest, I felt my breath steady against his heartbeat. This wasn't holding a door, walking street-side, or putting his blazer over my cold shoulders. This wasn't a gentlemanly act. Just two bodies.

DON'T EVEN
TELL HIM

When I was twelve, I got struck by the thought that reality wasn't real, that either I was dead or, worse, never born. When needed, I could push the thought to the side to act normal. I forced it to the back of my mind to do things like go to school, hang out with my best friend, Priya, see *Wayne's World* with our gaggle of girlfriends. But as soon as I was alone—which was more often now that my sisters had gone to college; now that my parents had moved on up, to a bigger and more spacious house in which their doctor's office was no longer attached—the thought came back. *This is all a lie.*

Two years before, I had seen a B horror movie during a slumber party with my cousins, *The Devil's Gift.* I came home scared and convinced that the movie was real. A doctor colleague told my parents to watch the movie with me to help me understand it was fiction. I sat on the couch sandwiched between my father and my sister Diksha, and my embarrassment was enough to break me out of the fears over the movie.

But this situation, at the edge of my teen years, was different.

There was no movie. There was simply a thought, a thought that reality wasn't real, that I was dead and stuck in a phantasm of life, a thought that seemed to overwhelm me in large spans of time.

A horror movie is the opposite of a lie. Sometimes they are rooted in myth, sometimes real-life events. Most pry at our psyche, letting the "anti-civilization emotions," as Stephen King calls them, out to play for a while. The best horror movies feel familiar. I've never had dinner with Leatherface, but that tormented dinner table scene in *The Texas Chainsaw Massacre* feels so real. I don't feel scared, I feel seen. Showing us *Rosemary's Baby* for a grad school class, the professor shrugged her shoulders and said, "That was New York in the sixties and seventies." And when *Get Out* came out, Justine simply said, "This is supposed to be a horror movie? I thought it was a comedy."

It wasn't just my waning belief in reality but the feeling that I was living a double life, donning a mask of an ordinary American twelve-year-old tween—that was what truly scared me. I began to cut school, but not in any *Wayne's World* cool white boy way. My mom would drive me to the psychiatrist. I'd skip last period gym to go, sitting on the steps waiting for her, hearing the sounds of the coach's whistle not far off, an alternate reality. Once, my mother was late and gym class was over by the time she got there. "You could have just stayed," the gym teacher said.

I was prescribed Prozac, which at the time was a fairly new drug on the market—released in January 1988, it was just six years old. I remember the pill crushed into ice cream. I hated that taste, the little bit of medical grime coming into something that could be so sweet. The ice cream holding its own deceit. I would remain on some pill and some form of therapy from that point on.

Throughout, I did my schoolwork. A year or so earlier, in fourth or fifth grade, my parents took me aside after a parent-teacher conference.

They held out the offending test—the letter B up there. If this was a horror movie, the test would be the MacGuffin: the insignificant thing that sets off a chain of events. "Work harder," my parents said: less scolding, more a statement of fact. I'm sure with two older daughters who got good grades without much prompting, this wasn't what they expected. But they didn't ever punish me for it, no real speech, no penalty, just "work harder," with more surprise in their voices than anything else, a bit of fear, their own B horror story.

"Work harder" worked but maybe not in the way my parents expected. It was the only thing that pulled me away from reality not being real—"work harder" to outrun whatever was getting in the way of being the high-achieving student they wanted me to be—that I wanted to be.

The term "model minority" would not penetrate my reality until decades later. In grad school, I would find W. E. B. Du Bois's *Souls of Black Folk* and his opening line: "How does it feel to be a problem?" At the Asian American Writers' Workshop (AAWW), through a coworker, I would find Vijay Prashad's *Karma of Brown Folk* and his addition: "How does it feel to be a solution?" I would find "model minority," and on cable, flipping channels, I would find *Evil Dead 2*. That scene when everything in the house, from the lampshade to the moose head, starts to laugh, starts to scream, made more sense than one might think. Living as a minority in America is living in a house laughing at you and living as a model minority is joining in that laughter.

But back then, the language of racial and ethnic identity came to me only in shared jokes: my South Asian friends and I impersonating the "work harder" voices inside our home or the "why are all Indian people so good at math and science" voices coming from outside. When a white boy asked me this, I shrugged. I knew that science degrees, in some part, were a means to an end—my parents used their MDs to immigrate to the U.S. But I also knew, in the way he asked, that he was not looking for an explanation, that he was not looking for someone to pierce the neat narratives of his reality.

I myself was contemplating stepping off the science track (if I was ever on it). My two older sisters had taken AP bio as juniors. I felt an expectation to do the same. I saw a life laid out before me: AP bio, a six- to eight-year dual BA/MD program, a life of science and math.

Just as I started high school, a young South Asian boy in a rival private school got expelled for trying to steal a standardized test. He broke a window with a bare hand. They found his dried blood on the safe where the test was kept. "I think he wanted to get caught," my tennis teacher, Pattie, would say to me. Pattie, a trim white woman who looked like Chris Evert, had a tennis court in the back of her house, and her driveway was often lined with the luxury sedans and SUVs of well-to-do suburban parents. We'd make small talk as we collected balls. I hadn't thought of this concept before—"wanting to get caught." Word had gotten around about the boy, but Pattie, not my parents, was the only one to say this truth most plainly. South Asian kids don't cry for help. Who is going to answer those cries?

I nodded politely, said nothing. I went back to hitting balls, inside imagining the hand through the window, the bloodstained safe. She brought it up several times, and after a while I wondered if she was using him to make a point about me, like the way she'd say, "I was thinking about your backhand this morning."

A few years later, at the end of the school day, I pack my things and start to make my way out, walking along the high school's narrow, windowless corridor with lockers on one side, classrooms on the other. With the overhead fluorescents off, the lack of light makes the space feel a bit smaller. It's just me and the bio teacher whose class is right by the stairwell exit, right by the Garbage Pail Kids locker—the last locker in the hall, with a ton of Garbage Pail Kids stickers smacked on its inside, the collage of bug-eyed, grotesque baby heads an image I cannot unsee. Even when the door is shut they seem to be peering. The bio teacher corners me right there. "You are forever cursed for not taking my class." He cranes over me with all of his very tall and wide body, his ever-reddening face. "God will smite you."

I stand there, my body frozen, everything except my smile. I want to turn to him. In what reality does a teacher say this to a student? I want to say, scream, right into his reddening face. Instead I smile. I smile because I have lost all other faculties. The lights have gone out in me and my smile is the trip switch. I smile until he walks away, until I can pass the rest of the bug-eyed baby heads and rush out of the building.

I'd really only feel comfortable, feel my mind drop the thought loop entirely, when I was with my best friend, Priya. When I was taken out of first grade on the teacher's advisement that I needed to repeat kindergarten, my mother found the only other Indian name in the class directory of our private school and circled it. Our parents became each other's only Indian friends. In any other context, our families likely would not have gravitated to each other. Priya's family was upper class in India where my parents were not. They talked with lofty accents that my parents once mocked while driving away from their house. And yet, in the wilds of white suburban America we clung on to each other for dear life. It was her house where I practically lived, where I'd feel most comfortable, maybe even more so than in my own house. I'd eat more family dinners there than at home. Her father, a gentle man who didn't even try to outmacho my father, always sat next to me, giving me doting attention and even praising my high achieving—"Priya, get some study tips from Nina." There I could table the terror of whether I was alive or not. Perhaps I felt duty bound to snap out of it and be with Priya. Perhaps I, too, knew our finding each other was a rare thing.

Priya and I joined forces, and as we entered the hormones of tween life, we'd argue, with her brother sometimes getting involved and taunting me. That's when reality started feeling unreal again: he had started to call me Norman Bates.

I knew the reference, the guy who dressed as his mother in *Psycho*. I loved Hitchcock and as a girl I would curl up in bed and watch *The Alfred Hitchcock Hour* on Nick at Nite with my father, guessing the plots before the denouement. And *Psycho* was one of the rare movies my mom saw in the theater, not realizing it was a horror movie until she was frightened to death. "I didn't realize it was scary," she'd begin, the opening line of her tale "The Weird Rare London Outing," told in a tone that would make Hitchcock himself feel guilty.

"Norman Bates with the butter knife," Priya's brother would snicker to friends. They were playing in one room, one slumber party over, and Priya and I were playing in another. Norman Bates—I wonder why he said it and why add a butter knife? Why swap a butcher knife for butter? I imagine that he thought I was creepy, quiet and creepy, which in this phase of my life—when I wanted to work hard and stop being scared about reality—I probably was. Maybe I wore my state of mind the way Norman wore his mother's clothes. I'd pretend I didn't get it, that I didn't watch *The Alfred Hitchcock Hour*, that maybe, much like my mother, I wasn't aware of what I was walking into.

In the horror movie, this is where our Final Girl checks for vampire bite marks or cuts or bruises she hadn't seen before or didn't remember; she wonders if she has been turned or if she herself is the one doing the turning. She scratches at an itch that ends up being more than that. She peels off a layer of skin, unwrapping a mad scientist's experiment gone wrong. She realizes she is the monster, yet still hopes against hope that it isn't true.

It was at Priya's house that I decided to drop it, drop this feeling that had its hold over me, this mask of normalcy. I distinctly remember the moment I made the choice. I called home and my sister Aria answered. I asked for someone to pick me up. She asked me how I was doing; she must have had some vague idea that I wasn't doing well. I told her I realized everything was real and not.

"It's all an illusion," I said.

"You're so brilliant," she said, hanging up.

I wasn't sure if she was dissing me or being sincere. I wasn't sure if she was really listening to me at all. Who knew that the B in "B horror movie" could stand for "brilliance"? I claimed to everyone that I was back to normal. But I was not normal, I was Norman.

Of course I knew I was not Norman Bates, I was not the great Anthony Perkins. But when normal did come my way, I was often afraid. "The doctor suggested we watch it together," my father had said as Diksha slipped the VHS of *The Devil's Gift* into the player. I realized Diksha, my frequent Blockbuster Video companion, must have rented this movie, this movie that had frightened me, this movie that I still believed to be true, this movie that is described thus on IMDb: "An evil demon that inhabits a monkey doll takes over the mind of a suburban housewife to carry out its plans."

We shifted uncomfortably, squeezed together on a tight love seat outside my bedroom, my dad expelling a brief laugh as the first sequences of the movie began, sequences that I can't even recall now. Watching the movie not at a cousin-filled slumber party but in broad daylight, with my father and sister flanking me, no less, I was filled with a different kind of terror. My father had talked to a doctor about me? My sister had taken the initiative to drive to a video store, rent the video? Please make it stop.

"We can take it out now," I think I said; I don't think we made it past the opening. Off they went back into their lives, and on I went with mine, happy to be relieved of this frightening family formation.

This is where the movie fast-forwards to act 2, our hero now an adult: professional, independent, and most of all normal. I had started grad school where not a soul knew of my mental hospital stays. I found community—AAWW—where, as luck would have it, a friend asked if I'd take over her full-time position as the director of events and calendar programming. I even committed to consistent mental health care, seeing a psychiatrist who was a family friend. I'd go to Uncle-Doctor's office in northern Jersey every week and then visit my parents' house, where my mom would make me not one but two turkey sandwiches. "Beta, they are small." All to say, I had found a life, a life I could believe in. This reality felt real to me.

I did very normal things like internet dating. For my profile picture, I chose a sultry shot with a downward glance. I just had to crop out that I was holding my newborn niece—a sliver of a bald baby head still remained at the bottom of the frame. Diksha helped me write my Match.com profile so it sounded less like the quirky vignette I had originally written and more generically flirty and fun. Bingo. I began to get dates, each normal boy like the others, a forgettable blur of first dates at bars, dates where the disinterest was mutual—one guy even falling asleep at the table. But I persisted in my pursuit of normalcy and went on a few dates with a boy who ticked off all the normal boxes my Punjabi Hindu mother could want: South Asian, check; lawyer, check; non-Muslim, check. Without meeting him, my mother began to call him "my handsome boyfriend," as if she was dating him and not me. My mother's approval making me go on a few more dates than I wanted to, no love pang, my heart blunt as a butter knife for him.

There were picturesque New York walks, there were fancy dinner dates, there were invites up to his place that I accepted and returned in kind.

But something isn't right. Something creaks in the normal night. Do you hear that? He doesn't. Something flickers in the corner. Do you see that? He doesn't.

I unplugged all the normal lights for a moment. "I have bipolar disorder."

I had long wanted to break up with him. Telling him did the trick. He said he had his suspicions for a while. The bright orange pill bottles on my dresser. "They were in plain view," he said almost litigiously. I will never forget the legalese of the phrase, my daily medication regimen framed not merely like an aberration but like a crime. And that's when I realized, we weren't ever dating. I was on trial.

Just as he is about to give his verdict, just as he is about to turn angrily to our Final Girl, search and seize her vulnerability, he's grabbed through the window and pulled into the netherworlds. The monster is real.

I was so scared to tell my family what had happened. I had worked hard for this normal. And yet now, if they wanted to know why my mom's handsome boyfriend and I broke up, I felt I would have to talk about bipolar disorder. I knew they would blame me for telling him. If

I only didn't tell him, I would have had a chance for normal. I decided to break the news first to my mother.

"What's wrong?" she said when she heard my sniffling hello. I heard kids in the background. They were all at my sister's white husband's white family's house in Connecticut.

"We broke up. He didn't want to be with someone who had bipolar disorder." I offered it up without asking.

"He's an idjiot," my mom said then. That added *j* always felt like an extra jab.

"Kirah—big bug—look." I heard her turn away distractedly from the phone, the shouting of "bug" not to alert me but to thrill, to delight my nieces and nephews. The spider in the WASP country house becoming their own horror comedy show.

Our Final Girl tries to move on like the rest of the family has, tries to see it their way, not hers. Our Final Girl tries to shrug off the lingering feeling. It's all over now. I told them I told him about my bipolar disorder and now it's all out there, as ordinary as sharing your astrological sign or some other dating fact. But why doesn't it feel that way?

In truth, there were a few more idjiots before I met Quincy. But for drama's sake (or theatrical run-time), let's introduce him earlier. Let's introduce him as a foil to lawyer boy. He is smart but not in a way that is superior. He wears suits but more in a rumpled, professor-rushing-to-class way than dry-clean-only associate attorney. Quincy is easy on the eyes and easy to talk to and makes me want to be open and easy.

One day, a month into our short-long distance, he came into my apartment, still catching his breath. This was not unfamiliar: on the days he was running late, it seemed like he would run from Penn Station clear to my apartment to try to make up for the lost time.

He opened up his messenger bag, a multiverse more than a bag, it often felt like, always overstuffed with student papers and teaching texts, his own writing, and tea bags for the spaces in between all these activities. But it was not any one of these usual things he was drawing out. A small plastic box—a cassette. I still had a tape player. I took it out of his hands—on the spine of the cassette I saw the words hand-written: "Nina Simone live."

"Did you make this?"

"Professor Shelly," Quincy said—this was his habit, to refer to people in his world as if we both knew them—"he gave it to me."

I imagined two kinds of people in his workplace—the white men who didn't give a shit about all the contributions Quincy was making to the university and just wanted to profit off them, and the white men who really saw him but didn't have much power beyond that. I imagined, or at least hoped, this Professor Shelly was in the latter category.

I popped the tape in. We joined hands, the August heat on his suit blazer. I nuzzled closer as Nina began to sing. It was a song I had never heard before. I cried. I was not sure why I was crying.

"I'm sorry I was late."

"No, it's not that, August is a tough time for me." I didn't mention the anniversary of my first hospitalization, how every August I wait for an ordinary hot summer day to show its true face to me, the summer breeze lifting a curtain and turning it into a hospital gown.

And yet, as we grew closer, I found myself getting more discreet. Waiting until he was asleep, then pulling the bright orange pill container out of a cabinet or a drawer. I wasn't ashamed. I didn't see taking meds like a crime. It was just out of plain view.

There were things I had been leaving out anyway. That after a weekend of our short-long-distance dating, I'd cry over spats with my family. They had disapproved of Quincy. This is the part of the horror movie where normal becomes too normal. There is no "he's my handsome boyfriend"; instead, it's their anti-Blackness keeping them from asking too many questions, from teasing or encouraging. They make it clear that they don't like this man who is not Indian. They do not like this Black man who I like very much.

And so, I talked to them less than usual. Took the train straight to therapy instead of stopping at home. No double turkey sandwich. I resigned myself to a peaceful non-coexistence with my family. But despite all my avoidance tactics, one day, maybe a year into dating Quincy, I had to speak to them. My parents were the only ones who could answer the question lying heavy on my mind. A question I could not push out of plain view. Should I tell Quincy about my bipolar disorder?

"Have you yet?" my father asked.

"No," I said. "Not yet."

"Good, don't tell Quincy, good girl."

Wait, what? If they didn't like him, why were they trying to protect him? I tempted fate.

"Even if we get married," I said, "how could I hide going to New Jersey for therapy every week from Quincy then?"

"So? Just say you are visiting us!" my mother chimed in on the speakerphone.

"Every week? At the same time? For exactly fifty minutes?"

"Don't tell him, beta. Don't even tell him."

Don't Even Tell Him! I see the movie poster: brown family, shifting eyes, two turkey sandwiches off to the side, everyone, including the turkey sandwiches, hoping that no one utters a goddamn word. Perhaps it is a bit like *A Quiet Place*. Perhaps it is a bit like Ripley hiding from the alien. Perhaps it is like saying "Candyman" five times. What happens next? To me, the rub is in that "even" in "don't even tell him"—it was not simply "you don't have to tell him everything, everyone has their secrets," but rather an imperative to steal away this whole entire part of my life, ages twelve through thirty.

This is the part of the movie where we realize the norms are in on it, the rescuers are actually the danger, the tannis root in *Rosemary's Baby*, the car keys in *Get Out*, the Last Chance Gas Station in *Texas Chainsaw*, the parents in cahoots with mental health stigma.

The final girl becomes Final Girl only when she is no longer naïve, when she realizes that reality as she once knew it was never real, that everything was a lie. It is a hard-won lesson. It will cost her everything to stay alive, and will she ever really be able to live in the midst of this horror movie? It's like Laurie Strode in the last *Halloween*, her house rigged and at the ready for Michael Myers (not the *Wayne's World* star). Strode made it through several Halloweens, made it from teen to seniority, but existing in this state of booby-trapped survival is not the same as living. It's not enough.

"Don't even tell him." I so desperately wanted to obey my parents' command. We were finally on the same page about Quincy. I so desperately wanted this moment to endure, to outlive, to survive. But I found obedience hard. I would have to "work hard" at it in a way I hadn't in a long time. I realized, in the time I took apart from them, almost a year, I had grown so much closer to Quincy than I was to them.

I was getting ready to read at a literary series, a short piece called "August." I left the side of a fellow reader. "Excuse me, I need to check in with him." I went to Quincy, I told him I was worried, stage fright, I debated picking something else to read, I debated backing out entirely. "You got this. Just breathe." When I practiced at home he didn't comment on the content, instead he noticed my voice straining. I wished for more of a critique but instead he just asked me to read with a hand on my belly. "You got this," he said now, hyped and peppy in a way I was sure he was with his performance poetry students before their big show. I went back to the fellow reader.

"Sorry, where were we?"

"That's really nice—what you have with him."

It was the first time someone else noticed our growing intimacy.

Quincy and I did things like watch VH1 Soul while completing our work. I was writing my master's thesis and he was prepping for teaching one of his five classes.

"You are the only one who can watch Destiny's Child videos while writing about *Invisible Man*."

He was reading a novel for his cotaught class Women and Men— *The Gate to Women's Country*. I would make fun of its cover, which made the book look more like the softest of soft-core erotica for the ladies' tennis club set than a novel about nuclear annihilation.

"You are the only one who can read a white woman's beach read while watching KRS-One."

We spent an entire year like this, his couch or mine, until I finished my thesis and he got through grading finals.

I couldn't imagine hiding my diagnosis, this part of my life, from Quincy, and at the same time, I had grown more comfortable leaving parts of my life out of plain view from my family.

"Don't even tell him" came from a place where I no longer lived—a place where, as a family, as a tribe, we kept each other's secrets, for we knew this was the best way to survive.

But why would we need to hold this secret? Why was my bipolar disorder so threatening? Was it as criminal as that lawyer boy made it out to be?

In "Why We Crave Horror Movies," Stephen King writes: "I think that we are all mentally ill; those of us outside the asylums only hide it a little better—and maybe not all that much better, after all . . . When we pay our four or five bucks and seat ourselves at tenth-row center in a theater showing a horror movie, we are daring the nightmare."

South Asian people do not have time to dare a nightmare. Maybe that's why my mother was surprised at Norman Bates, that *Psycho* was more horrific than she imagined it to be. It's not that she was scared. It's not that the boy who stole the exam wanted to pass the test. It's not that I wanted reality to be a lie.

The integration of South Asians into this country has always been predicated on believing a lie already—the lie of the model minority. The lie that if Asian Americans play by a certain set of rules, you can become white—or, more accurately, next-to-white. In that lie, there is no daylight viewing; Asian America is stuck in its darkened theater indefinitely. And in that theater, what do Asian Americans really see? That the monster is not mental health, but its stigma; the monster is not the act of revealing ourselves fully, but the fear of doing so. Asian Americans weigh what doing so would cost us: in white supremacy mental health is a privilege. White people can attend to their mental health, sure, but not us, not the next-to-white.

"Don't even tell him." I felt spun back into a nightmare that I thought I had escaped. How could I have been so naïve? Now it was the time to be the Final Girl, now it was the time to run for my life. But I just wanted to lie on top of Quincy. He came over the next weekend and as usual, like our short-long-distance clockwork, I jumped on top of him, peeling clothes off as I did. He lay down on the bed and I was still on top of him, where I remained until my legs gave out from under me. "Don't even tell him," I heard as we got our clothes on, a shiver and I turned away, my back to him as I was dressing.

"What is it?" He looked up at me.

But it was not me. It was the monster. I could feel the scales shiver across my skin as I opened my mouth. I could feel the room darken and fall away, exposing it for the underworld it really was. I could feel a swell in my breast, my heart racing through its own nightmare alley.

"I have this thing, I've had it for a long time . . ." Before I could finish I felt the stiff wrinkle of his blazer, his long arms reaching over to give me a hug halfway through my sentence.

But when I told my family how Quincy took it, my mom started on a new track: "You should be lucky that you scored someone like Quincy with your bipolar disorder and all." A bonus scene. A parting jump scare. A teased sequel. A lie.

JERSEY JAHRU

n Quincy's apartment, old student papers and handout photocopies were stacked in dust-caked banker's boxes against walls. Their multitude of bad student writing could not be contained. More papers and yellow legal pads with a list of grades or lines for poems or a little bit of both peppered the floor and tables. There was a plunger in the kitchen for the broken sink pipe, there was a plunger in the tub for the broken tub pipe. The paint all over was peeling, sometimes in large swaths that curled over and hung on. I wasn't sure for how long.

We spent most of the time on his bed.

Here, as he wrote or graded, I was watching the movie *Country Strong*, where Gwyneth Paltrow plays a tormented country singer. I provided color commentary. "I think she really thinks she's a country musician."

"Why don't you change the channel?" Quincy said.

I saw he had missed the point entirely.

"I'm hate-watching," I said. "I like doing that."

He got the hang of it and joined in. We made fun of White Country

Strong. We committed to a life in arts and letters that has room for broken pipes and peeling paint.

One day, I saw it while surfing the channels, a movie I'd first seen in a film class a few months before: Mira Nair's *Mississippi Masala*. My classmates were gone now and, free of grad student intellectual trappings, I took in a scene from the movie anew. The scene features two hotties, one Black and one brown, in their respective bedroom islands, the camera cutting back and forth between their bedrooms, spaces away from their messy, complicated lives, stealing a moment of sexy talk on the phone. It is an intimate, handcrafted, and Hollywood huge scene. I really wished we could hate it.

Eight months earlier, if I'd told the lovestruck girl—the girl who worried every date that she had said the wrong thing; who when the boy finally gave her his number with the flourish, "Number? I'll give you numbers," and wrote it down on a yellow sticky note, she snatched it with all her strength; the girl who analyzed his texts with her Asian American Writers' Workshop interns—that they had made it this far, to the sacred temple of her hate-watching, that she and him became an us, she would have been surprised and then relieved and then would have found something else to worry over. For this relationship came with layers of worry that I peeled away as promptly as clothing once Quincy entered the room. Then I was a woman without worries, a woman to whom he would say, "If I was a painter, I'd paint you."

In those early months, Quincy never seemed worried. He seemed curious. Did that curiosity mean he was into me? I was not sure, I was never sure, and so I worried, even as sudden summer lust settled into a steady fall short-long-distance flow. One weekend, he had to leave sooner than usual, early Sunday morning rather than late Sunday night or sometimes hustling out early Monday, driving right up to the first of his five adjunct classes.

It was his grandmother's birthday. The family was having a party in her honor. He had to head down to Philly to join them. I was barely awake as I climbed out of bed. I stretched my arms around his neck, pulling him into a sleepy, dreamy kiss. I could feel him linger there longer, his new Vans, the ones his students had noticed amid his well-worn teaching clothes and complimented him on, still stuck on the floor. "Don't forget to sign it," I said to him. I had asked him to sign my copy of his book, *The T-Bone Series.* Then I promptly fell back asleep. I woke up later in the day, opened the inscription. "Dear Nina, I don't want to go yet."

This was not a text message I'd analyze over kimbap with the AAWW interns. This felt personal. This felt like he had opened up something new to me, something more, those thoughts and feelings that occurred beyond our weekend trysts. What happened in those hours I didn't really know. I knew he taught for a living, I knew he created a warm and friendly-enough space that his students could comment on his Vans, I knew he went to family parties with my sex still all over him. I wondered if his family sensed a change. I wondered if there was a change.

A few weeks later, I was down in Philly. I asked him to drive me around.

"Take me to your favorite spot in Philly," I said.

He drove and I imagined the Rocky Steps or the boathouses, but instead he rolled up to a residential area.

"This, this is my favorite."

The sign over the house read "Yarborough & Rocke Funeral Home." It was his family's third-generation business, one of the oldest Black-owned funeral homes in Philly.

He clutched my hand. I took a sharp breath. I don't want to go yet.

It was exciting. It was not just our bodies. We were opening up to each other in new ways. Or at least he was.

I didn't tell him that I would go home on the way back from Philly to NYC. I likewise didn't tell my family where I had been. Instead, I would hide away in my mom's ashram-like bedroom, masturbating, thinking of all the things I wanted to do with Quincy next.

I felt like we had seen each other in new ways. I was not one to feel confident easily, but this felt close; I began to feel confident in this thing we were growing, relaxing into it.

In this relaxed state, I came home another weekend, another pit stop between Philly and NYC. We were sitting on the front steps, my sister Diksha and I watching the kids whiz around on Razor scooters catching the last of the sun. There was sex all over me, in my un-washed crotch, in my hair that held the memories of his bed. I was wearing nothing special, an Old Navy dress two sizes too large that I never got to returning. My earrings were a simple wire and stone pair that Justine got me from Ghana, that my mother with her penchant for gold everything thought was unfortunate.

"You look beautiful," Diksha said. And because I didn't yet know how to keep secrets from my family and because I felt like she had seen straight into my news, I decided to tell her.

"I met someone, I've been seeing him for a few weeks now, and he's Black." I made it the last in the list of three, tossing it in like a star sign (he's a Pisces) or a vocation (he writes poetry). But I didn't mention any of those parts of him, didn't even share his name, that basic dignity.

"What?" Diksha said.

My other sister, Aria, came out, could not have had better timing. Diksha whipped around without even asking.

"Nina's dating someone, and he's Black."

"What?" *What is up with these whats?* "Does Mom know?"

The whir of Razor scooters. I heard one of the youngest say, "Heeeey, wait for me!," the desperation in his eye matching mine. I was motionless. I don't remember getting up. I just remember still being there, being still, frozen maybe, when my mom marched out. This time the "what?" gained more articulation: "A Black man? What will my relatives think?"

Many months later, Quincy and I were trying to hate-watch *Mississippi Masala*. Then and now, I regarded it not as the first film to pose the question "A Black man? What will my relatives think?" but as the first one to do it in a South Asian context. Plenty of films have taken on interracial dating in America, but mostly in a Black-white relationship. And that might have been the fate of *Mississippi Masala* if Mira Nair had caved to the pressures from potential backers who were uninterested in her movie if it didn't have a white lead. What was a love story featuring a South Asian woman lead? Who was a South Asian person in the 1990s media landscape other than someone in the televised theater of the Gulf War? What was a Black man in an American love story if not a costar to a story of whiteness? Were there any other histories of interracial love in this country? No one was buying it, literally.

....

Nair got her funding after casting Ben Kingsley to play the Indian father. But when Kingsley pulled out, reluctant to play an Indian character after *Gandhi*, she was back to square one. As the actor who went on to take Kingsley's part, Roshan Seth, put it, "The Americans wanted to know who the American star was going to be if they were going to put money in it." Enter Denzel Washington, who said no before he said yes.

For Washington, "A Black man? What will my relatives think" wasn't enough for a movie on its own. Seth continues, "He wanted to know what else his character did in the film, other than fall for an Indian woman, and Mira said, 'Well that's about the size of it,' and he said, 'That's not enough.'"

For the character of Mina, Nair cast Sarita Choudhury, in what would be her film debut. Choudhury auditioned thinking if she didn't get the part she might at least be a PA for the film. Nair chose Choudhury after noticing she was someone who didn't care about appearances, what people would think: "For me, vanity is the biggest blow to performance. And she just was not interested."

The movie is equal parts love story and diaspora story. The film opens in 1972 as Uganda's nationalist dictator Idi Amin calls for the expulsion of the country's entire Asian population. Mina, Choudhury's character (portrayed as a child by Sahira Nair), is first seen spying on her distraught father, then asking innocently why her family must flee their beautiful pastoral Ugandan home. Mina's family becomes part of the wave of South Asian immigrants to the U.S. that are less model minority and more blue collar. From their idyllic home, they join their relatives who manage a run-down motel in Mississippi. There we see Mina grown up. No more neat braids and a bird-of-paradise perched on her shoulder. She is a scraggly-curly-haired adult-child in her early twenties. Mina's mother, Kinnu, runs a liquor store. Mina's father, Jay, writes letters all day asking Uganda for his rightful citizenship. Mina helps out at the motel, cleaning and working the front desk, but beyond doing her part to keep the motel going, she seems to hold her relatives in no more than a distant familiarity.

Because of the role they played in bringing family members to the U.S., my parents hold a kind of privileged position in the family. My cousins call my father "Big Daddy." It is a term of respect in the face of the unpayable debt of immigration, the debt we the children of immigrants could only collect interest on by having endless hours of white American fun. Those are my memories of Jersey as a kid. My cousins and I would play until sunset on the neighborhood block. Sharada Auntie would scream at us to come in as darkness hit, yet we would still spin the ropes of double Dutch, the wheels of our bikes and roller skates until it was nearly pitch-black. Sharada Auntie would give a second yell, and knowing that this time she meant it, we would rush in, gulp down glasses of strawberry Quik, night cool meeting our sun-baked brown skin. So many summers passed like this. But in those memories, I never remember the word "relatives." I remember Big Daddy. I remember Bua and Masi. I remember what my cousins called me (Nina Baby). I remember the one Barbie we all fought over ("India Barbie"), I remember Papa, my uncle's name for me. I remember that, in my family, Auntie would go after the woman's name but Uncle came before the man's name: Sharada Auntie, Uncle Dev. Those are the old familiars that I still can call up as easily as the pink sugar of strawberry Quik. "Relatives" seems foreign, hostile, like there are other words underneath that word.

"What will my relatives think?"

"Yeah, Nina. What will Mom's relatives think?" said Aria.

What will my relatives think? What will Mom's relatives think? The question marks were a farce. These were declarations. My mother and my sister declaring how they felt about me dating a Black man.

And so I gave my best nonanswer to their nonquestion.

"I'm leaving."

It was fierce and definite, and undercut by the realization that the train station was several miles away. "Can I get a ride?" I asked. I pondered stealing a Razor scooter.

My mother took me to the train station. She stopped the car and turned to me. "Please stay."

From where we were idling in the car pick-up-and-drop-off area, I saw the train platform—a long flight of stairs that led to a stretch of grime and concrete and rail looking desolate and hollow at this off-peak Sunday time.

"Please stay." The house was warm, full of laughing children and soft spaces for them to take their hard falls.

"Please stay, for your sisters . . ." The sisters that sold me out? The sisters that made me realize there was something to sell out?

"Please stay. You love him, right?" I could hear the platform shake as an Acela flew past, the whoosh accentuating its emptiness, a shuddering hollow. My words flew out just as quick.

"Yes," I said. "Yes, I do."

"That's good," my mother said to my avowal of love at the Metropark train station.

It was not a heartwarming moment. It felt as violent as that stupid too-fast Acela. I did not know if I loved him. Yet it didn't feel like lying. And as soon as I realized that, as soon as I knew I could possibly say those words to Quincy, I felt something I hadn't felt since I began dating Quincy—regret.

Not long after that conversation with my mother, we watched *Mississippi Masala* in my film seminar. It was one of the few classes I didn't miss while planning the Asian American Writers' Workshop's annual literary festival. We watched the scene where Demetrius and Mina talk on the phone in their respective bedrooms, Demetrius in tight shirt and skimpy shorts, Mina's crotch barely covered by a bedsheet. Their "what are you wearing" moment gets disrupted by a hotel ruckus that Mina must attend to. "What do you make of this scene?" the teacher asked. "Where does it fall on the spectrum of objectification?" I remember this moment clearly. I remember not having anything to say, a shrug of indifference coming from deep within. I wasn't invested in the objectification of their Black and brown bodies because I didn't quite feel protective of these characters. I wasn't pulled into the love story at all. I wasn't buying it. Where was the *When Harry Met Sally*-style meet-cute? It all felt so rushed. There was a car crash, Mina's car hitting Demetrius's, and later they run into each other at a nightclub, shortly after which they have their first kiss. Where was the enemies-to-lovers plot? The resistance? Where was the orgasm sandwich of it all? I hoped not to feel this way, I wanted to believe in their romance, I wanted to get caught up in *Mississippi Masala* the way I could with *When Harry Met Sally*. But I didn't say this to anyone. Instead of sharing my vulnerability, I framed my qualms as an issue of time: "It's so dated, right?" I said to a South Asian film school friend.

"There is still nothing like it," she said. "It's revolutionary."

My friend's comment irked me and I did my best to avoid thinking about it as I wrote my paper, "Mobilizing the Motion Picture: The Treatment of the Model Minority Myth in Asian American Cinema." Not thinking worked. My paper got an A in spite of my poor attendance record.

But when I watch the movie now, I see more. Not only does *Mississippi Masala* show the often underrepresented blue-collar Asian America, no one in Mina's family seems interested in the performance of integrating into white America. Mina's father, Jay, is obsessed with moving back to Uganda, writing letter after letter to get his citizenship back. A book called *The Concept of Human Rights in Africa* lies well-worn on his motel desk. And then there's Mina's mother, Kinnu, who, even as she hopes to marry Mina off to a suitable boy, seems to enjoy her life outside the motel their relatives run, seeming more herself making small talk with Skillet at the liquor store than with anyone else. As for Mina, she doesn't care about being a model anything. Jay says, "You are too intelligent to waste your life cleaning bathrooms," to which she replies simply, "Look, Pa, there is nothing wrong with cleaning bathrooms."

And for all my intellectual rigor I didn't mention the premise of the entire movie: interracial love. The word "love" appears in the paper only twice and only in relation to love and longing for home country. Never in relation to Mina's family's anti-Blackness, never in the way they took Mina's relationship as a threat to their upward mobility, and never in the way Mina's father, Jay, despite missing his Ugandan brother Okelo, despite his political consciousness, imprisoned in Uganda for speaking out against Idi Amin, could not overcome that question: What will my relatives think?

I didn't know then that exiting my mother's car, going up those steps at Metropark, that empty platform, the Acela flying past like a scissor through my heart, was a choice. It was not as big of a choice as that of Mina's father, fighting for his Ugandan citizenship to be reinstated rather than sorting out a life in the U.S. It was not even a choice in the way Mina later called her parents at the end of the movie to say she was not going back to Uganda with them. I was just angry and wanted to go back to my apartment where I could put on some pajamas and watch something comforting like *When Harry Met Sally* on E! And yet, even as my choice was neither as huge as Mina's family's immigration nor my parents' own, it was a choice of movement that would go on to impact so much other movement.

I started to go to Philly without any pit stops. I always thought of leaving my high-flying New York life and going home as something that grounded me, but the last visit revealed that "What will my relatives think?" was the shitty, insecure floorboard underneath the plush wall-to-wall carpeting.

On the way down to Philly, every time I passed the Metropark station I felt like I was doing something bad, like I was cheating on my family. I almost wanted to slink down as we passed signs for Little India, a pit in my stomach at all those familiar markers. It all flew past me now. I had made my choice. But if it was my choice, why did I feel so powerless?

Without the Jersey pit stop, the change from New York City to Quincy's place on the outskirts of Philly was even more dramatic. He lived right across the Philadelphia county line in a so-called "Main Line" suburb, the main part being the huge mansions that took up half blocks and looked like antebellum haunted houses. On the side streets were far smaller but stately starter homes and on corners, tucked away as best they could be between trees, were boxy apartment complexes that seemed perpetually stuck in the 1970s. He lived in one of those complexes, alongside many young Orthodox Jewish families.

And yet I kind of liked that he didn't live in a communal house in West Philly or something that seemed more "on brand." He said the location worked for him. He was equidistant from all his teaching jobs, far enough so he wouldn't run into a student but close enough that he could get where he needed to be even if he was running late. Likewise it was close enough to family in West Philly, close enough to poetry downtown, close enough to cafés, theaters, and bookstores, yet still it was tucked away. But on another level, it seemed like Quincy didn't mind, and even sort of enjoyed, being an odd man out. I noticed he liked to do things like "stop at the store"—an old phrase, as if it was a general store and not a Walgreens. He was the type of person who'd leave a poem on Marie Laveau's grave in New Orleans but also find passing a well-worn coupon to the cashier at the local Acme just as sacred an act.

I was touched that he shared his pseudo-suburban life with me—less trimmed hedges and more an untidy ground-floor apartment, blinds shut, sitting on the edge of the bed in his towel watching TV with a copy of an Etheridge Knight book by his side.

"What are you watching?"

He waved me over, into the crook of his still-wet body. It wasn't art house. It wasn't Black Power. It was *How I Met Your Mother*.

I had never seen it before. I wanted to be snobby. But then as this group of white friends got into ill-fated romances with other white people, the story told to the imagined audience of one character's future white children, Quincy's body let out one of his boyish giggles and I felt myself let one out, too. "It's kind of funny."

I found myself enjoying Quincy's pseudo-'burbs life, picking up routines like they were lawn toys. We'd walk to the Starbucks on the main street; we'd grab lunch at the deli across the way where sometimes we'd catch the local celebrity, a seventy-year-old local news anchor. If I'd lost my New Jersey suburb, I felt like I had found another one, if not a better one—a suburban existence that Quincy and I were building ourselves and in our own surreal design.

"I think I want to lead a kind of jazz lifestyle," he said one day as we were walking to the main street—and suddenly there was a crack in the design.

Though I wasn't seeing my family as much, we still talked enough that I wasn't surprised when Diksha invited me to a baseball game. It would have been my first game—a free Yankees box seat, no less. I even asked one of my AAWW interns, Simon, to join. My sister refused to take our payment. Simon couldn't believe his luck.

Diksha called me just before the game. "What will Mom's relatives think?" I was blindsided. I thought she was calling to talk about the game, but instead this.

I burst into tears.

"I get it." She started telling me about one of her friends, a Christie So-and-So. She was a lawyer in an interracial marriage: "My friend didn't like it when her aunt said, 'Aren't you worried about nappy hair?'" I found no comfort in the way Diksha told the story. Maybe I should talk to the friend myself? Did Diksha have the number for So-and-So & Associates?

Diksha is in an interracial marriage, too—to a white man. And yet, I knew that interracial marriage—of Indian plus white—meant something different to my family. My family's immigration, like many families', was not merely about inhabiting a place but about navigating a precarious relationship with white America—one in which there was a desire for acceptance alongside a threat of it being revoked. And while my parents initially pushed back against my sister's choice, it seemed to be more an anxiety about being accepted than accepting.

I texted Diksha later that I couldn't make it to the game. We pretended like our last conversation never occurred. "No problem!" she wrote back and I wanted to scream.

I told my intern Simon that I couldn't go to the game, giving some vague excuse. He deserved better. "No problem!" he said and I wanted to cry.

In the midst of a busy day at the AAWW, I got a call from my father. I stepped out from the cubicles and sat at one of our lunch tables.

"How are you?" my dad said.

"I'm fine, I'm busy but fine, what's up?"

Small talk. Small talk. And then: "You know, Uncle's daughter is married to a Black man, they have a terrible marriage, they fight all the time."

"What?" I began to cry. "I have to go."

I went to the bathroom. I burst out crying over the soap I hadn't filled yet and our sink that had trouble draining. Someone knocked on the door. It was the worst person to see at this time—my boss.

"You okay?" he said.

He and I did not talk like this. We generally just had fights about some high-stress nonprofit-related thing or another. Justine would liken us to the Bravo show *Flipping Out*—imagining our event planning and grant writing edited into dramatic camera zooms and cliffhanger commercial breaks. I couldn't believe I was telling him about how my parents disapproved of my relationship.

"It must be hard," he just said.

And I took it in, like an Acela clipping through the hollow of my heart, the fleeting comfort.

My father called back. "I was lying, they have a great marriage. Your mom put me up to it. She's worried about what her relatives will think."

I refused to share my family drama with Quincy. I wanted another genre for us, not family drama, not even dramedy. I wanted rom-com. I wanted *When Harry Met Sally*. I wanted the meet-cute, I wanted the will-they-won't-they, I wanted the orgasm sandwich. I wanted witty banter, not banal racism, not a love that was made to feel so literally relative.

"I think I want to lead a kind of jazz lifestyle." We were walking to the main street.

"What? Like be a musician?"

"No, I mean like . . ." I don't remember what he said. Jazz is hard to pin down, so many styles and traditions inform it, so much improvisation, so much happening in the moment. Did he want us to just improvise? Did he want to be hard to pin down, at least to me? I fumed in thoughtful silence for the rest of our walk, not even making a joke about the child-size cop car on the lawn we always passed. On the main street, we didn't eat at the deli as usual. Instead, I suggested we try the Asian fusion place that looked horrible.

"I love Miles Davis's *Kind of Blue*! Is that what you mean by jazz life-style?" The question mark was a farce. It's about the notes in between.

"Forget I said anything," he said as he pushed around too-oily rice. I didn't let up. "Using session musicians to create a specific sound!" Was this our first fight?

"I love the way you talk about music," Quincy said.

Jazz lifestyle. I hated the phrase. I began to say it all the time. "What do you think he means?" I'd ask my friends, my interns. *How dare you!* I wanted to say to Quincy. *After I said I love you!* But I had said I love you to my mom, not him. He had no idea what the past few months had been like for me. I did not tell him about "what will my relatives think." I didn't tell him about how once the phrase announced itself, the phrase never left.

And now, even after all the thought I had put into what I wanted, I realized I didn't think about what Quincy might want—maybe he didn't want a pseudo-suburban life with me but a "jazz lifestyle" with several women? Maybe I had thought I walked into a rom-com but ended up in another genre or even form entirely—not *When Harry Met Sally* but *Bitches Brew*. And like Miles Davis turned away from his audience when he played, would Quincy turn his back on me?

It was one of those periods of dating where I wished I could pick up the phone to call my mom or Diksha or go home and eat too many Nestlé Toll House cookies. ("I made them small, beta, have twenty.") But since "what will my relatives think," I hadn't given them much intel on me and Quincy. That's what it felt like—giving them intel, fodder for their next targeted anti-Black attack. All this talk about relatives, yet I felt so far away now from any real familial intimacy.

One of the unintended but most enduring legacies of the Hart-Celler Act, also known as the 1965 Immigration Act—the bill that opened the door to my parents and to many Asians to enter into this country in unprecedented numbers—was family, specifically the way immigrants, once naturalized, were able to sponsor relatives. This idea is now vilified by the Right as "chain migration." Back then, though, it was used to appease alarmists, those on the Right and the Left. A piece of Cold War–era legislation, the bill originally prioritized immigrants with special skills, namely science and engineering training. While that specification remained in the bill, it came third in the list of who gets visas—the first two tiers prioritizing relatives of those already settled. Representative Emanuel Celler said, "Since the people of Africa and Asia have very few relatives here, comparatively few could immigrate from those countries because they have no family ties in the United States"—a slight miscalculation, to put it mildly. The Hart-Celler Act transformed the ethnic makeup of the U.S. But if we were all in, all American citizens, if we all belonged, why did that question "What will my relatives think?" exist? Why did anyone care what anyone was thinking?

Another one of the unintended but most enduring legacies of the Hart-Celler Act was the way it reproduced caste. My parents were two of many upper-caste Indians whose qualifications fit with the bill's "exceptional ability in the sciences"—and they were granted visas accordingly. Their "exceptional ability" correlated with the ways that India's higher education system, which trained people in engineering and medicine, was itself casteist.

What is caste? It is who gets a visa and it's not. It is who are you related to and it's not. It is exceptional ability and it is not. It is "what will my relatives think."

The first U.S. scene in *Mississippi Masala* reveals the weight of relatives in South Asian American life, a literal weight—heavy as a cluster of milk gallons, one after another piled too high and precariously in a shopping cart, heavy as Mina, now in her twenties, trying to steer this cart. "Holy cow, you opening up a dairy?" the white Piggly Wiggly checkout guy says. His joke is met with her glare.

Those gallons of milk are for an upcoming wedding, Anil's—a relative, the one who runs the motel. It's his car Mina and an auntie are using for this errand. Everything is going to plan until the backseat-driving auntie gets on Mina's last nerve and causes Mina to turn around and crash, right into Demetrius's van. The meet-cute: they exchange insurance info as townspeople and police gather to take in the scene. No sparks, no hatred, just Mina's sincere apology. The auntie's is the loudest voice: "What will Anil say?"

Back at the hotel, we meet Anil, played with great comic sorrow by Ranjit Chowdhry. He is enraged. "Mina, what did you do!" He and all the relatives gather around the wreck. Anil's agita over the car is stoked by his two friends Napkin (Mohan Agashe), an uncle type named for the napkin he always has over the shoulder of his kurta, and Pontiac (Mohan Gokhale), the more desperate of the two to belong, full Western suit and tragic mullet. They become tribal over the car, framing the wreck as an us-versus-them situation—"Americans sue," they say. Mina's father offers the consolation that at least no one was hurt—"No use crying over spilled milk." Anil is not ready for humor.

"Your father can't feed your family," he says to Mina. "He can feed us just fine," she spits back—the slings and arrows that only relatives can shoot.

If blood relatives aren't enough, you can leave it to the adjacent community to express the thing left unsaid. "You can be dark and have money or light and have no money, but you can't be dark and have no money," says the gossiping auntie. Mina herself is aware of what the relatives think. Just before Anil's wedding, she goes into her parents' room wearing sneakers under her sari. When Kinnu wonders how will she marry her daughter off if she does things like that, Mina grins and says, "Face it, Ma, you have a darkie daughter."

Mina and Demetrius have a very fast romance—a dance at a club, a date at a family barbecue, some almost phone sex—then sneak away. They take off for a beach weekend only to be caught by Anil, Napkin, and Pontiac, who burst in on them while in bed. A scuffle and arrest follow. And that's that. There are too many other story lines to center the romance completely—Demetrius's bank loan and struggle to get white lenders to fund his small business, the family dynamics of the motel, Anil wanting Mina's family out as much as Jay wants the high court of Uganda to let them back in, the trauma of exile and assimilation, respectability politics. Where is the time for an orgasm sandwich when all that is percolating?

I set jazz lifestyle in the background, or tried my best to, and what do you know—Quincy and I made it to the half-year mark. It couldn't have been any more of a picturesque Valentine's Day. Paris, the City of Love, drinking wine and eating duck confit. Except I was with Justine. We had planned the trip long before. Quincy had asked me to wait to open his present until Valentine's Day—three interlaced copper bracelets from Boscov's and a card: "Sexy little Nina, what color are your eyes today?" He liked to say my eyes changed color.

No "I love you" yet.

I had begun to say it to him. Feverish whispers during sex or making out. I told myself I wouldn't demand it out of him the way it was demanded from me, the way my mother asked, "You love him, right?" But on this rainy day, in this love-soaked city, as I opened the gift and note, I felt my heart deflate.

Justine asked me what I got, and I feigned like I was perfectly happy. I know she wouldn't have wanted that. But I was scared to share the ugly parts of our relationship not only with my parents but with everybody.

I had a hard time shaking off this paranoia even as there were signs of change. During the Super Bowl that year my father called me, saying he'd expressly left his box seat so that he could talk to Quincy on the phone. And then there was my mother, who simply shared the reaction of her closest relative—her sister: "Sucheta Masi says Quincy Jones is a famous musician, can you play some of his music for me?" The tide was turning, but there was still no "I love you" and I was in Paris on Valentine's Day with a friend.

When I was twelve, my mother, picking me up from school, asked me what the N-word meant, why people said it. I asked her where she'd heard it. I told her not to say it. I felt so helpless, so upside down. She was the one driving, but I was the one trying to steer this conversation. She was the mother, but I felt like the parent. Why was I educating her on anti-Black racism? I didn't feel any more self-aware than her.

....

We were living through Rodney King and what the news was referring to as the L.A. riots, which I watched unfold from the comfort of a small TV area outside my bedroom. I was there more often than anywhere else in the house. When we moved, I had begged my parents for cable. I was seven and wanted to watch *Pee-Wee's Playhouse*. Now I was a tween watching a video of the police beating a man.

My eyes were fixed on that video, one taken before cell phones, black-and-white, shaky with zooms in and out. Yet very clear. George Holliday and his wife only had the camera because they were planning on watching a friend run a marathon the next day and were just learning to use it. I couldn't hear the helicopter overhead that woke Holliday up, that brought him to the window, but I could make out the body of a man underneath it, curled on the ground as police kicked and beat him, barely rising up on his knees only for the police to kick him down again, more and more gathering the more prone he lay. Holliday captured the beating, nine minutes.

The police beat King with batons, Tasered him repeatedly, and eventually dragged a handcuffed King onto the side of the street. Over twenty-one cops and a helicopter overhead, all for speeding.

Holliday first offered the video to the LAPD and when they weren't interested, he sold it to a local station for $500. That's how it reached me on my couch perch, that's how it became hate-watching for white America.

The bystander video of the police beating King was seared into my mind, but I never brought it up to my family. The date stamped in what would now be considered a '90s font—March 3, 1991—the time code running underneath it, Holliday's shaky grip, and the police's relentless assault, all of that an indelible memory. Then came the trial and the defense using the video to focus on King's behavior, on his movements, calling them dangerous, trying to turn his helplessness into something to hate. Then came twelve jurors—nine white, one Latino, one biracial, one Asian—all from Ventura County, a more suburban and less racially diverse county than L.A., finding the four charged officers not guilty. Then came the fury catalyzed not only by the officers being acquitted but by years of frustration against the LAPD and their aggressive paramilitary policing of Black people; by tensions between the Korean American and African American communities, especially in the wake of the shooting of Latasha Harlins by store owner Soon Ja Du thirteen days after Rodney King was brutalized by the police; by anger at being forgotten amid economic depression and insecurity, just as South Central was forgotten during the riots—the police slow to respond and retreating, the riots lasting five days.

And finally came King incanting, "Can we all get along?"—a year after his beating, three days into the riots, and yet it is all of one moment, one extended conversation to be had.

She asked me what the N-word meant, I told her not to say it.

My predominantly white private school wasn't any better at talking anti-Black racism and violence. The class hunk, a white boy, wrote the N-word on a blackboard, copying the *Doggystyle* album cover, and when the teacher told him to erase it and do not do that, the boy cried so hard his red saggy jeans seemed to weep with him. Black America had filtered into the suburbs through appropriation, through clothing, through objectification; but never through history, never through empathy or through social justice. Plainfield, a town over from me, had its own 1967 uprising, the result being white flight. About an hour south, Quincy would grow up in a majority-Black suburb just as mine was majority South Asian. I wonder how his town reacted to Rodney King. I never asked.

"Yeah, Nina, what will Mom's relatives think?" Aria said.

I noticed a slight grin.

I don't know why I was surprised. Anti-Blackness was always there in our lives even when it was not articulated. But I guess I wasn't aware of the grin that underpinned it, a hatred of Black people that seemed to fill my own family members with pleasure. My relationship had become fodder for their own hate-watching.

Through the "relatives" and the suburbs and the tears and the jazz, it was hard to believe this moment was coming. "My parents want to meet you."

"My parents want to meet you, too," Quincy said. "I was thinking we could knock it out all in one weekend."

What in the jazz lifestyle? Who suggests meeting all the parents in one weekend? It was the thinking of someone who was unaware of the fact that we had somehow managed the impossible. It was the thinking of someone who felt more serious than I thought possible. The kind of person who might not want a jazz lifestyle after all, or at least not a solo one, maybe one more like John and Alice Coltrane—a love supreme.

In *Mississippi Masala*, Napkin tries to convince Demetrius not to sue over the car accident. Demetrius and his business partner, played by the great Charles Dutton, are cleaning the carpets at Anil's motel when Napkin brings them chai and says: "As long as you are not white, you are colored, isn't that so? . . . All us people of color, we have to stick together."

This is a line Demetrius imitates later to Mina, in a mock Apu-like Indian accent, knowing Napkin's insincerity, knowing the allyship that Napkin feigned was impossible. Idi Amin himself spoke of its impossibility. He can be heard on the radio in the movie's opening scenes: "Asians are rich. Africans are poor . . . they refuse to marry their daughters to Africans."

And yet, I still didn't want Quincy to know why getting to the meet-the-parents stage felt like nothing short of a miracle. It was May, we had been dating nearly a year. I was happy that he was happy. I wanted to keep it that way.

"Okay," I said.

Of course, I immediately called Justine to complain. "He calls it 'knocking it all out in one weekend.' Who says that?" Though I knew there was no turning back—or that's what I insisted when Justine tried to reason with me, saying that I could just tell him I wanted to take our families on one at a time.

The weekend before "one weekend" I still had not shared with Quincy the pseudo–civil rights battle that I had waged for the last eight months. I told myself I chose to keep him out of the fray to spare him. But in reality I wanted to spare myself, to avoid more pain. Even so, I felt drained. And so I did what I always do when I feel drained—I put on the TV. Quincy and I lay back on his desert island of a bed, my hate-watching primo location, and took in *Mississippi Masala* together. We found little quirks in the film to hang on to, to make fun of—the way the music changes from on-the-nose African beats to blues as they migrate or how Mina and Demetrius wear ethnic apparel, a salwar and kufi hat respectively, in their embrace at the end. "How come we don't dress up in our ethnic apparel on our dates?" We watched them kiss, watched them near-phone-sex, watched them between the sheets before Anil, Napkin, and Pontiac burst in. We made play-by-play jokes. But it felt like we were looking at something that wasn't there. In my grad school paper I'd avoided talking about the love plot and now it was all I could see—or, more accurately, all I was looking for. But both feel like imprecise ways of viewing the film, love story or race story. And perhaps this is why it's an impossible film— impossible to pin down in its bothness.

That weekend, for the first time in a long time, I got off at the Metropark station. It was more than a pit stop en route to Philly. Quincy would drive up to our house, ostensibly picking me up to take me down to Philly to meet his family the next day.

But he got lost on the way and my mom, a nondrinker, got drunk on a half glass of wine as we waited.

Quincy finally arrived, his faulty Google Maps printout still in hand as he climbed out of his car. This was an era before ubiquitous smartphones or GPS, at least in Quincy's secondhand Nissan—my parents had car phones as early as the late 1990s. Now, his car parked behind their three Mercedeses, I saw him open the passenger door and pick up flowers. Little did he know he wasn't the only one with an offering, that an offering-off was about to begin.

I expected to be the only one to meet him at the door, but my mother came down the stairs to the door with me, a silver plate with prayer paraphernalia already prepared. Quincy came through the door. I often joke that Quincy takes so long to put on or take off shoes that I could go out and be back in the same amount of time. But this time he flung his shoes off so fast it seemed they might hit my mother, who was coming headlong toward us. Sweeping in, she pushed me aside and gave him blessing—a red tilak on the forehead with her vermillion powder. She did an aarti—circled a lit candle around his face and said Hindu prayers to offer blessings.

My father bellowed, "Leave him alone," but then also tried to direct the prayer action.

They say the opposite of love is not hate but indifference. The opposite of hate must be this—fervent, chaotic prayer.

Two incarnations of life later, we finally got past the front door.

"This is just delicious," Quincy said as he ate homemade tuna balls. He never talked like that. Where are his jokes? His "I got lost while holding a map" self-deprecation? I could feel his nervousness. "That was a great dinner," he said.

We informed him that it wasn't dinner. It wasn't even appetizers. It was a just-in-the-door snack. My mom took a tone like she was insulted by the very thought it was anything more.

There was a lot of talking in Hindi that I asked to stop. My father did a lot of talking in English that my mother and I could not stop. Quincy ate three dinners, confused about where the meal began or ended.

At the end of the night, Quincy and I got ready to drive to Philly. "You can stay over," my mother offered, but we declined. I went up to get my things and my mom offered me blouses to wear tomorrow when I would meet his family—one of her Macy's INC tops that none of her daughters had a good enough fashion sense to wear. She made a bag full of shawls and scarves from her India room, gifts for the women of Quincy's family. The offering-off was not over, apparently.

The next day, as soon as we entered Quincy's parents' house, I looked around and Quincy was gone—to his parents' backyard grill. I was immediately immersed in ways that I am not even with my mother's relatives. "Mom here had an issue with the fondue maker," Quincy's father said, already assuming a casual familial feel between us all.

"Can I help?" I said and though I didn't make it any better—I had never used an electric fondue maker—we did have fun.

"Meet my daughter," his mother, Celia, said to her sister.

I gave Celia the shawls.

"Tell my sister I said thank you," she said.

It was as if I had been there all along.

His mother said at one point, "What did they think of him? They must have thought he was funny looking with his hair and all." Quincy grimaced in a way that made me see for the first time in a long time that he wasn't just my boyfriend, he was someone's son.

"They loved you," he said as we climbed back into his car. Parent Palooza was over.

Or was it? I always mix up the first meeting of Quincy and my parents with the second, which happened just two weeks after. Quincy and I were going to visit my parents together. We didn't have several Indian dinners at my house but instead went to my father's favorite restaurant—not a joint in Little India but the Spanish Tavern on Route 22. On the way there, Quincy talked about used cars—something I worried my parents, with their penchant for Mercedeses, might not know what to do with. "Such a good boy," I heard my mom whisper in Hindi to my father. My father wasn't talking nonstop but this time put in a CD, which played spiritual music, not Hindi bhajans but instead Irish dirges care of a golf buddy. In the Spanish Tavern parking lot, still in the car, my father cried to the Irish dirge, thinking of his deceased parents. My mom tittered, making fun of him. I whined, "I'm hungry, let's go in," like a child. I didn't know what Quincy thought of all this, but I imagined he was horrified. It is this second meeting that feels more like us. Maybe that's why I always confuse it with the first. The first might be the more classic *Guess Who's Coming to Dinner* type of scene, but this second meeting was more the way we always are, our "mix masala," as Mina calls herself once, our Jersey Jahru—I imagine this to be the name of our film, our impossible film. Jahru meaning "broom" in Hindi, the title would reference Jumping the Broom—a Black wedding tradition where, after vows are exchanged, newlyweds hold hands and jump over the broom to make it official. This tradition has its roots in slavery. Having no legal right to marry before the Civil War, enslaved people would jump over the broom. It has come to mean sweeping out the old and making way for the new, but more than that, it is an acknowledgment to ancestors. I imagine myself explaining all this to a movie producer or exec. I imagine the same pushback Nair got: Who will play the American lead? Can one of you be white?

My filmmaking friend was right: *Mississippi Masala* is still revolutionary. Still no other film has broached Afro-Asian relationships and their geopolitical shadows. While *When Harry Met Sally* narrowly focuses on its main characters, their series of meet-cutes, Mina and Demetrius are drawn with their family and community histories in view. We experience all this biographical detail, the political backdrop of their lives, and the conditions that made it possible for them to be who they are. Mina wakes up after sex with Demetrius, jogged by a memory-nightmare from fleeing Uganda under Idi Amin's regime. It is a rom-com for us, for those of us who can't turn away, for those of us who find in a dark theater a place not for escape but for remembering.

It is an epic romance that doesn't have time for epic romance. There's rain, there's a car chase, but there's never a screaming *I hate you* morphing into a passionate *I love you*. They just leave together. Mina promises her mother she'll call with a "kiss Poppa for me." Demetrius concludes his call with "I love you" to his father. But to each other, Demetrius offers a more staid "I never thought I'd fall in love with you" and Mina responds with "I can clean rooms." How could Mina and Demetrius make such immense, life-altering decisions without saying the big words to each other? How can a rom-com not contain those words? That momentous declaration? It doesn't make sense.

This makes me think of my mom's question: "You love him, right?"—the subquestion to "What will my relatives think?" The two questions knock alongside each other in a way that does not make any sense. But it does to us—those of us nonwhite and in love, those of us who cannot turn away.

It was a nonchalant moment, months before Parent Palooza, a foot out the door on the way to the train station and all that jazz.

"Love you . . . and yeah, you got me saying it, too," he said, hugging me in the doorway of the apartment.

And as I sank into his arms, I felt relief and joy for a quick moment before dread crept over me. He didn't know how long ago I had said "I love you"—to the train, to my mother, to the Metropark parking lot— and in that moment, by the door, I realized I still didn't want him to know.

SACRIFICE

won't show his picture to my relatives until he cuts his hair," my
mother said, an ultimatum I didn't imagine. I imagined: "It's either
Quincy or us," not "It's either Quincy's dreadlocks or my relatives." I
was visiting my parents, just me. Her words broke into an otherwise
languid afternoon. We were sitting in the room we call the "sun room,"
more like a narrow nook off the kitchen; it is lined with windows on
one side and dotted with pictures of Hindu gods on the other. And
there, as she went on about Quincy's dreads, one was depicted in
peaceful repose right above her head—

Blue god. Hair coiled up. A spout of water coming out of the top.
The god of creation and destruction. Not the cutie butter thief everyone fawns over. He is the bad boy with a man bun. He is Shiva. And
he has dreads. His picture, along with the rest of the pantheon, is all
over my parents' house—in the linen closet my mother converted to a
prayer room, on the hallway walls alongside other gods that my parents pass and pray toward before they enter or exit the house. Shiva
sits cross-legged, eyes shut, serene, even as he holds a spear, even as
snakes wrap around one of his four multitasking arms, all this activity

leading up toward the pièce de résistance—dreadlocks, cascading down his shoulders, wound up on top with a spout of water coming out. Shiva is said to have protected the earth from the deluge of the Ganges through his hair, in which the Ganges water is retained. It's this scene my parents say hello and goodbye to as they enter and exit the house, to work, to golf, to things in between. And yet: "I won't show his picture to my relatives until he cuts his hair." My mother said this not once or twice but several times, a mantra of her own making.

"What about sadhus?" I was trying my best not to turn away from them, to be able to talk them through their anti-Blackness presented as chill afternoon teatime talk.

"What is she saying?" my mother said. She knows what sadhus, the holy men, are—this is a nonquestion question, another arm of "what will my relatives think?"

"It's a religious act," my father chimed in. I wanted to clarify to them that Quincy's hair wasn't a religious choice, but I also did not. I just wanted the conversation to stop.

"Maybe we can make a whole ritual about it. I'll shave him," my father said with a grin. Maybe he was making fun of Hindu hair-shearing ceremonies—like the mundans, shaving the baby's first hair on the head. My father was laughing. But I wasn't.

"I'll shave him" had me shuddering, the violence of that statement. I want to say I was scared. And I was. But being scared is my go-to when I feel discomfort with other feelings. I was angry, I was sad. We had only just gone public as a couple, but I was already bracing myself for the road ahead. What a brutal beginning. What a profane, godless start.

And I was conflicted. I loved his dreadlocks. They were how I fell in love with him, talking to them from the backseat of his car as he drove me and Justine to her friend's party. And yet they looked like they had seen better days. They seemed dry and were suffering breakage. I would find strands on the ground of our apartment. But I didn't want my parents to think I was on their side. I hoped I wasn't, that my concern was different from "I'll shave him."

In *Hair Story: Untangling the Roots of Black Hair in America* Ayana D. Byrd and Lori L. Tharps describe how head shaving was one of the first acts of enslavement. If not done by Europeans as they forcibly removed Africans from their home countries and onto slave ships, head shaving was done by slave traders once in the Americas and in the Caribbean. It was part of a project of cutting from enslaved Africans all ties to their place and people, all known markers of identity. It remained a consistent part of slavery—hair cutting became a way of dehumanizing, terrorizing, and punishing. And more materially, the shaved head was the first step in violating, exploiting, and extracting from a Black person's body for financial gain.

If a shaved head was used to "signal 'slave' status," as Jasmine Nichole Cobb writes in *New Growth: The Art and Texture of Black Hair*, then dreadlocks can be seen as a threat and defiance of that status, that history. And while I never asked Quincy the details of when and why he began to lock his hair I knew he was a poet and a professor with performance poet tendencies. I knew that in these highly visible, stage-loving roles, his hair did signal something. Quincy had grown and dreadlocked his hair over seven years, seven years of working upon it, seven years of making a statement through it, a statement about his relationship between self and society, between "Jones" (what his students called him) and Quincy.

His dreads are part of the project of him as much as his teaching and writing. This is what made "I won't show his picture to my relatives" hurt so much. My mother didn't just want a haircut. She didn't want them to know him.

....

What a brutal beginning. What a profane, godless start.

And yet this is the story of Hinduism to a certain extent. Some historians see Hinduism codified as a religion parallel to Islam in the period between 1200 and 1500. Others have traced its first mention as a term to the late 1700s and early 1800s by agents of the British colonial state in India. The latter intersects with the rise of orientalism in the U.S. and the ways that, even as Indian goods arrived on new American shores, Indian life was pictured as a simple and religious one. In *The Karma of Brown Folk*, Vijay Prashad writes, "The elevated thoughts of Emerson, Thoreau, and Whitman emerged in the first films on 'India,' just as they do in the world of popular orientalism. The first motion picture on India was called *Hindoo Faqir* (Thomas A. Edison, 1902). It was followed by a host of films that portrayed the subcontinent as the home of fatalistic spirituality and sensuality." It's not lost on me that this film, which follows the stage act of an Indian magician, which advanced the period's pervasive stereotypes of yogis and a mystic East, turning a blind eye to the complicated and painful realities of Indian life under British colonialism, was made by a man who bears the name of my hometown—Edison, New Jersey. This is an origin story for "Hinduism" that speaks most to me, finding its place and sense of belonging in a white world at the cost of any other perspective.

My first act of turning away, though, happened long before I was a white-assimilating tween/teen. Not more than six or seven, I remember walking out of my baby cousin's mundan, upset for the crying baby. Tonsuring, the practice of shearing one's skull, as an act of religious devotion and humility occurs across many religions and cultural contexts. For

Hindu Indians, it can occur at specific stages of life, but it can also occur anytime you want to entreat God. At Hindu temples, hair cutting is
either the beginning or the fulfillment of some holy pact. It is often the
resort of the poorest Hindu Indians, those who cannot afford to offer
money to God and so instead give their hair, a prized possession.

A few months after my mother requested that Quincy offer up his
hair, Quincy planned a trip to Cape May, New Jersey. It was ostensibly to celebrate his birthday. This was strange because he was generally not much of a birthday person and not much of a trip taker—I
was usually the Clark Griswold of our vacations, pulling him off his
stacks of grading to take in sun and skies. So as he planned this birthday beach vacation, I knew what was coming—a proposal. I knew it
because my mother had been calling more often and asking me for
"news." And yet, I didn't feel like I could be too sure.

The morning we were to go down to the shore, I woke up to an
empty bed in his apartment, which was now our apartment since I
moved down there. I saw Quincy was up before me, was hurrying me
out the door for a change, more worry on his face than a simple beach
weekend warranted. He got lost on the way down, taking an hour-long
detour into a sealess suburb, and when we finally arrived in Cape
May, just as the sun was setting, he hustled us into the hotel. It was a
beautiful place, so different from the chain hotels that we'd stay at for
weddings and writing conferences. I was nestled comfortably in the
sheets and "testing if the TV works" as Quincy went down to get the
bags. "You look so comfortable," he said when he returned. "Want to
get up and go to the beach?"

The water was endless and serene, though Quincy looked just as worried as he had in the morning. I clutched his hand. We walked and walked, getting farther from the throngs of people in picture-perfect sunset spots. His hand kept shifting grips and then he let go, he was kneeling in front of me. "I promise I will do my best to make you happy." A future clicked open with that box. I looked down too long. The ring. It was enormous and shiny. It was my mother's. She had given it to him sometime around when she gave me the ultimatum over his hair.

In the car back to the hotel, we called our parents to share the good news. "How about a June wedding?" my mom said.

"That's three months away," I said.

"So?" she said.

"Can I talk to Diksha?" I said.

"Mom keeps going on about a June wedding," I said to my sister.

"What's the problem with that?" Diksha said.

"I'll barely be done with school."

I had been daydreaming of a year-long engagement with the wedding the next year: same day, same beach.

"I see. How about July?" Diksha said.

I hung up.

I looked at Quincy. He looked at me. "I asked them to wait a day," he said.

I didn't cry when he put the ring on me. And I didn't cry as we talked to our parents. But when we returned to the hotel and Quincy opened a second gift, two simple but custom-designed necklaces, paid for on an educator's salary, I surprised myself with how much I cried.

....

In 1966, the year after the U.S. passed the Hart-Celler Act, the government did for Asian hair what it had just done for Asian immigrants. There had long been a ban on the import to the U.S. of any wigs containing Asian hair. But in 1966, the U.S. partially lifted the ban—allowing hair from Asian countries aside from Communist China, North Korea, and North Vietnam. At the time, post–Civil War, South Korea was one of the poorest nations in the world and, with most of the natural resources on the North Korea side, the government sought a different kind of natural resource: raw human hair. Destitution drove many families to participate in the wig trade— persuasive wig merchants gaining the long locks of women and children alike. By the 1970s one-third of wigs worn by North Americans were made in Korea and wigs became South Korea's third-most-exported product, next to plywood and textiles. So opened the door to the U.S. import of raw human hair from Asian countries that were not Cold War adversaries.

"Hello," my mom said, her voice over the phone ricocheting into the quiet of our bedroom. Quincy rustled but stayed asleep.

"Hey, Mom," I said.

"Did you just wake up?"

"No." I hobbled toward the door, sore from working out, working on my "bride body."

"Good," she said. "So, what did you think of the DJ?"

"He's the best so far, let's make this all paka finally," I said.

"Oh, great, DJ Mr Mike did such a good job at the Grover wedding," she said.

"Wait, I was talking about the other DJ, Desi Allstars," I said.

"What about Mr Mike?" she said.

"What about DJ Nandini?" I said. "I hope you didn't give a deposit."

"Oh, my god," she said. "So many names."

We were in agreement on this. The wedding planning was an overwhelm of names, of choices, of things that I did not know had names or were choices. I found myself more and more busy with them, and more and more invested in them. A simple beach wedding a year away became a wedding in six months' time, an elaborate South Asian–heavy affair in which Quincy would ride in on a horse and I would be carried in on a bejeweled litter.

As the details grew elaborate, "I won't show his picture to my relatives" seemed to fall out of our conversation. Not that she had given up the ultimatum. In the midst of sorting out DJs, horses, litters, and all that would come, she'd slip in the question—"Has he done that thing yet?"—a spectral presence in our planning.

When Quincy's parents hassled him about his hair, I did laugh. I wasn't sure why.

"Looking pretty raggedy there, kid," his mother would say.

"Your old barber is still working in the shop," his father would say. "He might remember who you are."

Their words were not so different from those of my parents. But they felt different. And maybe that is simply because they came from a different place. Not the cut-hair-or-we-cut-him-out anti-Blackness of my family but the small talk that comes from generations of navigating the politics of respectability.

Cobb writes in *New Growth*, "Violence is the chief imprint on textured hair's imbrication in struggles for Black liberation." In other words, "I won't show his picture" and "I'll shave him" are more than teatime microaggressions, more than a mother's nagging, a father's bad joke. Instead these statements, like the physical imbrication of scar tissue collected atop a wound, are layered with histories, rituals, traditions of violation of and control over Black people's bodies, all overlaying this country's original wound of slavery.

"I bet they didn't know what to make of him with his hair and all," his mother stage-whispered to me. I knew what Quincy's parents made of him, their son who had grown his dreads for seven years already, a son they could tease and yet whose pictures were on their walls, displayed proudly.

Hair for Black Americans has always been inextricable from economic and physical survival. Plantation owners favored those whose hair most closely resembled their own. As Byrd and Tharps write in *Hair Story*, "Those slaves living on plantations soon realized that lighter-skinned Blacks with straighter hair worked inside the plantation houses performing less backbreaking labor than the slaves relegated to the fields." This "hair texture hierarchy," as Byrd and Tharps continue, remained post-Emancipation in the lives of Black Americans, bound up with Black Americans' moneymaking potential, if not through the texture of natural hair then through a willingness to invest time and money in concealing or altering it. It makes sense then that most hair innovations that endure to this day were the creations of Black people, like Christina Jenkins, the inventor of the hair weave.

Working in a wig-making company in 1949, Jenkins noticed how wigs tended to easily slip off customers' heads. What's more, she wanted a means of altering hair without the damage of heat or chemicals. Two years later, Jenkins invented a process of plaiting the hair in rows that could easily be sewn on the wefts while making it look natural rather than weaving the hair and then trying to attach it to the scalp with clips. According to the patent the weave is described as:

> interweaving strands of live hair with filamentous material to permanently secure the filamentous material as a base on the head; and attaching a switch or like accessory of commercial hair to the base, by thread.

It is here where that once-banned Asian hair became "commercial hair" or, as it's more commonly seen on extension packages now, "true Indian hair."

My mom had thoughts on the where of the wedding as much as the when and how we should look. She and my father urged me to have the wedding at an event space in a mini-mall nearby their house.

"Just think of it as a kind of under-the-radar cool place, like that sushi restaurant in L.A.," Diksha said.

"But it's a strip mall. Not only that, it's the one I went to as a kid." I used to go to the Chili's in the center often, a cool thing to do when I was twelve.

"The best Indian restaurant in the world is there. Don't be such a stickler for details, Nina."

"So, what do you think?" I asked Quincy once about the mini-mall wedding.

"I'm happy with whatever you want, baby," he said.

"No, really, if your thoughts on this subject would save a nursery school sinking in a swamp," I said.

"Is there a nursery school sinking in a swamp?"

"No."

"Then I'm still worried about jumping over a column of flames while riding on that horse," he said.

In my heart I knew horse jumping would be nothing compared to the feat of cutting the dreadlocks he had grown for most of the decade.

South Korea was the first country to capitalize on the U.S. lifting of the ban on Asian hair. In the 1960s, in a hurting post–Korean War economy, poor South Koreans began to sell their hair right at the time this new market opened up. The South Korean government supported the development of this market, making it so there was no European middleman taking a cut. Korean manufacturers could sell directly to Korean American merchants. It became a common economic entry point for Korean American immigrants. As one wig retailer said: "Unlike meat and vegetables, wigs didn't go bad and were not bulky so I did not need a large storage space."

This direct trade channel meant merchants could get wigs at reduced prices, undersell department stores, and still make a profit. Moreover, they found a market white America did not: Black American communities. Retailers rarely set up businesses in Black communities, so Korean Americans did.

....

My mom and I began to talk every day. She asked me if I wanted to get the ceremony projected on a plasma screen. She asked me if we wanted our initials in a revolving heart on the dance floor. She asked me again if Quincy had "done it yet."

When I visited her, we sifted through business cards and flyers. She passed over a small glossy business card. On it appeared a woman in midgyration, wearing something more Britney Spears than Bharatanatyam. If it wasn't coming from her this would have seemed like a questionable handoff.

"She did such a great job at Rahul Patel's dinner—your dad and I were so impressed," she said.

"Mom, tell me the truth, is she like one of those dancers Uncle Champ used to hire? Those belly dancers?"

"No, Nina. Why are you so picky?"

Such a stickler for details, such a picky girl, I was being too difficult, making too big a deal of everything, especially Quincy's hair.

We traveled to northern Jersey to go into a warehouse that held Indian wedding props, fully constructed mandaps and garland samples. The cinder block mixed with the floral arrangement section gave it a cool, sweet smell. Huge, monolithic columns and frames were stacked against each other, looking like the unearthed ruins of a bygone empire. An Air India sign made out of red roses hung above, on a ceiling rafter.

"Here was one that I was thinking of." The warehouse owner pointed to a dark wood mandap; the wood was cut out and fashioned into floral designs.

"No," my mother and I said, in unison. We were agreeing more and more.

Another weekend, me, my mother, Quincy, and more pamphlets: "Oh, we must finalize the shenai player," my mother said, handing over one.

"Oh, yes, we must."

Quincy gave me a puzzled look. "What's a shenai player?" I had no idea.

In the corner Auntie Raj, my family's live-in housekeeper, motioned a horn with her body, craning it back and forth as if she was drinking from it as well. She waved a hand toward my mom, as if she was swatting an annoying fly.

"Oh, it's the horn-sounding instrument, like a thin horn."

"Oh," he said and edged over to peer at the Kinko's-type flyer the shenai player had made.

"It says he has a website," my mom said.

"I sincerely doubt it's any good, Mom," I said.

Quincy typed his name into a computer. We laughed at the page, which was an exact replica of the flyer. Quincy scrolled down and we heard his music play: it became the sound of the invisible instrument Auntie Raj played while taunting my mom.

After the pamphlet we played the DVD sent by a potential DJ. The video opened with the sound of clocks ticking, like the start of Pink Floyd's album *Dark Side of the Moon*. A man with spiked-up gelled hair was sitting with his head in his hand; a woman looked pained at the edge of the stairs. Then the DJ started playing, started emceeing and doing his thing. And all seemed right, though those two characters never came back into the screen.

"Seemed like the groom wasn't going to make the wedding. Did the DJ save the whole thing?"

I caught Quincy and my mom laughing together.

....

Another weekend, Quincy came up the steps into my family's home to visit. Instead of coming at him with prayer materials and vermillion powder my mother said, "Are you cutting it? When are you cutting it? I won't show your picture to my relatives until you cut it."

She finally felt comfortable enough to deliver her anti-Blackness directly to Quincy.

A small group of young Black people are seated at a lunch counter; they look about the same age as the college first-years I teach, just kids. Behind them, a throng of white kids pour food and drink and condiments into their hair. The Black students remain seated, goopy white messes congealing to their hair and clothing. Cobb writes, "In preparation for harassment, activists of the Student Nonviolent Coordinating Committee (SNCC) practiced having their hair pulled (figure I.3). Eventually, and for practical reasons, many of these same women let go of straightened styles."

The efforts of activists culminated in the landmark passage of the 1964 Civil Rights Act, legislation that ended public place and employment segregation and brought about the Equal Employment Opportunity Commission. And yet hair remained a wound, an imbrication, the pressure to alter one's hair to get a job, to keep a job, that racial capitalism remained in place.

Ten years after the Civil Rights Act was passed, the 1976 case of *Jenkins v. Blue Cross Mutual Hospital Insurance* was one of the first natural hair discrimination cases. The U.S. Court of Appeals agreed that workers were entitled to wear afros under Title VII of the Civil

Rights Act. But in 1981, when American Airlines was sued by an employee who was told her cornrows didn't meet their grooming policy, the court sided with the airline. The idea that the grooming policies are "race neutral" became legal precedent.

Forty-three years after *Jenkins v. Blue Cross*, in 2019, then California state senator Holly J. Mitchell authored the CROWN Act (Creating a Respectful and Open World for Natural Hair).* According to the CROWN Coalition website, "Black women are 1.5 times more likely to be sent home or know of a Black woman sent home from the workplace because of her hair." In summer of 2019, the CROWN Act was signed into law, making California the first state to ban hair-based discrimination. As of 2022, nineteen states have adopted or are in the process of adopting similar laws. On the federal level, the CROWN Act passed in the House in 2022 but remains stalled in the Senate, actively blocked by the GOP, as of January 2023.

I didn't come out and say it. Slowly, as we were seated on the couch together, what came out in fits and starts was: "Justine thinks your dreadlocks need shaping up." She had said this long before, two years before, only the second time we all hung out together. That night, Quincy charmed us both as we talked into the wee hours. It was late, he had to go home, she showed him to the door, and when

....

*As per their website, "The Official Campaign of the CROWN Act is led by the CROWN Coalition, founded by Dove, National Urban League, Color of Change, and Western Center on Law & Poverty." This movement to legally prohibit race-based hair discrimination "was created by a team of Black women leaders, in partnership with a coalition of organizations and individuals actively supporting the movement."

he shut it she flipped around, back pressed against the door, both of us still laughing, still smiling, her charmed eyes meeting mine. She said: "I would date him, but he'd need to get his dreadlocks retwisted." I was immediately jealous. Then I remembered she was a lesbian. And now, two years and an engagement later, I was using her as a patsy.

I suggested we try what Justine had imagined, the retwisting. I booked Quincy a trip to a salon in Philly that, like lots of Philly landmarks, boasted Jill Scott and members of the Roots as customers. The salon had a dedicated, specifically priced service to get locks retwisted, but Quincy came back looking like a sad dog after a haircut, no longer the wild poet or beloved professor, but like someone had given him a slick Wall Street comb-over while he had dreads.

I wished they could go back to the way they were.

In 1991, thirty years after those first Korean American wig shops found their way into Black communities, and thirteen days after Rodney King's beating, fifteen-year-old Latasha Harlins was shot by fifty-one-year-old Korean American convenience store owner Soon Ja Du. Du, who accused Harlins of stealing orange juice, claimed she did not see the money in her hands. The gunshot, after a scuffle, was caught on camera, a bullet into the back of the head. Much like King's beating, the footage played on the news on repeat, sparking greater attention and awareness. When Du's ten-year manslaughter sentence was reduced to five years' probation, four hundred hours of community service, and a $500 restitution, uproar ensued. The shooting is often thought to have factored into the 1992 L.A. uprising, during which large sections of Koreatown were destroyed.

What rose from the ashes?

White people discovered hair extensions.

In the 2000s, America started embracing the twin toxic mix of the early internet and reality TV, and things started to get hairy. Paris Hilton wore weave extensions in *The Simple Life*. The extensions became so much a part of her brand that in 2007, after being released three days into her more than three-week prison sentence for a drug-related parole violation, Hilton immediately called for a hair salon van. Victoria Beckham ditched her Spice Girls bob, donning weave extensions as a breakout star of the group, proudly and openly discussing them. As Posh could put it: "My extensions come from Russian prisoners, so I've got Russian cell block H on my head." These are the two events that are often referenced when discussing the surge in interest in extensions—a point of entry that belies the truth. Celebrating white celebrities' long straight hair extensions, celebrating hair ideals traditionally associated with white women, all while failing to acknowledge that Hilton, Beckham, and their fans were all culturally appropriating from 1990s–2000s hip-hop and R&B, is a means to keep whiteness as the center of beauty.

It took a week, but Q's hair worked its way back from stock-trading executive to paper-grading poet.

I came home one day and Quincy was listening to Paul Simon. This was a first, and the *Graceland*/Africa phase resonated:

> *She's a rich girl*
> *She don't try to hide it*

Diamonds on the soles of her shoes
He's a poor boy

We had picked out a wedding song, "I Only Have Eyes for You"—timeless, but I wondered if "Diamonds on the Soles of Her Shoes" should have really been it.

As white America searched "how did Posh get long hair so quickly" on AltaVista and Internet Explorer, business boomed. Indian hair as "true Indian hair" became popular as it had its own advantages, a different texture from Korean and western European hair extensions both. It was durable, malleable, able to be bleached and dyed, and affordable. As Sana January, one Black American beauty salon owner, simply put it: Indian hair is the "Bugatti" of Black hair extensions.

At three hundred people, our guest list was considered modest by Indian standards. Then the Hyatt gave us a larger banquet room than expected. "We need to invite more people," my mom said to Quincy's mom. My mom had begun knocking on neighbors' doors like a wedding Jehovah's Witness. *Do you have a moment to talk about the glory of Nina and Quincy's wedding?*

I overheard Quincy talking on the phone with his mom. "How many do we have?" Quincy said.

"Ten," she said.

"With plus-ones, that's almost twenty," he said.

"Your in-laws are inviting hundreds of people."

"Okay, make it plus-twos."

The talk over Quincy's dreadlocks had dissipated or at least been usurped by the half-filled banquet hall. Two years after I set eyes on Q's hair from the backseat of his car, six months after "I won't show a picture to my relatives" and that failed Wall Street retwist, the ongoing conversation in my head over what I really wanted him to do with his hair (tabling if I had any say in the matter at all) and how to separate my desires from the racism of my family had puttered out, too. I didn't altogether notice this, my mind quickly filling up with other fretful parts of preparing for the wedding.

We practiced dancing:

I could feel myself falling asleep on his heartbeat, lulled by the soothing melody of our beautiful song. It can't be that easy.

"Honey?" I said. "When are we going to twirl?"

"Baby, we work up to that. Just relax," Quincy said.

"But what about the flourishes?" I said. "The twirls, the dips."

"How about I tap your back when it's time to twirl," he said.

"We should have done dance class," I lamented. "All these couples go to dance classes to learn some special choreography."

"Don't worry about it," Quincy assured me. "Just get comfortable."

"But everyone will be watching."

....

I decided to go out on errands. Not really for anything necessary. More to quiet my mind. Wedding planning was getting to me. We were three months in and had three left to go.

On a conference call with the Hyatt Hotel wedding coordinator, I swear I heard my mother say: "You can't just give me an answer to my easy question?"

To which the coordinator said, "Meet me on the grassy knoll."

I think we were talking tablecloth colors. In any case, I needed to get some air.

"I'm going out," I said, "need anything?"

"I'm good," Quincy said. I heard the bathroom door shut.

The Rite Aid was nondescript heaven. After a while, I wasn't thinking about the wedding. After a while, I wasn't thinking about anything at all. I floated through aisles to the sound of Hall and Oates until I forgot what brought me here.

I wasn't there when he took up scissors, our oldest pair, metal going from tip to grip.

I wasn't there when one by one Quincy placed his severed locks into a can.

I wasn't there when he got light-headed as he cut the largest one.

I wasn't there when he weighed himself. Five pounds lighter.

I wasn't there when he took a shower.

I wasn't there when he shaved his face.

I came home with a bag of unnecessary things.

I fiddled with our sticky lock and opened the door to someone standing in our living room, a man, a stranger, a young boy—maybe all of nineteen. This was what I saw. All of Quincy's marks of recognition were gone. No dreadlocks. No professor scruff. I burst into tears. There was nothing to hold back the waters.

"You don't like it," he said.

"No, it's not that . . ." I said.

She got diamonds on the soles of her shoes. She got diamonds on the soles of her shoes.

That night Quincy went to pick up sushi for us from our neighborhood place. He put a cap on to cover his new shaven head. But he still flipped up his jacket like he was making room for his dreads. He did this for months on end and each time I felt it again. This hurt.

"You don't like it," he said.

"No, it's not that . . ."

I never completed the sentence.

The next day Quincy went to get shaped up. Not at the Jill Scott–touting salon but a barbershop in a neighborhood that city planners hadn't figured out how to gentrify yet. The barber cleaned it up and said, "There are going to be lines on your head for the rest of your life."

After the barber, Quincy never really talked about his dreadlocks, though he chuckled at his hands flipping ghost hair every time he put on his jacket; though he paused when he found a black hair band or three in his pocket; and though Philadelphia at the time was experiencing its fifth-warmest summer, he often declared, unprompted: "I feel cold."

....

At the wedding, Quincy wore a sehra, a turban with bejeweled strands, over his just-growing-in curls.

I wore my hair in a low bun and then, at the reception, in bejeweled clips. "You look like Sheena Easton," Diksha ribbed.

I didn't have diamonds on the soles of my shoes. My masi commented on my shabby Nine West pair and my mom made Diksha give me hers. She handed them over immediately—the Indian wedding equivalent of giving the shirt off one's back.

A DJ didn't come to our rescue, didn't have to. The wedding was a well-oiled machine with day-of event coordinators. As per Indian wedding tradition, my cousins successfully stole Quincy's shoes. Quincy played along so well that Sharada Auntie waved other girls in to join, asking for a ransom. He offered them first a dollar, then two, and then his brother. It wasn't that he was simply enjoying himself, he *was* himself. Our friends mixed and mingled, traded numbers, Aisha and Axel reuniting. As for the elders—an uncle literally danced his pants off.

We succeeded in filling the hall. Too well. At dinner, Quincy and I didn't make it to all of the tables.

There was a table for my mom's relatives. There was a table for my sisters and their families. There was a table for my sisters' in-laws. There was a table for my parents' medical school buddies. There was a table for the financial planners—yes, plural. There were tables, multiple, for the Indian community of greater New Jersey, neighbors and feuding uncles and aunties placed strategically. There was a table for my high school friends. There was a table for my college friends, both Brown and Barnard. There was a table for my and Quincy's mutual friends, from New York and Philly, and all our chosen family in between. There were but two tables for Quincy's family—one for the immediate, which in fact also had some of my parents' friends, their oldest white friends, a couple who had great Christmas parties. Sitting at their other table was Quincy's cousin Lauryn and her full crew of friends, the ones who were close enough to call Quincy's parents Mom and Dad or Uncle and Aunt Cee Cee, a crew of people that more than any other table gave Quincy West Philly cred.

The next day my sister Aria mentioned my faux pas of not going to all the tables. "Don't worry, I went around for you (you are welcome)."

Aria arrived at Lauryn's table in all her aspirational identities— Good Eldest Daughter, Model Minority, Assimilated Private School Doctor-Mom.

Lauryn was done up in evening dress and makeup and hair and even though she was a businesswoman and author, that night it was all laughter and fun with the crew: *West Philadelphia, born and raised* . . .

The interaction went as expected.

This is how our families connected. This historic and ongoing tangle of racism and colonialism summed up in a brief exchange that Aria relayed breezily the next day in our postwedding debrief. It was quick. It was chaos. It was ours.

"I love your hair," Aria said.

"Well, you should," Lauryn said. "It's yours."

SHITHOLE COUNTRY CLUBS

Wedding planning is a constant weighing of choices. South Asian weddings in America are a constant wait for choice—to find out what choices, if any, we have. My wedding venue was one of my own choosing. Well, of my own choosing and one that checked off all the boxes I learned to consider when venue hunting:

- ☐ Will this place allow outside food (meaning non-white-people food, Indian food—or, as we Indian people called it, food)?
- ☐ What about the fire codes? Can a havaan be lit there? Do we need to get a fire marshal involved?
- ☐ Can its grounds accommodate a baraath horse? If a horse is too much, how about an elephant?
- ☐ And perhaps most important, how close is it to my hometown of Edison, New Jersey? This wasn't for any sentimental reasons, but rather in case, as my mother put it, "we forgot a sari."

I chose a local hotel where the white lady who worked in events impressed me with her pronunciation of Indian wedding customs. She guided my mother and me through the hotel parking lot, "our baraath parade route" up into the lobby, where "we normally have our milinis," describing it all with neither a pretentious white-woman-at-a-yoga-studio flourish nor a callous I-can't-be-bothered butchering. A few months later, in October 2011, our two-day Afro-Indian wedding followed the path the white lady laid out. It was an action-packed event: there was a horse to mount, a fire to circle, a broom to jump over—and Quincy and I did it all.

But even though the wedding album so clearly shows us baraath-parading all over the hotel courtyard, and the men of the bridal party and the groom's party exchanging garlands in the lobby; even though Quincy and I walked around a fire in a marigold-decked conference room and later, during the reception, jumped a broom on the dance floor before commencing the traditional electric slide; even though my mother still complains about how a suitcase filled with turbans could go missing in the hotel halls ("Who would want so many turbans?"); even so, despite all the in-person, photographic, and videographic proof otherwise, my father still says, "Remember your wedding at Trump?"

Technically, my father had arranged a postwedding event honoring us at Trump National Golf Club Bedminster. But the gathering was unconnected to the wedding itself. It took place weeks after and was not listed in the invitation. My mother was not involved, as both of us were maxed out from planning the actual wedding. My father was, essentially, the non–wedding planner of this nonwedding. He asked me to pick out the foods I wanted, with options like salmon and chicken—none of the "outside food" that would otherwise prove a deal-breaker. There was no fire code consideration, no horse route, no need to be within a ten-minute driving distance of the "forgotten sari." None of the checks and balances of venue hunting were factored in. Even the guest list was different: no uncles or aunties, just my father's golf buddies.

An 8.5-by-11-inch sheet of paper with roses printed at the borders listed the menu options, but I knew neither Quincy nor I would be there to choke down dry salmon or cut around chicken bone, or to make polite conversation with whoever responded to the RSVP at the flowers' edge. It wasn't so much *if* we'd get out of going but how.

"You can blame it on me," Quincy said.

"No, I don't want to make you the fall guy," I said.

"It's a husband's job to protect his wife at all costs. It was in my vows."

"You really believe that?"

"I don't know. My vows were in Hindi."

The day of the party, the arrival of a big storm provided a great excuse for our no-show. While the weather was merely seasonal, I called my father to say we couldn't make it, as if the wind and rain held us back and even the floral menu page was waterlogged in my regretful hand. My father put me on speakerphone in front of his guests. Later he told me, "Trump dipped his head into the party." I couldn't tell if my father was humble or bragging.

I hung up the phone. I sent the obligatory thank-you notes. And that was that.

Four years later, in June 2015, Quincy's hair growing back from its prewedding cut and me no longer caring what was said about it, Trump came gliding down a golden escalator in Trump Tower to announce his presidential bid, and all I could think was *Phew, that was close.* How could I ever have lived with that man's name emblazoned on my wedding invitations—letterpressed, no less? How would I have ever looked back at wedding photos, romantic shots of me and Quincy staged on that man's greens? That man who with his birther conspiracies kept barking for Obama to show his birth certificate. That man who, once off the escalator, launched not only a presidential campaign but a vicious attack on Mexican migrants. That man who, when the PGA and ESPN moved major tournaments away from his clubs, still claimed that the golf industry supported his views on Mexico: "They know I'm right."

I was relieved I didn't have my wedding at that man's club. That is, until my father said, casually, wistfully, and between bites at a family dinner in July 2016, "Remember your wedding at Trump?"

It's one thing for my father to say, "I had an additional party celebrating my daughter's wedding at the Trump National Golf Club a month after the wedding." But to say "your wedding at Trump" is, I daresay, an (*gulp*) alternative fact.

Why did my father say it? What made him insist—straight-faced, without hesitation, between bites of salmon—that we got married at Trump National Golf Club?

Perhaps just as much as country clubs, Indian weddings in America are a fantasy of place and privilege.

How many Indians have encountered white people who've described an Indian wedding like a visit to Disneyland? Its opulence, its decadence, its ancient rites and rituals so stunning to behold and worthy of a monorail ride. Indian weddings are the safest and most nonthreatening way to talk about Indians in America, through this sort of noble savage rhetoric. And it is perhaps the most fraught and potentially toxic way for Indian Hindus to affirm their identity—Indian diasporic weddings become a way to conflate religion and cultural identity into a pageant, an exhibit that upholds one of the most time-honored and oppressive of Indian practices: caste.

What is caste? It's race but it's not. It's class but it's not. Caste is story.

Here is a story, a love story, one that guided my life, one that I thought informed my own union in so many ways, one that I took pride in telling. My parents met in medical school. According to my father, he was singing in a band. My mother went to watch them and became a lovestruck fangirl. "I got a love letter, but it wasn't signed," he told me. "I had to go around campus looking for the woman who wrote this letter."

They had a "love marriage"—I'd say this to friends, to anyone who asked. I'd mention "love marriage" casually, a humble-brag. What I always left out was the conclusion of the story, the part Dad seemed to relish the most:

"And when I met your mother's side of the family," my father would say, "your mother's family disapproved of me, even though I am a higher caste than her, just because I'm from the countryside. But I'm a Brahmin, the top, the holy, the most learned. Your mother, a merchant caste—she's the lower one!"

But I'm a Brahmin. A strange twist to my parents' love story, one I never wanted to hear and one I never repeated. Love conquers all, I hoped to express when I shared my parents' story. Love conquers all except caste, I knew and never said.

Instead, I grew accustomed to saying Quincy and I had a love marriage, much like my parents did. And that our giant Indian-Afro wedding would be part of a tradition of defiance, wherever it was held. I think of black-and-white photographs of my parents early into their courtship, ones that looked like scenes from a high school play. "We were acting out moments from our favorite Hindi films," my mother once told me. Movies, I now imagine, might have emboldened them to pursue forbidden love. I think of the theatrics of my own wedding: the bigger and more traditional we went, the more I truly believed I was giving the middle finger to all those who said love between a Black man and a South Asian woman couldn't be.

In April 2011, the month after Quincy and I got engaged, Barack Obama released his longform birth certificate. The certificate was to put an end to birtherism, a movement designed to tug at white America's most racist, go-back-to-Africa heartstrings. But its splash on the screen felt bone-chilling. In so many ways it felt like the birthers had won. Obama's hand had been forced. Trump himself boasted that it was a proud day. "So, just in finishing," Trump said ten minutes into a thirty-minute speech, "I'm really honored and really proud that I could do something nobody else could do." He went on to say, "Experts will check it." His fight wasn't quite over.

By this point, my father had been part of Trump National Golf Club Bedminster for five years. He first interviewed there in 2005 and was rejected. "Someone on the board thought he talked too much," my sister Aria told me.

When my mother told me that my father had suggested Trump National Golf Club for the wedding, I could have said: "Hell no will I marry Quincy at the place owned by a man who questions the citizenship of Black men."

I could have said: "Would Quincy be asked to produce a birth certificate? Citizenship papers? Would our marriage certificate even be
honored?"

I could have said, "Exonerated Five," and hung up.

But in reality, I didn't say anything. I laughed.

"Ha ha, no," I said, assuming the conversation was dead on arrival.
I thought it was a joke.

When I was seven, we moved from one central New Jersey suburb
to another, from Fords to Edison. It was 1987, and our new town felt
largely white to me: the India Day Parade wouldn't make its mark on
Edison for another seventeen years, and even the grocery chain Patel
Brothers hadn't yet made its way from Chicago.

Every day, turning the corner to go to school, I would see the Plainfield Country Club, a whites-only institution near the border of Edison and Plainfield. Hedges lined the periphery and kept most of the
club out of view, but I could make out the street-side tennis courts
and a hill rising toward a majestic colonial Big House. The club's sign
lay at its entrance, a simple white wooden placard. At the top, the letters "PCC" were nestled in a small blue-painted crest that rested on
two crossed golf clubs, like a coat of arms. At the center and taking up
the length of the sign, the full name of the club was etched in blue, in
a distinguished, chunky Times New Roman. At the very bottom, be-
neath a margin made by a small gold line, lay in smaller blue letters,
this time in all caps: "MEMBERS ONLY."

While I couldn't see much else of the club, I imagined that our
house didn't look so different. It, too, was a Colonial with rolling hills
and was as old and storied as PCC, previously owned by a textile-rich

family who in the 1940s designed for themselves English-countryside-style estates. That an Indian family had come into one of the estates so many years later was always funny to me. The joke lost its humor, though, when I'd reach the end of the block. I don't remember having to be told what "members only" meant—it felt like I had always known.

"PCC," the kids called it at school. Many of my private school classmates were members. PCC sounded to me so much like PC, '90s shorthand for personal computers and political correctness. Here is a sentence we'd never say: I saw a kid in the computer lab working on a PC while wearing PCC clothing, which is so not PC. We'd never say it, not because it's a tongue twister, but because our country club and our private school seemed to share an admissions policy. It was not uncommon to see white children wearing a club shirt or hat to school. Baseball hats, I came to understand, aren't so many generations removed from white pointy Klan hats. The kid who I most often saw wearing PCC gear had a locker right next to mine, and in it was a giant bumper sticker for a metal band called W.A.S.P. He was a blond white boy with a dizzying name along the lines of Van K. Van Dyke III or Whit V. Whitman V or Mils P. Millions the Millionth. He went by Trip.

I had one friend whose family went to the club, but I never went with them. They did once take me to Rhode Island, to a town called Watch Hill. I was shy there. I could have fun with my friend when we were on our own, but I would shut down when the rest of the family was around. I remember them joking together as a family: "You need to have blue eyes to be a resident in this town— it's the way that you apply for residency." Did they see that I was there?

....

Some of my earliest memories were mealtime conversations in our dining room. The way we talked as a family sounded like we belonged in the country club, just no one knew it. At the dinner table, I'd hear my father and sisters talk about the word "Arayan"—how it was first an Indian word before Nazi Germany, how swastikas were born out of religious swastiks.

As high schoolers, my older sisters, Aria and Diksha, would press my father to talk about his green- and blue-eyed relatives. He liked to tell us about his hometown, a northern Indian hill station "where the British loved to vacation." All the while, he continued to tout his upper-caste Brahmin lineage. Soon, my sisters would show up to the dining table with green and blue contact lenses in their eyes—to connect with their ancestry, of course.

I was a decade younger than my sisters and I didn't quite understand everything. I didn't say much. Listening, sometimes I'd get stuck on the tone, stuck in the rhythm of what was said.

"Members only, members members only."

"Only?"

"Yes! Members only, only."

"Only, only, only members."

"Members, yes, members only members."

Suburban New Jersey tends to sprawl, with country clubs segregated along race and color lines. We navigated this terrain like pros, like it was part of our Brahminic birthright. While I was in high school my parents joined a Jewish country club. The club's name—the Shackamaxon Country Club—derived from the Lenni Lenape. "Shack," we called it.

We spent almost every Thanksgiving of my high school years at Shack. We didn't socialize inside, no one besides my father, that is. I tried to keep my head down, staring at my food. I felt overwhelmed, not from the Thanksgiving feast but from self-scrutiny: there were no other brown faces. Well, technically there was one lone brown face we passed before we entered. On a small signpost just before the car valet, painted in a green as vivid as putting grass, was a spare profile of a man's stoic face, atop of which lay a row of feathers.

In the dining area, Dad held court as fellow doctors came up to our table and shook his hand, thanking him for a consult, referral, or favor. My father expertly played the part of a rare and benevolent brown king, telling a joke or ribbing club members kindly, his thick gold Rolex glinting as he shook their hand and wished them along to their happy Thanksgiving.

I remember seeing kids from my high school there, but we never talked about these encounters, passing each other in the school hallways as wordlessly as we did in the Shack buffet line.

Once when we had no water in our house, Mom took me to shower at the Shack. I remember her calling out to the groundskeeper with all the force of her lungs as she tried to find the ladies' locker room, and how he just drove past us on a golf cart. I felt so hurt. I'd rather have stayed dirty.

Many years later, sometime between Quincy and I watching *Mississippi Masala* and walking around the wedding fire, we drove past PCC with my family, and we finally talked about the place openly, or as openly as one can for a few seconds at a stoplight. Quincy, Diksha, and I were together in the backseat. Diksha and I spoke separately of our fantasies of wanting to vandalize PCC's white placard as we passed it every day on the way to school. "You, too?" I said aloud, surprised that she felt the same way. She told me how she wanted to write about PCC for the school newspaper but that our English teacher disapproved because of how many families at the school were members. I was impressed that she had tried to say something at the time. And I was angered that our teacher shut her down. He taught me as well and would make the very same joke he had made to my older sisters at attendance, likening our last name to the toilet paper brand. "Sharma as in Don't Squeeze the Charmin." Later, he would be caught trying to flirt with a minor.

Even past the corner, Diksha and I continued plotting our spray-paint-and-buzz-saw revenge on PCC. "I'd make copies of their entrance sign," Quincy later said. I couldn't understand it—vandalism not by destruction but by replication. A PCC wooden placard posted at the entrance of the local mini-mall, another flanking the sign for the Parkway, another eclipsing the closest rest stop. Perfect well-constructed replicas—painted golf clubs crossed like swords, "Plainfield Country Club" plainly etched and "MEMBERS ONLY" in a finer print—popping up like advertisements of exclusivity, like the markers of Jim Crow from which they came.

"Trump" we began to say simply. In 2006, my father got in. From then on, Mom could say on any given day, "No, your dad went to play golf at Trump," or "Do you want to join him for a meal at Trump?" or

"He doesn't care to be home, he loves his life at Trump." Last name and place conflated, a caste of its own.

My father talked about taking my five-year-old nephew to the clubhouse for lunch. "Trump stopped by our table. And he snagged Rohan's chicken nugget. 'Hey, he took my chicken nugget,' Rohan said. And Trump just smiled." My father smiled, too.

My father talked about seeing Trump's balls being knocked, kicked, ushered closer to the hole, only adoring him more for it. "And he says to me: 'I cheat in business, I cheat on my wife, why wouldn't I cheat on the green?'"

"Your mother doesn't like him," my father added.

"Evil man," she chimed in.

Only in the midst of Trump's campaign, sometime in November 2015, did my father hesitate in his ardor. Trump asserted that the "heavy Arab population" of Jersey City "were cheering" during 9/11 as "the buildings came down." "He went too far then," my father said.

I wonder if my father remembered the bumper stickers that my mother bought just days after the attacks, American flags and soaring eagles slapped on their German cars. Maybe he recalled the Dotbusters terrorizing Jersey City in the 1980s and early '90s and was angry at Trump's erasure of this history. Or maybe his mind went further back, toward hardships from his first year in the U.S., when during his medical residency he broke down in front of his supervisor over a fellow resident's continual taunts and aggressions. Or maybe he simply knew, no matter what caste he was himself, he could always be mistaken for a "cheering Arab."

At the time, I thought this might have marked the end of my father's affiliation with Trump. He would quit, just as he quit Shack. He'd find another golf club, maybe he'd drop the sport entirely, take up tai chi or join my mom's meditation group or attend one of those

Bob Ross seminars painting happy trees. But when Trump won the Republican Party nomination in July 2016, my father initiated his own robocall campaign.

"It will break my heart if you don't vote for Trump, Nina."

Just before the election, in October 2016, Trump came to Edison to attend an event of the Republican Hindu Coalition, an organization run by Shalabh Kumar, one of Trump's largest South Asian donors. There, in the New Jersey Convention and Exposition Center, Trump said, "I'm a big fan of Hindu." We might mistake this phrase as an ignorant slip of the tongue, but I would argue the phrase is blindly clear. "I'm a big fan of Hindu" signaled the bold-faced racism and religious discrimination to come from a Trump presidency: a racism that is putty in the hands of many Indians, those who set their horrors— traumas of home and migration—behind a "members only" religious piety, men like my father who, as he says, is "a much better caste than your mom," or Shalabh who, when asked why he forgoes more inclusive terms and instead uses Hindu American, simply said, "The word 'Hindu' has caught fire."

Trump first used the term "shithole countries" in January 2018. He was speaking at a bipartisan meeting to debate a plan proposed by the Democrats to end the diversity visa lottery in favor of providing visas to more vulnerable groups, such as those from Haiti, El Salvador, and some African countries, and to keep DACA—Deferred Action for Childhood Arrivals—going with "concession."

"Why are we having all these people from shithole countries come here?" he said.

He went on to say:

"Why do we need more Haitians? Take them out." The new year had just begun and the next day would be the eight-year anniversary of the 2010 earthquake in Haiti.

The year 2017 had been filled with legal fights over travel bans, threats to the existence of DACA, and the rescinding of Temporary Protective Status. In November 2017, he rescinded protections for nearly 60,000 Haitians. Just three days before shithole day, he had rescinded similar protection for nearly 200,000 Salvadorans. In June 2017, Trump was reported to have said in an Oval Office meeting that Haitians "all have AIDS" and Nigerians would "never go back to their huts."

It was an Indian American man, White House Deputy Press Secretary Raj Shah, who came out fighting for Trump in the wake of "shithole countries." "Certain Washington politicians choose to fight for foreign countries, but President Trump will always fight for the American people," began Shah's statement, the first public response from the White House.

Shah's response was filled with words such as "merit-based," "assimilate," and "legal pathways." They appeared in article after article, articles most often titled something like "White House Does Not Deny Shithole" and in which Shah was referred to simply and directly as "spokesperson"—the mouthpiece for Trump's "shithole."

Every immigrant wants to claim that they came here through a legal pathway. But the truth is, the more you look at those legal paths, the more you see their ever-changing, ever-conflicting racist contours. From the Naturalization Act of 1790, which limited naturalization to immigrants who were free white persons of "good moral character"; to the Chinese Exclusion Act of 1882, the first time federal law proscribed entry of an ethnic working group; to the Immigration Act of 1917, through which the "Asiatic Barred Zone" was created and literacy tests were implemented; to the National Origins Formula, quotas used and adjusted from 1921 to 1965 in service of keeping America WASP always, with restrictions tightening under the Immigration Act of 1924 when the post–World War I recession led to yet another rise of "they will steal our jobs" xenophobia; to the Immigration and Nationality Act of 1965 where, while the national origins quotas were abolished and the country let in Asians in unprecedented numbers, the bill, passed during the height of the Cold War space race, largely brought in those trained in specialized skills—like my parents.

These continual reroutings of so-called legal paths shifted with white America's racist wit and whimsy. This is how we knew what my father "talking too much" during a country club interview really meant.

I first stepped into the Trump National Golf Club a year after the wedding. I had slept over at my family's house and as I was waking up, everyone was getting ready to go to "Trump."

"I don't have a bathing suit."

"You can borrow one of mine," Diksha said, passing me a one-piece with maternity control top, a clump of excess nylon resting heavy on my already-knotted stomach.

The ride from Edison to Bedminster was long, or long enough for the children to fight as a Chipmunks movie entered its second act on the Mercedes's backseat TV. When we were finally off the highway, we entered into an unlikely part of New Jersey, vast farmland with hay bales, horses, and even cows.

We slowed at a gatehouse, a tiny stone-and-columns cottage that seemed more Hobbit home than entrance checkpoint. Waved in, we made our way up a tree-lined drive, rolling golf course hills on either side. A larger version of the Hobbit gatehouse came into view. This was the clubhouse: a two-story brick building, with many wood-shuttered windows painted white and a doorway fashioned like a Greek portico, columns and all. In many ways it was much more a classic wedding location than any hotel. How manorly it looked took me by surprise. There was no sign of gold-plated Manhattan high-rise Trump.

In the pool area, recliners were laid out in rows across a large sun-dappled deck. On the left were tables and a poolside bistro. Tucked in the right corner, farther away from the main pool and closer to the kiddie pool, was a cozy white cottage, out of which I would later see Melania emerge. Holding a tube of sunscreen, she marched toward a kid splashing in the pool with my nieces and nephews. "That's my friend Barron," my niece would say later.

The pool space was enclosed by a building, another majestic brick, the center of which was an arched entryway, a portico without columns. Instead, the arch held a split staircase. A verdant golf course appeared just beyond. This building made an idyllic stage picture, the perfect symmetry of neoclassic design.

"That arch is pretty," I said.

"See?" Diksha said. "You could have done the wedding here."

I didn't realize I had said it out loud.

....

Trump went to his golf club during the funeral of the Parkland school shooting victims. He went to his golf club after declaring a "national emergency" at the southern border (though he gave no evidence of said emergency). And after telling four congresswomen, four women of color, all American citizens, to "go back to where they came from," he went back for another round of golf. He went to his golf clubs far more than he condemned Obama for, so much so that there is a website called Trump Golf Count, tracking how much it costs taxpayers—$144 million total, with the last recorded outing on December 30, 2020.

We might say he went there so often because the club was a small-scale version of an America he saw as great. But in reality, the club is more like the America we know.

In a December 6, 2018, profile in *The New York Times*, Victorina Morales and Sandra Diaz, two of thirty-eight fired undocumented Trump workers represented by lawyer Anibal Romero, broke their silence on the use and abuse of undocumented workers at Trump National Golf Club Bedminster. In February 2018, investigators with the New York attorney general met with thirty former employees of Trump's New York golf courses. A few of the interviewed workers had publicly come forward to reveal that golf club managers were not paying undocumented workers for overtime, sometimes after working over-sixty-hour weeks, or were denying promotions or health care benefits. Hundreds of contractors had come forward with unpaid bills for work done at his clubs, resorts, and casinos. In a June 9, 2016, *USA Today* report, Marty Rosenberg, vice president of Atlantic Plate and Window Glass Co., said he was owed $1.5 million for work at

Trump Taj Mahal. He went on to informally represent 100 to 150 unpaid contractors, some of whom Trump offered as little as thirty cents on the dollar. "Yes, there were a lot of other companies," Rosenberg said in the report. "Yes, some did not survive." And in those very same structures built by devastated contractors, we see our familiar, ungreat America reflected in how the staff are most often from those countries Trump targets in his hatespeak. At Mar-a-Lago, a majority are from Romania and a country Trump deemed a shithole—Haiti.

In this way, country clubs are not a MAGA utopia filled with "people from places like Norway." They represent the United States at its shittiest, a place where economic disenfranchisement and racial hatred are sanctioned, bound together, practiced on rolling hills and open air.

When we spilled out onto the march starting area outside Grand Central Terminal, I was unprepared for its sheer mass and size. The Women's March, as all organizing can be, was contentious before it began—getting pushback for its whitewashing and white feminism and, when veteran nonwhite activists were brought in, criticized for too much of the credit going to the big shots. And yet, what started out as a Facebook conversation ended up being the largest single-day protest in U.S. history.

We were being carried along in a current. Our sign swimming alongside a sea of signs: "Women's Rights Are Human Rights," "Love Trumps Hate," and toddling little girls with a preschool-like cheery floral patterned "Fuck Your Fascist Bullshit." "This is what democracy looks like," the call and response went. I was surprised by how loud Quincy yelled, as if he had been storing up his shouting voice for threats to democracy. The chants changed up as we went. "What do we want? Justice! When do we want it? Now!" And most simply, "Resist!" I had my period and was wearing a cup for the first time. I didn't know what to wear to a protest and so I wore workout clothes and the thin coat I wore sometimes when I ran. "This is what democracy looks like!" I shivered.

In 2016, just after the election, I talked with my father over the phone:

I don't think you will like hearing this, but . . .

Trump held an event at his golf club . . .

The event was for people who had been members for ten years . . .

That's me, I am a member for ten years . . .

It was a dinner where he gave a speech . . .

That he is misrepresented . . .

That he will take care of minorities and that they like him . . .

He pointed at me—you are the one who told me to run for president so many years ago . . .

Brought me and Mom up for a picture . . .

I didn't want to go up . . .

But . . .

That African Americans shouldn't even be called that . . .

Just Americans . . .

"No," I said. "Dad, do you read the news?"

Yeah, the way they treated Mike Pence . . .

"No, Dad, do you read the news?"

I don't like Trump, but I also don't like parts of Obama or Hillary either . . .

I really don't like this one thing Hillary did . . .

"Dad, I don't agree with you. I would like to stop talking about this for now. I don't want my precious time talking to my mom and dad to be about this."

He pointed at me—you are the one who told me to run for president so many years ago
    Brought me and Mom up for a picture
    I didn't want to go up
    But

MAD MARRIAGE

W hat are you going to do with your name?" Quincy's mother asked.

It was a few weeks before the wedding. We were sitting at his parents' home bar. Smooth jazz emanated from his father's surround-sound speakers. Two glasses of white wine rested between us—the type of wine people who don't drink keep on hand for guests. And because I still felt like a guest, I had a glass.

"I'm not sure . . ." I took a sip.

"I might hyphenate it?" I took another sip.

She began to discuss her time as a school registrar. It was a job she held for most of her adult life to the point of earning retirement that very year.

"Kids with parents who have different last names are always caught in some paperwork bind . . ." Her talking points glided with the smooth jazz sax.

"Then there's the hyphenated name misfilings . . ."

I poured my second glass.

"And sending out communications can be tricky . . ."

I finished my glass, waited until she wasn't paying attention, and started drinking from hers.

"And under different last names, the two of you would have trouble booking flights."

She had worked as a flight attendant at Pan Am in her twenties. But by my age or likely well before, she had two feet firmly on the ground—a wife, a mother, a school registrar, a Jones.

". . . so much trouble with flying."

A year before, we were lying in a hotel bed in Canada. Quincy was asleep. I was awake. The blare of Delta's on-hold music didn't get to him, passed out after a full weekend of someone else's wedding, a full weekend of man of honor duties. He and the bride had known each other since they were seven years old.

"Hello, yes? I'd like to change our tickets to a direct flight."

Quincy and I were still dating . . .

"No, I did not make the reservation."

. . . no discussion of marriage . . .

"I'm his wife."

. . . barely out of the jazz lifestyle era.

I nudged him awake.

"You did what?" he said.

"Changed the ticket."

"What about our lunch in the nation's capital?"

"Our lunch in the nation's capital's airport."

Quincy took a brief pause because he knew I was right. "Wait, how did you change the ticket?"

"I just said I was your wife."

"You did what?!"

Wife—this word, this title, this power to change tickets, I could feel it going to my head—the clarity, the certainty with which the world met "wife." It was a magical power. I thought, *What else could I wield with my wife wand? Wife wand? That sounds like a vibrator.*

This was before any intimations that we might one day share a last name, before I moved down to Philly to live with him, before Quincy raced the sun to propose on the beach, before he chopped off his locks.

I didn't realize then that Quincy had thought of these tickets as significant—it was our first trip together. As I helped him navigate the Canadian highways, I didn't realize he used this as our first test as a "real couple." And as I hung with the bridal party, ordering a coffee / hot chocolate mix in a Tim Hortons, I didn't realize he had been cornered by the bride and all her bridesmaids and told, almost in unison, "Marry that girl."

He fulfilled their edict the following year.

The day before his proposal to me, Quincy proposed to someone else—the chair of his English department. Quincy had held semester-by-semester adjunct appointments at a small university on the outskirts of the city. This was a university where he worked the same teaching load as full-time faculty, where he was one of but three instructors of color in his department, where he always held his ID nearby for the latest security guard who didn't know him and would mistake him for an intruder. Quincy had been trying to level up. He had been there for ten years.

He asked the chair if the department would be interested in him proposing a creative writing concentration for the English program. In this concentration, he dreamed of crafting an expansive curriculum, giving his students something diverse and inclusive. He dreamed of giving himself something more lasting than his semester-by-semester appointments at the school. And then there was a dream beyond his educational aspirations, a dream to simply be a husband who could provide for a wife.

Once the chair said yes, Quincy started to put those dreams to paper, or in this case, a fresh manila folder into which his five-page program proposal grew.

I had been dreaming, too.

I had my eye on the Mansions longer than I wanted to admit. I saw it from a distance, across the county line, back in Philadelphia proper—a soaring high-rise apartment complex complete with an enormous gate and castle-like main house at the front. So different from the stubby, fading '70s-era two-story apartment complex complete with field mice where we'd been living. This was not the ground-floor former bachelor pad that the girlfriend squeezed herself into, blinds shut not only for privacy but because if you tried to open them the whole contraption would come down. This was a husband-and-wife place, where tall French windows let in plenty of sunlight on my husband-to-be's freshly shaven head, a place with crown moldings and ceiling fans and a built-in bookcase that would hold only a quarter of our entire collection, but no matter because husband and wife do not read, really, husband and wife are too busy with the stuff of husband and wife.

But could we afford it? We had only two conversations about money, early on into dating. Once after a night out on the Upper West Side, going from party to party, to doormen and high ceilings, he turned to me and said, "You know I'm poor, right?"

Granted, "poor" was a flip term. We'd grown up in comparable Jersey suburbs, gone to the same college. But our middle class was different. My sisters often joke that they were of the generation that ate out of Campbell's soup cans and got stuck in stalled cars with my parents while, a decade later, my newborn body was chauffeured home in my dad's brand-new Mercedes. I threw up in it.

I'm not sure what kind of car Baby Quincy was brought home in, but I know his family drove preowned, not new, and put Quincy in public school, not private. I know his family worried about tuition when Quincy got into college, and worried that he would feel ostracized among the rich kids at Brown. I know I was one of those rich kids likely doing the ostracizing.

And I know one of America's favorite weapons in its anti-Black arsenal is economics. In March 1965, between the passage of the Civil Rights Act and the Voting Rights Act, Daniel Patrick Moynihan, then President Lyndon Johnson's assistant secretary of labor, published *The Negro Family: The Case for National Action*, commonly known as the Moynihan Report. The report aimed to be a close and focused study of African American poverty. Moynihan placed blame not on the socioeconomic systems that disenfranchised Black Americans but a "tangle of pathology" that Black Americans brought on themselves. "The object should be to strengthen the Negro family so as to enable it to raise and support its members as do other families. After that, how this group of Americans chooses to run its affairs, take advantage of its opportunities, or fail to do so, is none of the nation's business."

Moynihan encouraged a rhetoric in which race is pathologized—the plight that African Americans suffer can only be remedied through personal rehabilitation. Black poverty was not rooted in structural inequity but individual dis-ease. Soon after, in a 1966 *New York*

Times article, "Success Story, Japanese-American Style," William Petersen spread this prosperity gospel, writing about how Japanese Americans rose up from unjust mass incarceration during World War II, saying, "They have established this remarkable record, moreover, by their own almost totally unaided effort"—this "unaided effort" being a "success style" in direct contrast to that of Black Americans who, marching for equal rights, endured fire hoses, police dogs, and billy clubs. Such protest and uprising would be unthinkable to Asian Americans because, to quote Petersen, "These nisei were squares."

Never mind that "model" minorities benefited from the "trouble" that "problem" minorities caused. Were it not for the passage of the 1964 Civil Rights Act, the passage of the 1965 Immigration Act, within which national origin quotas were abolished, may not have come to be. Never mind that the 1964 Civil Rights Act outlawed segregation in business and employment discrimination no matter your race or nationality, and that incoming immigrants would not experience the Jim Crow that preceded them. Never mind that the "model" minority and "problem" minority were narratives to diminish the gains of the civil rights movement, and as of 2020, "the median wealth of Black families is nearly ten times smaller than the wealth of the median white family."*

The second time we talked about money was on vacation. Walking downtown through the fancy tourist shops I asked, "Is there anyone like a 'rich activist'? Do you know of anyone like that?"

Quincy paused. "Batman."

....

*Dante Disparte and Tomicah Tillemann, "A Pandemic of Racism." *The Great Correction*, Washington, DC, 2020: New America, pp. 15–17.

....

In May 2011, a few months before the wedding, we moved to the Mansions.

"Wow, the light just bounces off the wood floors," Quincy said when we first got our keys.

In our blinds-shut, ground-floor life, we were not accustomed to the sun having its way, let alone bounding around an empty space. And then we realized the shimmer wasn't only the alchemy of sunlight hitting fresh hardwood. The floor had just been waxed. Too late. Our footprints, his Vans, my bare feet, remained there etched like babies' first steps.

Quincy was working now nine to five between teaching and concentration planning, while I had scaled back.

I rejected the renewal of my teaching appointment, and the PhD programs I had applied to when I first moved to Philly had all rejected me. But it didn't feel like a setback. I had other things to do. I already felt behind on all things wedding and house planning and threw myself in with the same intensity as everything else I had done in my life. My mother had offered to fund a wedding planner and put one on the phone.

"Your invitations were printed out incorrectly," the woman said without much of a hello.

I had known this. Indian weddings are three-day affairs and day two was placed where day one should have been—right-hand side of the opened side-fold card. My invitation designers agreed to reprint for free.

"I'll get back to you," I said.

What I wanted to say was: "I planned the first all–Asian American literary festival in NYC, bitch."

I told my mother, "I got this."

....

We would explore the flagship store of the mini-mall across the way—Acme supermarket.

"I need to buy my cotton balls."

"I can get them for you."

"But I like this brand and type—I should go. They're called Swisspers."

We wandered through the supermarket looking for the beauty aisle.

"Swisspers . . . where are you?"

"I feel like we are looking for our pet ghost wolf dog named Swisspers."

"Swisspers?" Quincy patted his leg and whistled.

We began to do that every trip.

We'd make fun of the strip mall's stores. We'd pretend like we were eager to eat at Qdoba. We promised ourselves we never would.

We slipped rather unintentionally into daily routines.

"A kiss while I still have good breath," Quincy would say in the morning, coming back to bed for a moment after brushing his teeth.

"But *I* don't have good breath."

"Your breath is always good."

And before I could come up with something snarky, he was gone, back to the bathroom for a quick shave or to the kitchen to make a cup of tea he wouldn't have time to drink.

"Love you!"

"Love you!"

The door shut.

One more "love you!" through the shut door as if I was married to a doorframe. I could hear his Vans thud down our paved stone hallway.

Then I got to my day, turning off NBC10, pouring out the tea

Quincy made, all while seeing what wedding or house setup work I could get done before Quincy came home again. It all felt very *Mad Men*, a show that Quincy and I had begun to watch in the last few months.

Mad Men had been on TV for four years already, had won four years' worth of awards and critical acclaim. But we didn't start from the beginning. We didn't even watch every week. We breezed in and out of the show, the civil rights era barely seeping into Sterling Cooper's climate-controlled Madison Avenue high-rise offices or into the home life of Don Draper and his wife, Betty. Our favorite part was the "On the next episode of *Mad Men*" segments, which were filled with cliff-hanger lines like: "I have to tell you something," "Hello?" and "So . . ." said in serious monotones by stylish white men and women in elegant mid-century looks while a spare but hypnotic piano and drum track played.

"Do you know what's happening?" I'd ask Quincy.

"No, I'm just watching for the 1960s style and manners. Oh—and I think Don's passing." Quincy had a theory that Don Draper, played by the certifiably white male Jon Hamm, was actually a Black man.

"I really liked their whiskey tumblers, shouldn't we have whiskey tumblers?"

"Neither of us drink whiskey."

We approached watching *Mad Men* like watching a *Seinfeld* episode, a bunch of white people making something out of nothing, making "I have to tell you something" out of nothing. But where *Seinfeld* built comedy out of nothingness, this show constructed something dreamy, aspirational, filled me with a longing for a way of life that I didn't know I wanted. It wasn't just the whiskey glasses or the sharp outfits, but that other thing—the nothingness of whiteness.

The Mansions' freshly built, empty apartments held that nothing, too, offering a literal blank slate.

I had wanted that spaciousness for longer than I realized. No more ghosts of girlfriends past. No more signs of academia having its way with him—the wall next to his grading chair scuffed up from when he fell asleep, the banker's boxes full of old papers, attendance and grade reports in case a student challenged him and the mostly white faculty took the student's side. No second room that was so full of stuff that I could only open the door a crack.

In the Mansions there was just Quincy's thin manila folder, beige with the promise of a reliable future. That manila folder was wherever he was: in the crook of one arm as he entered the house, a bag of Acme groceries in the other, Swisspers at his side; on the couch with us as we ate dinner and watched TV; on the bed when I woke up in the morning.

"Did you sleep at all?"

"Not yet," he said, though it was almost time for him to teach.

As the folder grew thicker with more papers, it was the one thing that didn't enter our banter. It was too much something.

A few days after we moved, I went to meet a potential wedding photographer with my mother. We met Mr. Hari in his studio, a thirty-something Indian man who my mom found through word of mouth on the Indian wedding circuit of the greater New Jersey area. He gave us his sample album. My mom flipped through the various pictures, pausing at the bride. "Who is she? What does she do?"

"She moved to London; she is an economist."

"Oh," my mom said. "She must be a put-together girl." My mother's tone was not entirely complimentary. There was something gruff in her voice. I thought of my own job prospects, still nothing between leaving my job and getting rejected from PhDs.

I started passing this gym in Center City, and one day, curiosity getting the better of me, I opened the Pandora's box. Pulling at a heavy door, I walked up a flight of stairs, toward the thundering sound of feet pounding treadmills, an instructor shouting commands as a bad up-tempo remix of Rihanna's "Umbrella" played.

Entering the hallway, I glanced through a picture window into the class in progress—the room was lit like a wine bar. In the dim mood lighting glowed white people on treadmills who seemed to multiply in numbers with the mirrored walls. I saw just one woman of color.

"She must be a put-together girl," I could hear the disembodied voice of my mom say.

I arrived in a reception area where the words "heart muscle mind" were emblazoned on a wall.

"Do you have personal trainers?"

"What are you looking for? Pilates? Strength? Cardio?" the receptionist asked me while bouncing on a stability ball.

"I'm looking for someone who isn't . . . mean," I said.

I hadn't expected to be so vulnerable.

"I know just the person for you."

Coach Mari was Afro-Latina, the only trainer of color I had seen so far in the gym. She was an enthusiastic soccer mom with a metal-head past. We bonded over our shared love of Chris Farley's *Tommy Boy*. Between reps, we traded quotes from the movie. I felt like we could have been cousins except that she was a decade older than me and infinitely more energetic.

"I woke up a half hour ago, sorry," I'd say, coming still groggy to our "early morning" workout.

"What?" she would cry. "It's noon! We got to get you up bright and early!"

I was on an antipsychotic at the time that put me into a sleeping stupor at night. It was often used as a street drug alongside coke or meth and would leave me sick with diarrhea and chills if I didn't take it. With the guidance of a psychiatrist, I would wean off of it in a year's time.

Between tapering meds and increasing exercise, I started waking up earlier and more alert. One day I was bragging to her about how energetic I had become in so many different facets of my life.

"I shower in like five seconds, put some clothes on, and am ready for the day!"

"No, no, you got to take some time, lotion the body."

The thought crossed my mind—if I lotioned, would I ever have had manic episodes?

Everything seemed to be working in sync—heart, muscle, mind; Nina, Mom, wedding vendors; Quincy, papers, Swisspers. Over the next few months, I lost all my post-smoking weight, hitching up my old exercise clothes in Club Treadmill to the point where Coach Mari treated me to some fancy exercise duds. I felt like I was finally fitting in, nearly indistinguishable from all the fancy-panted white people in those multimirrored rooms, me and my reflection running alongside me, running into the everything and nothing of my new life.

Quincy told me that he, too, was preparing to be a groom. He said he pictured himself in his Indian kurta, like his own positive visualization, he pictured it on and underneath his teaching outfit, Superman-like.

"It's my spirit journey," he said.

"Your what?"

I looked over . . . he was talking to me with his face on his manila folder, completely asleep. I pried it off his cheek, the manila no longer a steady shade of beige, grimy with tea stains, scuff marks, creases from a rubber band to keep the growing stack shut. It would need a second rubber band in about two weeks.

Just as July brought us to three months in both our Mansions life and our wedding planning, I found out about a writing workshop in a bookstore in Mt. Airy. It would start two weeks before the wedding. I really wanted to take it, but I felt like I would be cheating on my wedding planning and Project Bride.

"Go for it," Quincy said.

"I don't have anything to write about. All I have been doing is wedding things."

"How about writing about those wedding things?"

I wrote a bit when I wasn't wedding planning or tending to my beauty and/or fitness regimen, but just as often, I found myself just lingering in the strip mall across from the Mansions.

I would go to Lord & Taylor and get my makeup done even if we were just going to a small gathering with Quincy's family. I visited the nail salon so frequently that they kept a box with my personal nail supplies in it. I got blowouts at Supercuts and pretended like it was a trendy NYC salon.

I kept these activities like appointments, like I imagined Betty Draper would, bopping in and out of a series of stylish locales as that elegant *Mad Men* instrumental played behind me.

Then I would come home, open my laptop, and write. I was playing with a humorous how-to format—how to prepare for trying on Indian wedding outfits, how to find a venue with a horse permit and/or fire ordinance—but the so-called jokes never quite felt funny to me. I could hear my mom floating amid the punch lines I was trying. "She must be a put-together girl."

By the time Quincy came home, not only was dinner not ready, it wasn't started. I didn't cook very much while we were dating, and when we got engaged Quincy didn't expect that to change. The women in my family were another story. Quincy's mom encouraged me, saying, "You'll cook during Eagles games." Diksha mocked me, saying, "Mom says you can't even boil water!" And at a family dinner, my sisters and mother said in near unison, "You *still* haven't made him chai?"

"No," I flatly replied. A few months later, my mother showed Quincy how.

In any case, Quincy insisted on cooking dinner, deeming it our way of challenging gender norms. I agreed to this, less because of a feminist inclination and more because I was usually dead from Coach Mari and my fitness classes. He'd come in, drop his bag and his folder, and move right on to filling our open-plan kitchen with smoke while cooking some healthy dish Coach Mari told me to try. We'd bypass the secondhand West Elm dining table and instead eat on the couch. We'd eat quickly, hungrily (at least I would), and Quincy would set the dishes to soak in the sink. Then we'd get in bed, where Quincy would work some more.

What we lost in waking hours, we made up for in pillow talk. I would tell him about my day of bridal prep, of weight training, of floral arranging, of discovering kale cookies, and I'd ask him about his day. I waited for him to tell me about the open houses he led or the meetings where he pitched his ideas and revised them based on notes.

"What did you do today?"

"Nothing," he'd just say.

I wasn't sure if he was awake or sleep-talking.

Quincy and I returned to Mr. Hari's studio for the engagement photo session.

He showed me to a seat where his assistant prepared to do my makeup. She pulled out a contraption she told me was all the rage—an airbrush machine for makeup application. As the mist dappled my face, I thought of those car ads where they show automated machines spraying on the paint: building a bride was not that different from building a car. Quincy and Mr. Hari sat on a couch nearby.

Upon discovering Quincy was a writer, Mr. Hari showed him a book he was working on, telling him how he wanted to be the next Eckhart Tolle.

I tried to interject—

"Hey, I have to give you a shot list, right? We hired coordinators and they told us that."

"Your coordinators can pass it along. That is all."

He turned away and continued to ask Quincy for advice about his self-help book.

The first part of our photo shoot took place at my parents' house. We sat and hugged under a large oak tree in the yard.

I couldn't bring myself to perform for the moment. Mr. Hari gave some side coaching.

"Are you shy?"

"A little," I said. I wasn't.

I liked being watched—at workouts, at facials, at Supercuts. All that gazing was to prepare me for this moment: my debut as a bride, my launch into wifedom, my creation of my very own aspirational nothingness for others to glimpse in envy.

But now the magic hour ticked by as my body, my face, my very being refused to comply with Mr. Hari's lens.

"What are you going to do with your name?"

Four weeks before the wedding and I realized in all my many months of bridal preparations, I did not think about the taking of the husband's last name. Quincy's mother went through her list of reasons not to hyphenate—paperwork, misfilings, airline tickets—but then she concluded, "Just don't let anyone go persuading you."

Driving into Mt. Airy for the writing workshop was like driving to Sesame Street—except it was populated by mostly white people, no Sonia or Luis. There was a garage that fixed and sold furniture and antiques, a co-op market, a yoga studio, and the bookstore.

Our teacher, Mave, asked us to go around and introduce ourselves.

Everyone's names left me as soon as they said them. I was rehearsing my intro in my mind, moving my lips discreetly, preparing something they could hopefully laugh at.

"Hi, I'm Nina," I said. "I'm working on some stories about my wedding. I once Googled 'how to plan your Afro-Asian wedding without losing your mind' and nothing came up . . . so I decided to write about it."

No laughs.

"Wow!"

"Amazing!"

"I've always wanted to go to one."

"Ever thought of putting a directory of vendor contacts in the back?" one white woman added.

"That's a great idea," another tagged on.

This wasn't what I had in mind. I envisioned a parody of a "how to plan a wedding" piece. Either I didn't pitch my idea right or they had missed the point.

I kept my eyes on Kara, a Black woman, the only other woman of color in the workshop. She said nothing.

When it was her turn, she shared her origin story: how her family would put a pencil and paper in front of her as a child—her toy, her playtime becoming writing time. I had been the same way.

What brought her to this place? What brought me to this place? What brought us together? In this overwhelmingly white space it felt like I could think about nothing else.

"He ran away, didn't he?" Priya had been my bestie since my Norman Bates years. She already had her big Indian wedding, so she knew a thing or two about its dramas.

After a paparazzi-like team of photographers followed us around during the wedding, after my mother had paid him in full, Mr. Hari was nowhere to be found, radio silence. It had been a month since the wedding.

I reluctantly called my mother. I felt like I would get in trouble.

"He hasn't called me back or returned any of my emails about the photos."

"I will handle it."

A few fretful days later, I picked up the phone on the first ring.

"Be quiet," my mom said.

"But you called me."

This fact did not faze my mom, deep into our hunt for Mr. Hari. He still hadn't turned up, but my mother became her own two-for-one, mother of the bride and detective of the wedding. She had managed to track down his neighbor in his office suite.

"I'm going to talk first. Hello! Sophia? Are you here?"

"Yes . . . I'm here."

"So what happened to him, what were you saying again?"

"Well, he said he is not in a space to do his work, you know, creatively."

"Is he in the hospital?"

"No," she said.

"Well, then, he is a grown man, you know."

"He says he has to start rebuilding a business in order to finish up his previous projects," she said.

"I can help him get out of this. I am a doctor, I do psychiatry."

My mother is a radiologist.

"I'll pass that on to him, but for now, I can't give you any definite answer."

"Well, at the very least, we need the raw material back, at least that."

"Okay, I will ask him about that."

"It's just handing over the footage, we're not asking for anything he'd need to spend any money on," my mom said.

"Yes, I understand that and I very much sympathize."

"She's my last, you know? Do you have any daughters? Can you imagine that?"

In a coffee shop down the road from the Mansions, a very white shop typical of Philly's so-called Main Line, I admired the photos hanging up. One was of mehndied hands. I asked the cashier for the photographer's name: Karin. I called her, and when we finally got the raw materials from Mr. Hari, I gave them to her and asked for her thoughts.

"No one is looking in the same direction," Karin said.

The number of photographers on Mr. Hari's team, their paparazzi-like presence throughout the wedding, ended up making it hard to figure out where to look. The start of our married life seemed like a struggle to share a focus.

She color-corrected, cropped, and put stuff into soft focus. She edited and edited until they, too, looked like they could hang in a white Main Line café.

A month after the wedding, I stared at my first submission for Mave's class on my computer screen, my cursor going back and forth over my name—Nina Sharma or Nina Sharma Jones. I wasn't sure which way to go still. No one had persuaded me.

I called my mom. Over the past few months, we had deliberated over so many wedding matters together. It was the closest we had been in a long, long time.

"I should take it, right?" I asked her.

"Of course, sure." She hung up. We debated table napkins for longer.

My name change on Facebook got more "likes" than any other news I had ever posted, eclipsing any job news or literary successes. I loved how it was celebrated. And I loved surprising people with it. Surprise! A reply from Nina Sharma Jones. The timpani of the wedding seemed to echo through its syllables, each word carrying its own little buoyant bhangra beat.

I showed Quincy, very pleased with myself.

"Are you sure you want to take it?" Quincy said. "It's 'Jones.' It was probably just a name made up during Reconstruction."

I realized I'd forgotten to ask him. I realized we hadn't talked in days. By the time he'd come home from a full day of teaching and ramping up his concentration planning, I'd already be asleep.

The practice of a woman taking a man's name is a vestige of a centuries-old English law. Sometime after the Norman Conquest, the Normans introduced the idea of coverture to the English. Henceforth, under English common law, coverture asserted that, once married, a woman's identity was "covered" by her husband's. From the moment of her marriage, a woman was known as "feme covert," which, while it sounds like some cool *La Femme Nikita* superspy, actually means she and her husband became one. Her identity is erased, meaning she could not own property or enter into contracts on her own. Husbands controlled their wives legally and financially. Women had no recourse in rape or domestic violence cases and they had no legal rights over their children. At the end of the day, coverture actually is kind of like a spy movie, except it's that classic big Hollywood flick where the woman is beautiful but powerless.

Coverture laws were never formally overturned, and while the practice fell out of favor with the rise of the suffragist movements, some of its effects endured: for example, prior to the 1970s women could not get passports or other legal documents until they adopted their husband's last name. Even more glaringly: until 1975, a married woman's right to vote was contingent on whether she took her husband's last name.

English common law is only part of my and Quincy's story. Among Hindus, last names signal caste. "What is your last name?" a fellow South Asian writer/teacher asked me at a mixer. I heard it not as "Remind me of your name again?" but rather, "Where do you fall on the hierarchies of power and status?" And as Quincy so casually mentions over couchside dinner, his last name was "probably just a name made up during Reconstruction." I wondered over the word "probably." Quincy hates adverbs, but here "probably" was fitting, holding the complexities of naming post-Emancipation. Cutting off an enslaved person from their last name was part of the obliteration of slavery—to render someone without any connection to family, to community, to one's history, stuck in the perpetual present of the enslaver's control and dehumanization. Enslavers sometimes assigned a last name, sometimes they didn't, sometimes in the place of a last name there was nothing.

A year since his first meeting with his chair, Quincy got an email: "Your proposal has been accepted."

It was a very short email.

How could Quincy's tower of Babel manila folder be reduced so?

Not long after this, the department chair walked into the office Quincy shared with three other adjuncts.

"How many classes have you taught?" she asked.

Quincy offered his CV.

"No, just count your classes. I think with your experience and time here, you have been underpaid."

That same month, I began to take a writing workshop in NYC with an old friend. That meant I was in two now—I was still taking every cycle of Mave's Life Writing.

I went every week, leaving Quincy huddled over his manila folder, which had grown to require two rubber bands. He was working as an unofficial creative writing coordinator by that point, meeting with students who were interested in the concentration, keeping the folder as his guide.

The NYC workshop was a stark contrast from Mave's; we were all people of color, all people who sought this place out not for its nothingness but for its specificity, its very something.

It was a poetry class. I wasn't a poet. Quincy was. I imagined him here with them as much as me, as we read poets of color in the class, as we discussed shared experiences and themes, as we joked the way Quincy liked to joke, telling stories through jokes. I began to think: they all need to know him and his work.

I wish people knew you there in NYC as much as they know you here in Philly.

I wish I said that to him.

More often, though, it was, "Did the chair get back to you yet?"

"Baby, you asked that yesterday . . ."

I knew I had. I knew what I was doing.

"Still nothing."

....

By May we had been in the Mansions for one year, married for just over half that time. One year is long enough to settle into the household duties each member of the couple likes to do. Quincy liked to do the dishes.

"It helps me think."

I would go to bed, knowing the dishes were just the start of his evening, to be followed by some writing and grading.

He had a whole system—soaking them first, doing a bit of work, and then pulling them out of the water to scrub, rinse, and dry.

A system, a ritual, a habit, whatever it was I figured it was helping him cope with things: scrub, rinse, dry.

With Quincy's number in hand, the chair nodded. "I think I'm right. You are underpaid. I'm taking this to the board."

Ten years. Ten years of a semester-by-semester adjunct load, ten years of composition conferences, creative writing conferences, integrating himself in the Philly writing community, pulling that community to this school, publishing every year, coming out with a book, designing an entire creative writing concentration—it was finally all paying off. Quincy could nearly see his Vans morphing into *Mad Men* wing tips.

No more than a week later, the chair returned. "They agreed that you are being underpaid. They're okay with it."

Quincy took a beat, a few days or a week, and then tried to re-approach.

He knocked on the chair's door.

"I was happy to plan the concentration for free, but I'm wondering now: is there any chance for upward mobility?"

"Don't think so, Quincy, no."

"How about something like a creative writing coordinator position?"

"Sorry, Quincy, no."

"I don't need more financial compensation. Just something more than a year-long contract would be fine."

"No."

So that was it. Quincy turned his Vans, walked back down the hall, and slumped down into his chair. After a long pause, he finally turned to one of his fellow adjuncts. "This is why offices used to come with minibars."

I came back from New York after what was supposed to be a fun girls' weekend with a friend. I didn't have my meds and couldn't sleep. I drove home exhausted and plopped in bed and cried myself to sleep. I slept through late into the next afternoon. I had been suggesting New York to Quincy, who replied, "But I hear it's hard to get adjunct work." I was even thinking of graduate schools for him out there. "But I already have a degree." But even as I lay in my passed-out state, Quincy, on the phone with his mother, said, "We are thinking about moving."

One day it rained, a lot, across the entire Northeast. Watching the rain from the gorgeous French doors of our apartment was peaceful. Watching the rain come through a hole in the ceiling—not so much.

I put on my wifely best voice to call the super. "Excuse me, there is a hole in our ceiling. Can you please come fix it?"

"Not in a rainstorm," the building super said.

"Of course not, it's pouring outside. And now it's pouring inside, too."

One day the fire alarm went off without any cause and kept going off about once a week for two months. We'd file out to the parking garage in our pj's with the other neighbor-strangers. Quincy would always bring our passports, "in case it was the real thing."

I stopped going with him.

"If it's a real fire, I'll come back to save you."

"Uh-huh," I said and went back to sleep.

And one day, deep asleep, I didn't hear that little creak, didn't see that little quiver to the pool of suds, less dishes and mostly suds at that point, I didn't hear the crash of the whole sink just dropping, the whoosh of suds and soap flung up with the force, a volcanic quantity, shooting right into the middle of Quincy's face.

The counter ate our kitchen sink.

I woke up.

"What did you do?"

Not *are you okay?* Not *what just happened?*

"What did you do?"

The next day was Mother's Day. Our sink was still sunk, but I got my makeup, hair, and nails freshly done and we went to a family party at Quincy's grandmother's house, one neighborhood over.

By the time we arrived, the house was already buzzing. Quincy's older cousins were cooking in the back. The evening news was blaring on the flat-screen, its plasmatic clarity at complete odds with the retro charm of the rest of the house, its older, faded woods and shag carpeting. Quincy's parents shot up like soldiers or actors in a play, enveloping us in hugs and cheeky humor.

"Are you still there? You're thinner than at the wedding, Nina." I felt pleased with my upkeep.

"We'll be saying happy Mother's Day to you soon enough." I felt a knot in my aerobicized stomach.

Grandmom came over and put a red, thick cable-knit cardigan over my body—"You look cold," she said. I didn't think I was. When I looked down, I could see my arm hair on end. Maybe I was cold, maybe my goose bumps were something else: while Quincy had talked to his family about our move, I had not. Had I misled them with my Mansions life?

"Can I help with anything?" I said, more an overture than a real offer. Everyone knew I wasn't a cook, but I thought this was part of some holy trinity of daughter-in-law duties—asking to cook, offering to set the table, and chanting, time and again, Does anyone need anything?

"No, no, you just sit and relax," Quincy's mother said.

I took a seat at the dining table, half set already with appetizers. Quincy posted up by the stairs, in what seemed like deep communion with his aunt's lapdog.

While Quincy's brother and father settled into watching the evening news, his mother joined me at the table.

"How are things?" Quincy's mom said with a sporty hand on a chin. I could see how she would be great on bumpy Pan Am flights.

"Okay. Just working on grad school applications, planning the move," I said as steadily as I could.

A quiet beat followed; someone forgot their stage cue.

Quincy's father's voice came in then, though his gaze stayed on the TV. "How does that famous song about New York go? Something like leave before it changes you."

Quincy's mother added, "I thought the girl goes where the boy is in Indian marriages."

"What about the apartment?" Quincy's brother said.

"Maybe you can move in!" his father said.

"You can take it all, even the kitchen sink." I didn't mean to make a joke—the first time in a long time I wasn't trying—but they all were laughing.

"That was fun!" Quincy said as we waved goodbye from our car.

But when we turned the corner, I began to cry, catapulting into a full-on howl as we drove, smearing my Lord & Taylor makeup job, streaking the wife right off of me. I had taken his parents' ribs about us moving to New York personally. I thought I had violated some edict in a how-to guide for newlyweds—don't go against the norms and approvals of in-laws. Flying past blocks of row homes, I felt the dawn of my life not as a cool *Mad Men* character, Betty Draper in pearls, but as a wife of plain old suburban desperation.

I cried so hard. I had been holding the Betty Draper mask so close. I had told myself if I just kept up my gym and beauty routines I'd somehow take to married life. I wasn't. I kept crying.

Later that night, we were in the worst of all bedroom positions— opposite edges of the bed, me a never-stopping fount of tears and him all head in hands.

"I want this move as much as you," he said.

"Why didn't you say anything, then? Why did you just keep holding the dog?" A moment passed so quiet and long you would think we were trying to divine an answer from the Mansions ceiling fan.

"I didn't realize how long it had been since I talked," he finally said.

It felt like our biggest fight yet, but calling any of our fights a "fight" wasn't quite right—it was mostly me talking, my anger its own crackling strip-mall neon met by Quincy's quiet, steady as a dark blanket of night.

That quiet was maddening to me. I didn't want a quiet marriage.

One day I threw a cup against the wall: a green plastic tumbler I had bought from the Target that had just opened up. The cup was one of a set of four—neon blue, red, orange, and green—like a rainbow of whiskey tumblers. Neither of us drank whiskey.

I didn't know where it came from, this urge. So far away from the Betty Draper perfection I was chasing. And yet strangely familiar.

Crash.

"I'm sorry. Please just tell me what I did," he said.

It was plastic, it didn't break.

"I know I did something."

Just a slight lightning strike of a crack on the side.

"I'm going to New Jersey. My sisters are home anyhow," I said.

A few days later, I returned.

"I wish you could have just told me then," Quincy would say. "I wish we could just talk about things."

I honestly don't remember what I told him: that it was the way he arrived late, left the dish. Behind my words was all that was left unsaid, all I really wanted to say: all the open houses he attended while the white man cribbed his speech and fed it back to the faculty, all the meetings he had where he had to reexplain his curriculum and the white man didn't, all the times when Quincy's fellow adjuncts had to point out the double standard, all the ways the school disregarded him for nearly ten years. It was frustrating, the math never adding up—Quincy seemingly established, steadily working toward a future, but it was always just out of reach.

I didn't want to talk about that. I wanted to go back to Swisspers and imaginary Qdoba meals. I wanted to go back to our nothing.

I tried so hard—I still kept up all my appointments. I went to the hair salon where sometimes they'd say, "Why'd you get your hair blown out? It's so nice as it is." I'd go to the nail salon where I'd hear a harried mother say, "Can you please just do one coat?" and the nail tech would roll her eyes at me as if we both knew to judge her on her poor upkeep.

"What did you do today?" Quincy would ask.

"Nothing."

One day he screamed.

Aisha and a few friends were visiting us at the Mansions. "Wow," our friends said as I opened the door to our place. I was pleased. The perfect picture of the start of married life. While Quincy was at work, I took our friends out and we came home with even more friends. As I walked in, I saw Quincy doubled over his school papers, grading. He had fallen asleep but had almost fallen out of his chair in the process. As I opened the door, he snapped his head up and screamed a wild, long bellow, as if from a nightmare. But his eyes were open now. And then I screamed. I forgot about all the people behind me. I forgot the Mansions and all my bride-wife posturing. I ran to him. I made sure he was okay.

"I just fell asleep," he said.

But he woke up screaming.

"I just fell asleep."

But when his eyes opened, he was still screaming, and that felt bigger to me.

I collected myself and him. I put on a smile worthy of a Mr. Hari photo and welcomed everyone in like nothing had happened. They responded in kind. Except for Aisha.

"You ran right to him," she said.

Mad Men addressed critiques of their depiction of an all-white 1960s America by saying that it was in fact historically accurate—they weren't erasing race, they were simply representing the whiteness of Madison Avenue.

"What do you think white people would make of us, an Afro-Asian couple, in the 1960s?" I asked once as we watched.

"I don't know if they'd care." Quincy shrugged. "We might mean nothing."

In 2012, *Mad Men* creator and showrunner Matt Weiner responded to criticism that the show didn't do enough to represent the civil rights era. Earlier that year, the show had brought in two Black woman characters, but both were ultimately little used.

Weiner said, "I feel like the expectation that introducing a black character means you have to tell the civil rights struggle is in a way racist. I use her character the same way I use all the characters on the show. She is there. I'm sorry if people were disappointed."

On the Mansions website, there is exactly one Black person—a sliver of a face, barely in the frame as three white people cheer over a cocktail. There is an interracial couple—a white man and a woman of ambiguous ethnicity, smiling wildly as they are on their respective electronic devices. She is there.

In October, the hole in our ceiling not yet fixed, Quincy gave his notice to the university. This would be his last semester. No send-off. But immediately after Quincy told them he was leaving, a job posting went up. Interoffice hire only—the description matched everything Quincy did for them for free.

Early in the morning, Quincy rode with me in a cab to LaGuardia Airport, the NYC skyline in the rearview mirror. Three days earlier we had driven in from the turnpike, that skyline hitting me hard: those buildings like glamazons compared to the Mansions.

"It feels so good to be here." It had been a while since I had said that about any place.

I had been accepted into a writing residency in Vermont. After multiple rounds of Mave's Life Writing, my essays had won me a fully funded month in January, starting three days after our move.

We were nothing but a bunch of winter layers. Not a stitch of makeup, not a suit or dress in sight. My curly hair was in a ponytail that I only fiddled with as I tried on winter hats. Quincy's hair was finally growing back after cutting his dreads, and as we kissed good-bye in the airport his wild curls mixed in with my hat-head frizz for the first time in a very long time.

"Don't touch any of the boxes," I said.

Our would-be apartment was a labyrinth of unopened boxes.

"You said that already."

"Go out and take in the city!"

"It's nineteen degrees."

I was leaving him like this—finishing up his applications and look-ing for a job. He'd left his job of ten years and home city of fifteen. He'd done this all for his wife, Nina Sharma, sometimes Jones, board-ing the 9:50 to Vermont, direct flight.

THE JOKE LIMIT

I asked myself, what else was there to sustain our will to persevere but laughter?

—RALPH ELLISON

February 8

Coming back to New York City following January in Vermont, thirty degrees feels like nothing. "This would be a warm day up there," I say while unzipping my winter coat. I push the open coat flaps behind me like a cape, as if I've returned with some new superpower. I feel different, not just from being up against the elements. I keep thinking about Ralph Ellison, who, "shortly before the spokesman for invisibility intruded," saw a poster for a blackface minstrel show in Vermont. Residencies are filled with the racism of the well-meaning. In my case it was a white man who lectured me for not liking Quentin Tarantino's *Django Unchained*, who made our friend group, a necessity to a month-long writing residency in near-zero temps, markedly less fun. But I wrote. But I felt like a writer. Now I'm back in New York, where I have long wanted Quincy and myself to plant roots together as writers. Neither one of us has heard back yet from the grad schools we applied to. We are getting some financial support from my family. I am okay with the support. But Quincy, who still holds on to faded coupons and stashes money in the back of freezer bins, struggles with it.

Quincy is holding on to some remote teaching, but barely. We live near Columbia and students are returning for the spring semester. Their bundled-up faces make me wince. All our problems seem bundled up with the students' start-of-the-semester glee.

February 21

The Upper West Side still maintains its Nora Ephron, rom-com charm. The café where Meg Ryan's character gets stood up by Tom Hanks's character in *You've Got Mail* (and where Dave Chapelle as the magical Black best friend watches her and reports back to Hanks what she looks like); the 72nd Street subway station area where Hanks and Ryan walk around, Ryan's character still unaware that Hanks's character is catfishing her; the Gray's Papaya where she meets Hanks's character and he gaslights her—"Maybe I've seen him and I don't even know it." You know, classic rom-com. Then there is Ephron's own real-life Upper West Side love story, which is not about a man but Ephron securing an apartment in the historic Apthorp building. She wrote once in a personal essay for *The New Yorker*:

> In February, 1980, two months after the birth of my second child and the simultaneous end of my marriage, I fell madly in love. I was looking for a place to live, and one afternoon I walked just ten steps into an apartment on the Upper West Side of Manhattan and my heart stood still.

What Ephron called a "famous stone pile" is unforgettably majestic—I always considered it the Upper West Side Buckingham Palace, complete with a doorman-guard at the archway that leads into a gorgeous courtyard.

Where are our Upper West Side rom-com moments, me and Quincy? We had them when we were dating—those walks with the "long walk facts," getting "married" by the cigarette-bumming man as we passed the church on Seventy-Ninth Street, postsex breakfasts at my favorite old-school diner, and gripping hands (or more) during big blockbuster movies at the Lincoln Square AMC. But now, even out of work, it seems like we're too busy to have such moments. Quincy gets dressed as if he is going to work every day, full suit, only to scan job boards with NY1 on in the background, until laptop and flat-screen seem to bleed together. I just want to catch up with friends whom I haven't seen in two years. Quincy always suggests I go on without him, offers to stay home so my friends and I can talk. I insist he joins. I remind him my friends are our friends. I want to put things more bluntly, meanly even. I feel like Quincy's life is a little isolated—no friends, no interest in a social life.

One friend has recently become vegan, and we go to a restaurant in the West Seventies he picks out, Peacefood. Not a Nora Ephron haunt, but not a trendy vegetarian place like the type that feels part Meatpacking club, part restaurant. I have managed to drag Quincy out. He seems to be doing okay. As we wait for our food, Quincy tells a joke. We laugh. See, getting out of the house does a body good.

But then he tells another and another and another. A joke about the menu, a joke about the stew. A joke about the subways, today's politics, and reapplying to school. He's less my husband and more Quincy Live from Caroline's. We're just catching his evening show.

After we part ways, as we walk home, I drop the veneer of peace.

"I feel like you weren't with us," I say.

"I feel like I couldn't relax," I say.

I want to say, "I feel like this is a bad idea, moving to New York," but I don't.

Instead, I offer a proposal:

"What if you gave yourself a limit? A limit on how many jokes you can tell in one sitting?" I say it with such authority.

We pass by all the rom-com spots, all the spots where we once traded "long walk facts" full of boundless curiosity.

Five jokes. He agrees.

March 1

I think it is the cable company calling me, but it is Phillip Lopate, the head of the Columbia Writing Program. I got in! I tell him I'll be in Boston for the Association of Writers & Writing Programs conference, too, and would attend his panel. "Well, come say hi to me." I say I will. I got in. I'm having trouble registering it so I do what I do whenever I can't put a finger on things: I text Justine. She calls me right away. "This is amazing news." I mention some older worry: won't Quincy's family think I'm some clever career woman? "Let those days be over now," she says simply.

At the conference in Boston, I see friends I haven't seen in a while. I see people who treat me like a stranger. I see people to whom I want to say, "Do you remember me?" Quincy is just as flustered. He goes to an event for Black poets. He sends me a text—"They want me in the photo!"—and then sends me another: "Scrap that, not in the photo." I go to the event with Lopate.

"Hi," I mutter.

"You remembered to say hi to me," he says.

Sometime between events, I check my phone—voice mails from the heads of two more schools and a few emails. Acceptance from every school I applied to except for one.

Quincy has heard from two of his four schools—the two he wanted to go to the most because of the teaching that came with it—no from both. "I fought for you," a faculty member from one of the schools says to him at the conference book fair. "I'm sorry."

Returning home, the networking continues and along with it our fluster. Justine is part of an event on the Barnard campus that features one of Quincy's old teachers, the type of teacher who made him want to be a writer. "I don't want to go up to my teacher and say I'm a loser," Quincy says. But I argue with him until he turns away from the double screen of higher ed job boards and NY1, puts on his kente-patterned vest that is reserved for special occasions, and turns to go. We walk to campus practicing the thing I've gotten sick of doing, pretending like we haven't been arguing all day. I wear the mask of my blowout, a holdover from my Philly putting-on-appearances days. We only see Justine and Quincy's teacher from afar. For Quincy, it seems as if everything this year is just out of reach.

March 22

Winter is beginning to thaw, snow melts into gray city-dirty mounds. But Quincy is still out of work. I make him go on a model casting call. I go to Walgreens and print out what I think are stunning pictures—a mix of wedding photos and some gems I took myself. I am proud.

Even so, he doesn't fit the casting agency's needs: "They told most of the room to try again in six months," he tells me, "but they just handed back my pictures and laughed."

"I'm so sorry."

"So I asked if they'd consider taking me as a comedian."

"Did you really?"

"No, I just left."

I realize that I do not know much more of what is going on with him beyond that.

"What do you want for dinner?" I ask.

"What do *you* want?"

"What do you want to watch on TV?" I ask.

"What do *you* want to watch?"

I want his awareness, but it seems to boomerang right back at me. I realize it has been this way between us longer than I want to admit.

"Ladies' choice," he sometimes adds.

"No, men's choice," I counter.

He laughs at my bad joke.

April 4

The dance party has changed locations. Back when I lived here, it was in a spacious club that was right outside the Holland Tunnel—a location perfect for the bridge-and-tunnel Jersey kids like myself to find something better, the new world that a dance party, if done right, could be. Basement Bhangra is one of those parties, perhaps wrote the playbook of that kind of party. DJ Rekha made a space that is equal parts fun and transgressive, to honor our roots and to challenge boundaries.

The party is now at a club in the West Village, Le Poisson Rouge. The crowd is a mix of Indian intelligentsia and people who just want to dance. Rekha supports young artists and a couple go on before their set. We watch a short, humorous film by a music critic. "I would love to do that!" I say.

"You do!" Quincy says—he reminds me of the blog I keep occasionally where I post music reviews, *The Bass Slaps Back*.

We run into the filmmaker afterward. Quincy does that thing I have noticed he has started to do since we moved—introduces me instead of himself. "Nina Sharma of the *Bass Slaps Back*." He sounds like a manager of a bygone era, almost paternalistic. The filmmaker looks flummoxed. I try for something more human—"Loved your doc."

"You sounded like some 1980s high-powered manager. It was weird," I say as we leave the club, the DJ set still underway, people still entering.

"I just won't talk next time," he says.

"That would be even weirder," I say.

That night I have a dream. I'm sitting with a friend of mine: maybe it's a friend catch-up, maybe it's Basement Bhangra, most of the world is unseen. We're talking about "the new guy."

"So how's the new guy?" she asks.

Oh, it's my new guy.

"You mean Q?" I ask.

"No," she says, lowering her voice and widening her smile, "the other guy, the newer new guy."

I wake up.

April 10

Out of all the places to get pizza in NYC, why Midtown? I consider
that a red flag. But Quincy goes anyway. He's meeting the head of a
new MFA program in Brooklyn. He is a friend of my Philly writing
teacher, Mave. The program head offers him a spot in the inaugural
class with the promise of teaching at some point. The teaching offer is
vague, but it's the best he's gotten so far. Quincy's goal with an MFA is
not to blossom his writerly identity—he feels pretty secure in that—
but simply to get a terminal degree through which he might avoid more
de armento cacas Academia* and get secure teaching. And it's nice to
be wined and dined, Midtown or not. It's nice to be wanted.

A few weeks later, we find out about a letter that was sent to his
parents' house instead of our apartment. A thin letter. Could have
missed it. It is an acceptance. The school is Sarah Lawrence, a place
that doesn't have teaching attached like all the schools Quincy got rejected from. But it is the school most steeped in a literary history that
matches Quincy's own vision, with a stellar present faculty to boot.

Quincy doubles down on joining the new school, the offer made
during the Midtown pizza seeming too good to refuse. "I just want to
get back to work," he says. I find the offer dubious, but I'm tired of
fighting him so much. I realize I'm beginning to use the word "tired"
when I really mean angry, *I'm tired of everything*, a code.

But then I meet up with a writer friend who makes the decision for
us, putting it bluntly, "No, he's got to go to the name school," meaning
Sarah Lawrence.

"No," I parrot later to Quincy, "you've got to go to the name school."

....
*Academic bullshit, loosely translated.

May 18

We go to a friend's art opening, a friend from Vermont. The gallery, in Greenpoint, Brooklyn, is so small that it seems like an art project in and of itself. Only five people can step inside at one time. Mostly everyone just spills over on the steps and drinks beer in brown bags. We all migrate to a dance party that reminds me of the ones we had at the end of our working days in Vermont. Almost our whole residency cohort is there, minus *Django* man. I watch two women dance with nervous self-consciousness and spurts of abandon. Me and a Vermont friend smile.

"They aren't so bad," Quincy says of my group of friends as we leave.

I realize I had more fun that month in Vermont than I let on. I worry what other fun I'm missing out on while I'm still having it.

June 12

We go to the High Line. It's not like us to take advantage of the nice weather, but I don't want to be us. I get Quincy off his side of the couch. At the High Line, I remind Quincy that I came earlier this year with a guy friend.

"And then he kissed you! I will kill him!" Q shakes his fist playfully in the air.

"Hey! I don't like that."

Little white kids prance around the High Line with artisanal ice pops while I fume.

"I'm sorry," Quincy says. "It was a joke."

"I'm leaving."

I walk off the High Line. He walks off behind me.

"I'm so sorry."

It's too late, I'm angry and at more than just his comment. I hate feeling angry.

"Please talk to me. I'm sorry."

I take the train back uptown. I ignore him when he enters the train car with me.

I get off at Fifty-Ninth Street and begin walking through Central Park. He says, "Mind if I walk next to you? I won't say anything."

I always feel like I'm in trouble when I'm angry.

We somehow have landed in our third park, Morningside Park. We sit on a bench opposite a giant pond and twenty-foot waterfall. It's hard to believe it is here. It was built on what was once an abandoned gym project by Columbia University.

In our quiet, the waterfall rushes, the geese honk, the turtles make strange clicking noises—are they humping?

"I hate jokes about cheating," I say finally.

"I know," he says, "I'm sorry."

July 4

Nothing interesting happened today.

August 23

We take a walk to get some evening ice cream. I'm thinking Cherry Garcia or Sweet Cookies and Cream. We notice the street feels busier, younger. The kids are coming back to the dorms. Now I'm thinking of my own orientation just a week away.

Quincy is looking at the sidewalk. "I've never been this close to fall without a job." Way to kill my Coffee Coffee Buzz Buzz.

August 28

When Quincy tells me he got a job, I climb on top of him. He got two classes at CUNY Staten Island. The commute would take him over the George Washington Bridge, through New Jersey, and back across another bridge to Staten Island or he could take the subway to the end of the line, then the ferry, then a bus to campus—ninety minutes one way on a good day. He would have to do this on top of starting grad school at Sarah Lawrence. People think he's crazy. He takes the job in a heartbeat. Printed-out lesson plans and photocopies of readings soon scatter across all the surfaces of our apartment. His teaching papers. I realize how odd our life was without their presence. Our apartment decor feels complete.

August 30

I go to the orientation for Columbia. As we chitchat with faculty, I correct all the teachers who read my application—"I know it says Nina Sharma on my name tag, but it's Nina Jones on my application." I want to tell them the whole story of first taking and then dropping Quincy's last name, but I'm not sure where to begin or to end.

I mostly keep to myself at the orientation so I'm surprised when a spry blond girl comes up to me. "I met you at the open house—you got off the wait list, right?"

We have never met before. I realize she might be mistaking me for someone else—another Indian girl.

"No," I say, but it sounds more like "no?"

When I come home, even as I tell myself I don't want to get into it, I tell Quincy about this blond girl. Some part of me is angrier than I want to admit.

"Are you okay?" he asks. I hate when he asks this. I think it means I *should* be okay.

"How do you feel?" he asks. I hate when he asks this, too. Maybe more.

To say how you feel is to make something real and to make something real means making it susceptible to judgment, to criticism, to being told by feeling this you made a mistake.

I just want to take my Nina Sharma name tag off and change into something more comfortable than the blazer-dress academic costume I'm wearing.

October 2

Quincy and I venture out again; we're building a bit more of a social life. We meet up with old friends, some like us who have come and gone and now returned to the city. We take the C train home from Brooklyn to the UWS. It's a long trip and we settle into each other, holding hands watching the train car change character as we make our way up and up. At Columbus Circle, we get out to change to the 1 train.

"I had fun," I say, sleepy on our last stretch home.

"Me too," he says. It was the first time in a long time we had been on the same page in that way.

"And I was under my joke limit," he adds.

"What? I can't believe you took me seriously."

But he moved to New York for me. He chose the name school for me. He, before anyone or anything could validate my writing, took my words seriously.

"I still have two left," he said.

"You wanna tell me one now?"

He said he couldn't think of any.

NOT DEAD

When I started watching *The Walking Dead*, I thought the show needed flashbacks. Based on Robert Kirkman's comic of the same name, *The Walking Dead* follows a group of survivors banded together in postapocalyptic Atlanta, where the dead walk around—"walkers," they're called, never zombies. It is a world with no preexisting zombie lore. No George A. Romero, no Zora Neale Hurston, and no flashbacks.

"You know, flashbacks like they do in *Lost*," I told Quincy as he set down our Sunday dinner.

He's the one who got me into the show. We had begun to watch *The Walking Dead* together each Sunday evening over plates of his signature salmon and sweet potato fries, the menu unchanging, our own ritual of black-and-brown nerddom and nourishment. The show premiered just over a year into our dating; we watched from the start. Our married life felt like it paralleled the track of the show, a knockout start, a sophomore slump, and then finally growing into itself.

But still, no flashbacks.

"You know how in *Lost* they cut back to periods of their lives before the plane crash, those origin stories?"

"Different show, baby," he said, cutting another piece of salmon.

I quietly fumed at this logic. There are rules that govern any science fiction or fantasy universe, amid any and all chaos and wildness. Unlike *Lost*, in the rules of *The Walking Dead* universe there is no time for the past. Or, more simply put, there is no time-past. History, like water, medicine, food, and life itself, is a scavenged thing. Take what's necessary, what's useful to the present. The rest is a luxury.

Even the word "past" is a luxury; most often on the show, it is referred to as "before." Characters ask one another: "What did you do before all this?" or "before it all changed." One survivor, Sasha, is even more efficient. She recounts a portentous dream, simply saying: "We were at the beach, but it was before." Sometimes the word holds on its own like that, no more time stamp needed.

Can I even like a show like this? I wondered then. What are we but the past we carry? What constitutes our stories? Our survival?

And then came Glenn.

I woke up in the middle of the night not so much with a start but with a gnaw, like when you become aware of your own hunger, as if something has been eating at you for longer than you had realized.

Seven years and many servings of salmon and sweet potatoes later, I not only had fallen in love with this flashback-less show, but was now also grief-stricken over the brutal killing of one of its most beloved characters: Glenn Rhee.

The Korean American Glenn was the only character of Asian descent within the core group of survivors in the first seven years of the show. Anger swelled among the show's fans after Glenn became one in a long line of characters of color to get the ax. There was anger because the death scene was incredibly gory: Glenn was bludgeoned to death with a baseball bat by yet another big bad white man villain, Negan.

Glenn's final episode, the season 7 opener, titled "The Day Will Come When You Won't Be," earned the nickname "The Day Will Come When You Won't Be (Watching)." On social media, fans professed that they were turning away from the show. *The Verge*'s popular weekly recap column "The Walking Dead's Quitters Club," which was premised on the fact that one day the "Quitters Club would actually quit," effectively ended its run that week, and show numbers did in fact drop.

"The Day Will Come When You Won't Be" was directed by *The Walking Dead*'s longtime makeup special effects supervisor, Greg Nicotero, whose first major special effects makeup job was on Romero's 1985 zombie classic, *Day of the Dead*. Under Nicotero's supervision, gore is a cast member unto itself, and "The Day Will Come When You Won't Be" is an exemplar of his style. The episode debuts Negan, the brutal leader of a community called the Saviors. In previous episodes Negan's name is invoked, but he is never seen. The Saviors often made appearances without Negan. "I am Negan," members of the Saviors often said cultishly during confrontations with our survivor group, assuming this white man's name regardless of their gender or race. Loyalty trumped personhood.

In this episode, Negan has most of our survivor group down on their knees, not merely to meet their death but to meet "Lucille." Echoing the name of B. B. King's beloved guitar, Lucille is Negan's barbwire-festooned baseball bat, his go-to weapon and, sometimes, instrument of mercy—a blow to the head from Lucille prevents zombie resurrection. Negan begins to wave Lucille in his hand and sing.

"Eeny, meeny, miny, moe . . ." he hums as he points the bat toward the members of the group. At the end of the rhyme, he lands on the lovably smarmy Abraham and swiftly bludgeons him to death. We think he's finished. But then the group's longtime bad-boy heartthrob Daryl lunges at Negan. Negan in return goes after one more. Not Daryl, but Glenn.

The best we can say about this scene is that Negan goes for the head. We do not see Glenn return as a zombie. But the killing is long and protracted. What I remember most is seeing Glenn's eye pop out of the socket, hearing him tell his wife, the pregnant Maggie, how much he loves her, talking from someplace beyond sight and sense.

"I'm not sure I feel like eating," I remember telling my husband, looking down at the sweet potato fries and salmon he had so lovingly made. Our Sunday ritual. It wasn't that my hunger was gone. I'd just had enough.

That night we managed to finish our food, but we did break another tradition. We did not watch *Talking Dead*, the Chris Hardwick wrap-up show that followed *The Walking Dead*. I had often looked to the aftershow to situate the past. It was where the actors and crew could reflect on that night's victories and losses and where callers and audience members could ask questions. Hardwick once joked that the show served as a form of therapy, complete with a couch.

"No way," Quincy said. "There is no making sense of this."

Waking up in the middle of the night, I turned and watched Quincy, sound asleep. I appreciated that he took Glenn's death to heart as much as I did. I loved his refusal to watch *Talking Dead*, which to me felt less like mere refusal and more like an act of resistance.

I couldn't get back to sleep. Something drew me up out of the dark and made me open my eyes—a gnawing at the corners of my mind that, with the quickness of a flashback, turned into an image:

First the baseball bat, then the dead man rising again. Not Glenn, but this time, Vincent Chin.

The bat that Vincent Chin's murderer, Ronald Ebens, used thirty-five years earlier also had a name. It was a Jackie Robinson model Louisville Slugger. This was Detroit, 1982, thirty years after Robinson had changed the game, twenty years since he had been inducted into the Baseball Hall of Fame for doing so. And Asians were in the eye of a violent racial storm. American automobile plants were shutting down, and the rise of the Japanese-made car was being blamed for cutbacks at auto plants. In Detroit, people routinely demolished Japanese cars with baseball bats in a show of frustration and force. The United Auto Workers union even took part; UAW locals marched into town one Labor Day and battered Japanese cars with sledge-hammers.

At first it seemed like another barroom scuffle. The barroom was Fancy Pants, a strip club. Ronald Ebens, a local auto plant foreman, and his stepson Michael Nitz were sitting directly across the dance runway from Vincent Chin and his friends. Ebens had his eye not on the runway but on Vincent.

I imagine Ebens watching him—Vincent surrounded by his buds laughing, ordering another round, the vodka they preferred, tipping the dancers every chance they got, Vincent using the tip money he had just earned from his shift at the Golden Star restaurant.

"It's because of you little motherfuckers we are out of work," Ebens hurled across the runway. And then the words "nip" and "chink."

Ebens says Vincent dealt the first blow. Interviewed in the 1987 documentary *Who Killed Vincent Chin?* Ebens laments: "He come around and sucker punched me, and that was the start of it all right there, I never even got a chance to stand up, never seen it coming, that's the way the whole thing started." This affront warranted Ebens hunting Vincent down long after Vincent left the club. Nitz held Vincent's arms back as Ebens struck Vincent again and again until, as one cop put it, "there was brains layin' on the street." Ebens swung the Jackie Robinson bat with such force that it broke the handle.

Vincent's mother, Lily, caught him on his way out of their house. He was heading to Fancy Pants for his bachelor party, a party with no more than Vincent and three friends. She didn't like him going to strip clubs.

"Ma, just one last time," he said.

Maybe Vincent meant it. Maybe "last time" just fit the occasion for the outing, his bachelor party, a party with no one more than Vincent and three friends.

Bob heard "chink" and Jimmy heard "nip."

Gary's the one who heard Vincent reply, "Don't call me a fucker, I'm not a fucker."

And later, long after the club, it was just Jimmy in earshot. Jimmy, who followed the route Vincent took after he caught a glimpse of the bat in the Fancy Pants parking lot. Jimmy, who suggested the fluorescent protection of the Golden Arches when he caught up. Jimmy, to whom Vincent yelled out "scram" when he saw Ebens coming with the bat in hand. Jimmy, the only other Asian person in the group. Jimmy, to whom Ebens turned and said after the cops came: "I did it, and if they hadn't stopped me, I'd get you next."

Jimmy heard Vincent's last words emanating out of his disembodied head: "It's not fair."

"T-Dogging," it is called—when a Black character on *The Walking Dead* is killed. The phrase was coined by *The Root*'s Jason Johnson and takes its name from the original lone Black survivor of the group, season 1's Theodore Douglas, nicknamed "T-Dog," who was killed just as his character gained depth. Most often the "depth" is earned through sacrifice—assuming the position, albeit momentarily, as the group's moral compass and then risking death for the greater good of the group. In his final scene, T-Dog heroically charges toward a herd of walkers so that his companion, Carol, can escape.

Glenn stands out for the lack of blood on his hands. Over the course of his seven seasons he takes only two human lives, and one on behalf of Heath, a young Black male, so that Heath can keep his hands blood-free.

Glenn outlasts nearly all the Black characters on the show. Only Michonne, a Black woman who joined the group full-time in the third season, outlives him in surviving BIPOC death on the show, still alive even as Sasha, Gabriel, and others have come and gone. Michonne is most identified by her katana, a weapon with which she slices through zombies and human enemies alike.

Glenn, by contrast, is most identified with the pocket watch bestowed upon him by group elder Hershel. If you look closely, there is a small compass set within it.

Unlike the T-Dogged, Glenn survives and thrives. But his belonging seems to require unparalleled goodness, requires a steady grip on not a weapon but the group's moral compass.

> **The SHOT HOLDS, and just when we think there's nothing left to break the silence . . .**
>
> A SOFT CRACKLE OF STATIC. A voice.
>
> > VOICE
> > (filtered) Hey, you. Dumbass. You in the tank. You cozy in there?
>
> END CREDIT MUSIC begins, as:
>
> CAMERA CLOSES IN as RICK turns his head, stunned. Staring toward the forward compartment at the radio . . .

These are Glenn's first words, at the tail end of the pilot, introduced as a disembodied voice emanating from the radio of the army tank that our hero, Rick Grimes, is stuck in.

Rick was late to the apocalypse; shot and in a coma before the epidemic had begun, he woke up to a vastly different reality. We calibrate to the new world order (or lack thereof) with him.

By the end of the pilot, Rick is failing pretty hard. He has taken refuge from walker-swarmed streets in an army tank that, as the shooting script describes, "will very likely be his tomb."

Unless you have read the comics, there is no way to know whose voice bursts into Rick's catacomb-tank. We just know the voice is re-sourceful, radioing in, direct, and, indicative of a most underrated aspect of survival, unabashedly smart-mouthed.

To Rick's "we're not in Atlanta anymore, Toto" innocence, this voice sounds proficient in apocalypse.

And there is something about the casual banter of "hey, you," "cozy," "dumbass," that is even a bit nostalgic, the ambling swagger that one would think is more befitting of before.

In that way, Glenn's voice sets the tone for the show. A present that is forever channeling the past. A soft crackle of static.

There is no time-past—that, above all else, seemed to be the verdict in the case against Roger Ebens. No time for a past with any trace of Vincent.

At the trial, not one representative from the prosecutor's office or any advocacy group was in the courtroom. Only the defendants, Ebens and Nitz's legal team, were able to present their case before the court.

There was no jail time, not even the thirty days you'd get in Detroit for killing a dog. Just probation, a $3,000 fine, and court costs.

There was no mistaking what really guided the verdict, dealt by a judge who ignored the psychological evaluation that concluded Ebens deserved not only prison time but treatment for alcoholism, a judge who had been held in a World War II Japanese POW camp, a judge who said the murderers "weren't the kind of men you send to jail," adding, "You don't make the punishment fit the crime: you make the punishment fit the criminal."

There were no witnesses or family called to testify—not even Lily

Chin, who responded to the judge by way of a local paper: "These men wanted my son to die. They did not hit him in the body. They hit him in the head."

Sometimes, though, time moves in two directions. A verdict becomes a flashpoint, last words turn into first words.

"It's not fair," the protest placards read at the march organized in Detroit in the wake of the verdict. Vincent's last words were taken up as a rallying cry by Asians across class and cultures: by waiters, restaurant workers, chefs, laundry workers, housewives, engineers, and scientists; by business owners who shut down their stores so they or their workers could participate; by Chinese, Japanese, Koreans, and Filipinos; by scurrying children and seniors in wheelchairs alike.

The phrase was honored with precision: the signs all uniform, the words all in straight lines, chants and movements choreographed in twenty-second intervals. The joke went that because the planning committee had so many engineers, GM scientists among others, this had to be "the most precisely planned demonstration in history."

But if you looked closely, there was only one primary calculation to determine all that followed.

His words stood in English, with no other language in sight.

English only, they said, making clear their intended audience, white America.

His words not a luxury, a scavenged necessity.

"It's not fair."

....

When the verdict of the Chin case came out, it was almost exclusively picked up by local news outlets and smaller Asian American community publications. The *Los Angeles Times*, though L.A. had a sizable Asian population, ran only a two-paragraph wire service story on the judge's decision. *The New York Times* ran nothing.

Things picked up steam in the most unlikely of places for the beginnings of a movement—a car rental shop. Helen Zia, a longtime activist and cofounder of American Citizens for Justice, a new Asian American advocacy group that was working to challenge the judge's decision, was waiting in line. She noticed that the tall Black woman in front of her had copies of *The Detroit News* and the *Detroit Free Press* open to articles about the Vincent Chin case. Then she spotted a small notebook embossed with the words "New York Times."

She made good use of her wait time. "Are you interested in this case? I have some press packets right here if you'd like."

The reporter turned out to be Judith Cummings, the first Black woman to head a national news bureau for *The New York Times*. She was in Detroit visiting family and looking for a story to do while she was there.

Cummings's piece included details that had not been mentioned in previous national coverage outside of ethnic news media. She made sure to mention how no law enforcement officials had come to the club to question employees or investigate the case. She included voices from the prosecution, including lawyer Liza Cheuk May Chan, who said Judge Kaufman's decision was based on "'material errors of fact' in the information he considered, including the question of how the fight began." And she made room for a discussion of race, referencing an "ill feeling against Asians" in Detroit due to the losses of the auto industry.

The story led to national attention that spurred other reporters to delve into the case with more nuance and depth, examining particularly the yellow peril inscribed in the auto industry: the United Auto Workers parking lots with "Park your import in Tokyo" stickers and the union's sledgehammering of imports on Labor Day, the comparisons workers tried to draw between the "auto war" and Pearl Harbor, the aggression embedded in "Buy American."

By 1984, all this public pressure, and the joint work of Helen Zia and Liza Chan, led to a federal civil rights hearing—the first time a federal court would hear a case involving a civil rights violation of an Asian American.

A red Dodge Charger is coasting down a highway that looks a bit like two kinds of afterlife. There's the side that looks more like hell than heaven—the side clogged with a wreckage of cars, an evacuation that never came to be—and there's the one free and clear of any signs of the epidemic.

Before we even see the Dodge coming on the clear side, we hear its car alarm. As the red speck grows, a backbeat slips in, a Bo Diddley cover with a bass line moving in time with the alarm blast, and then a yell, a cheer—it's Glenn's voice. This is how the second episode of *The Walking Dead* ends. Glenn, not the sheriff, rides into the sunset in the most American of transports, to the most American of songs, and in the most American of outfits, a baseball cap and matching jersey. His unabashed smile as the engine's roar reveals that he is well aware of what this car can do on an open road.

The "supply runner" of the group, Glenn has always been skilled at finding the best way into and out of a crowd of walkers. It is the way he navigates Rick out of the tank. It is the way he continues to organize others to get out of the mess Rick started. It is something he does without apology, without deference, and with a little bit of annoyance—"I don't get in this trouble when I go out on runs on my own," he says. "You better just trust me," he says with growing impatience. It is a clue to what life looked like for him before.

"Hey, kid, what did you do before all this?" Daryl asks him in the fourth episode.

"Delivered pizzas, why?" he says.

I was surprised by this detail. And still craving flashbacks, I hung upon it. It pointed to a "before" free of the tiresome types of before that emerge around Asian characters. It is the detail that kept me watching, if only to follow this character a little bit further.

Maybe it was that Glenn, beyond the familiar banter, had a type of knowing that seemed relatable, applicable not only to combating an onslaught of a horde of zombies, but also to handling the everyday things that press against Asian American survival.

This is a type of knowing that seems embedded in Glenn's first words on-screen: "Not dead!"

Glenn's got his hands up and Rick is pointing a gun to Glenn's head. Rick, who has made a walker shooting gallery out of the escape route Glenn has given him.

"Whoa! Not dead!" are the exact words.

Whoa! Not dead! and I think not of Rick's gun or whatever the hell is on the other side of the highway at the episode's end, but all the other ways Glenn has had to stay not dead.

Of the five-year court battle that followed Vincent Chin's murder, there is one detail that stuck with me: Lily Chin stuffing and pulling cotton out of her ears so that she did not have to hear the gory details again and again, her own kind of before and after in this eternal present.

"Every time she saw a camera, it reminded her of the tragedy and . . . she got very emotional," said Renee Tajima-Peña, who, alongside Christine Choy, codirected *Who Killed Vincent Chin?*, which aired on PBS. "Off camera, she was the funniest. She loved to cook. She was always trying to set us up."

That humor, I imagine, is what Vincent inherited from her. He and Jimmy were laughing in the McDonald's parking lot when Ebens pulled up.

"[Ebens] was humiliated because Vincent was laughing when he got to McDonald's," said a witness, a man Ebens paid to help him track Vincent down.

A killer's "humiliation."

It must have been words like these that were worth a piece of cotton. Not just the gore. Words that make me wonder, What was it like for Lily to hear all that quiet?

"Walker bait," Maggie calls Glenn in the sixth episode of the second season, "Secrets."

Earlier in that season, Maggie, new to our gang of survivors, watches a few of the survivor group usher Glenn down a well to fish out a walker. The rope they're using to lower Glenn down goes loose, and he almost hurtles to his death. They scramble to pull him out. "Back to the drawing board," Dale says in resignation. Glenn, climbing out of the well, is panting but smiling. "Says you," he rips, passing the rope that was once tied around him to Dale. Turns out he managed to lasso the walker.

Maggie isn't as ecstatic as the others. In a quiet moment alone, Maggie says to Glenn, "You're smart, you're brave, you are a leader. But you don't know it. And your friends don't want you to know it. They'd rather have you fetching peaches. There is a dead guy in the well, send Glenn down. You are walker bait."

"Walker bait," my husband and I would say sometimes to each other, mostly in moments where we thought we were being used by someone or another. Mostly in the context of white America.

Walker bait when we find ourselves to be the only person of color on a panel or committee and are asked to be the spokesperson on race and ethnicity.

Walker bait when a white professor questions my experiences of racism and tells me, "Like us Irish, your people, too, will soon assimilate."

Walker bait when in 2019 I still find myself screaming "Indian!" at a lone brown face on the TV screen with just as much excitement as my mother did in the 1980s.

Walker bait when the federal trial is stymied by accusations of "coaching" witnesses, while the prosecution has only asked the questions the police never cared to.

Walker bait when the retrial is held in a city where only nineteen of the two hundred potential jurors had ever seen an Asian American person; where evidence of Ebens's racist statements was deemed inadmissible because the jury might be "repelled" and "resentful" of the person who said them; where the judge ruled the autopsy photographs "not relevant."

Walker bait when the defense takes the position that Ebens's extreme aggression was understandable in light of his job loss; when the phrase "bar brawl," as in "just a bar brawl gone wrong," is used again and again, until the killer walks away without a day in prison. When Ebens, decades later, millions behind on his fine plus interest, takes issue only with the price.

I sometimes think about why we found Glenn's death so surprising. It echoes a question I often ask myself—why do I find racism so surprising? And a question I have been afraid of asking—why did Vincent find Ebens and Nitz so surprising, enough at least to throw a punch?

Then I think of my coworker, a white man, who spied me doing my *Walking Dead* research at work. Peering into my cubicle, hovering over my body, he told me how much he hated Glenn. "Don't you?" he said. He told me that he wished the writers had left Glenn and Michonne, the Black swordswoman, alone. The writers should not have let them find love and a sense of place. They were better before—when they were not two human beings, but a gopher and a "killing machine."

In that moment, I felt the weight of a rope around my middle, guiding me down a well. I felt my hands tense around an office chair, wanting to scream out, "Don't call me little, motherfucker."

I did neither. I laughed nervously. I changed subjects quickly. I knew on some level that I was fetching peaches in my majority-white office.

I thought of Vincent's two white friends and Glenn's majority-white survivor community, and all the newspaper reporters who didn't call Vincent slurs but did call him "oriental" like a rug, a carpet, an object, a machine.

I thought of the PBS higher-ups who didn't "trust" Renee and Christine as they made *Who Killed Vincent Chin?* PBS funded the project but only under the condition that they work with a "Caucasian script consultant."

I thought of all the white cameramen who kept quitting on them until Renee and Christine learned to operate the cameras themselves.

And I thought of Lily Chin, who knew better than to trust a white camera, prying white eyes, with her whole, funny, and vulnerable self. Lily who knew that, even though we can be so many things at one time, a world under the bat-grip of white supremacy wouldn't know what to do with all that.

And maybe the day will come when this mistrust will no longer be.

Until then, I ask you. You in the office. You in the strip club. You on the couch. You trapped in the armored tank that is white America. You cozy in there?

THE DAYS THAT HAVE COME

(Or, How Is This Not a Hate Crime?)

At the end of the first season of *The Walking Dead*, our group of survivors journeys to the CDC's Atlanta, Georgia, headquarters in search of a cure for the zombie virus. There they meet virologist Dr. Edwin Jenner, holed up alone. Dr. Jenner regrets to inform them that they have no cure and also, by the way, he's blowing up the CDC in order to protect the world from other deadly diseases an abandoned CDC could potentially release. They all race for the exits. Our fearless group leader, Rick, hangs back a minute. In the finale's closing sequence, before he blows both himself and the CDC up, Dr. Jenner whispers a deeper, more shocking truth into group leader Rick's ear. The secret is so juicy, so incomprehensible, that they hold it for the season 2 finale, when Rick finally divulges: the virus is airborne.

Ten years later, March 8, 2020, I'm teaching writing to first-year college students. I take my two sections, forty students, on a field trip to a comedy show in Midtown. As we wait for the show to start, I see them pick up their phones one by one. They have all gotten this same email from our school: due to the novel coronavirus we would be going remote for this next week.

"What about after?" a student says to me. "How long do you think this will last?"

"I'm guessing three weeks," I say.

Then we go into the theater, no windows, no distance between our seats, a person coughs, but I'm not sweating it. My mind is fixated on my "three weeks." Way to scare the poor kid! So dramatic, Nina.

We are remote for the next year and a half.

But that first week, we continue to struggle with what airborne means. That week, students tell me about mass gatherings on the lawns and steps. That week, Quincy goes into the supermarket without a mask and gets stares from the employees. That week, I say to Quincy, "I just know I have antibodies," not because I think I ever got the virus, but because I somehow just have them, like good cholesterol numbers.

We tell ourselves stories to block out the truth. The day of the comedy show, CNN and NBC reported growing numbers of positive cases in the U.S., 550 and counting. By the end of the week there will be more than 3,000. By next Monday, on March 16, Trump will call this airborne disease with an ever-escalating, incomprehensible death toll the "China Virus" on Twitter.

March 16, 2021, exactly one year after Trump tweeted "China Virus," in Atlanta, a gunman, a white man, went into three Asian American–run massage parlors with a 9mm semiautomatic pistol and killed eight people: Hyun Jung Grant, 51; Suncha Kim, 69; Soon Chung Park, 74; Yong Ae Yue, 63; Paul Andre Michels, 54; Xiaojie Tan, 49; Daoyou Feng, 44; and Delaina Ashley Yaun, 33. Six of the eight victims were women of Asian descent.

And yet, the course of deeming something a hate crime never runs smooth. Authorities took the gunman's word that he was motivated by "sexual addiction." Advocates for the victims pushed back, noting what might not have been clear in the perpetrator's own words: the history of Asian women being hypersexualized.

"There were no cries. That means he shot them as soon as he saw them," said one survivor, Eujin Lee, recalling the deaths of two of three colleagues in an NBC Asian America report. Lee hid behind a box that had stored charcoal for an unused sauna.

Lee, who was once held at gunpoint, talked about what was different here: she noted the gunman's silence, no demands, no instructions, the plain and clear target—*he shot them as soon as he saw them.* "So how is this not a hate crime?" she said.

The gunman's lawyers did not respond to calls for comment. Their law group is situated in Canton, Georgia. There is a Canton in Vincent Chin's Detroit, too. According to Peter Ho Davies in his stunning historical fiction *The Fortunes*, which recounts Vincent Chin's story in "Tell It Slant," Canton was named "in the 1830s, when the nation was fascinated by all things Chinese, before any Chinese had arrived . . . there are Cantons dating from the same period all across the country."

In May 2021, just over a year after Trump's tweet, the *American Journal of Public Health* published a study that found that anti-Asian bias was apparent in half of the more than 775,000 hashtags with #chinesevirus. Timing here is key—the number of hateful, racist anti-Asian tweets associated with #chinesevirus grew much faster after Trump's March 16 tweet.

This is how we come up with the convenient mythologies like "sexual addiction." This is how we spread hate.

This is what we do even when we didn't know we were doing it. One of the first studies of language "virality" was done in 1964—a study in *Nature* that used epidemiological modeling to reveal that "a rumor can reach a large fraction of a population even if it is transmitted at an infinitesimally small rate."

We live in a time best described as a fusion between television and real life, a reality show president and his real-life impact. The confluence of Glenn and Vincent reaching its fulcrum. The merger of marks forming a hashtag.

The other day I saw on Instagram a self-care kit for Asian people; it contained a spiked stick to ward off attack.

The other day my student said her parents asked her not to travel too far from school.

Glenn knew the best routes. Vincent ran through Detroit. Lily Chin returned to China.

So many people are dead, not everyone from the virus.

HOW CAN WE TALK ABOUT INTERRACIAL LOVE WITHOUT TALKING ABOUT THE LOVINGS?

like making people laugh. It's in my blood. My father, too, loves joking around. Growing up, I almost never saw him without his joke book in his back pocket. He seemed to favor writing in out-of-date weekly planners, but even a stray piece of paper or napkin worked. Wherever the day's events took him, he wrote down one-liners, which he then delivered at "Indian parties" or weddings, an unscheduled performer, sometimes to the annoyance of the bride- or groom-cousin. My dad nonetheless made all the aunties and uncles laugh. His jokes at their best are cut from the cloth of one of his favorites, Rodney Dangerfield—"My wife and I were happy for twenty years. And then we met."

Jokes never come naturally to me the way they do to him. But the exalted space of laughter, making people laugh, having them in the thrall of our comedy—that was something I learned from my father and have kept in my back pocket.

I tried to dip my toes into theater with this impulse. I was twelve, a fan of Umbro nylon soccer shorts. In my after-school theater program, we did an exercise where we circled up and one person had to step in to play a character. I stepped in. I started walking wobbly, my purple Umbros swishing as I arced my right hand around an imaginary cup (my first attempt at object work, not too shabby). The teacher, a very Jersey white woman, stopped me. "What are you doing, dear?"

"I'm a drunk man," I said.

"We don't do that here," she scolded.

I never went back.

Twenty-five years later, in 2017, I took an improv class. I found it very difficult. I wanted to jump into the scene and be part of its magic. I wanted to be present and have as much fun as everyone else. But present and fun Nina receded every time I got onstage. Still, I continued to go, making it all the way to the class show. And somehow I just kept going.

By 2018, I had cofounded my own indie improv team, an all–South Asian women team. We called ourselves Not Your Biwi, meaning "not your wife" in Hindi. We opened for comedians, performed in showcases, put on off-off-off-off-off-Broadway Tuesday night shows. With them, I never receded. I flourished. And then the pandemic happened.

We went from the Newark Improv Festival, our biggest show, in January 2020 to doing nothing in March, or the only-slightly-better-than-nothing that is practicing improv on Zoom.

It's Tuesday, June second (that's what Governor Cuomo tells me in his daily briefing on TV), four months into lockdown. I have done the things that get me through my pandemic days: I have worked out, showered, checked the growth of my coarse chin hairs in the bathroom mirror (they are flourishing). I have arranged a weekly online Zoom-prov practice for me and my Biwis. I have been awaiting this practice. I need the relief.

....

A week before, May 25, George Perry Floyd Jr. was murdered by a police officer, Derek Chauvin, in Minneapolis, Minnesota. Darnella Frazier, a seventeen-year-old Black woman who happened to be walking with her nine-year-old cousin to buy candy, captured on her cellphone the arrest and the ensuing murder.

Floyd was accused of using a counterfeit bill at a local convenience store. Four police officers were called in. The officers forcibly dragged Floyd out of his car. After handcuffing him facedown in the street, Chauvin pressed his knee into Floyd's neck. For nine minutes and twenty-nine seconds, Chauvin kept his knee there. Two other officers further restrained Floyd and the fourth prevented onlookers from intervening, all the while Floyd said repeatedly, just as Eric Garner said before him, "I can't breathe."

Beyond the murder itself, one of the most chilling parts of the crime was Chauvin's awareness of the camera. Unlike the police in the Eric Garner bystander video, unlike countless other bystander and bodycam videos, Chauvin looked straight into Frazier's camera as he crushed Floyd's airway. And he kept going, fully aware of the camera, as Floyd said "I can't breathe" about twenty times, kept going as Floyd began to narrate his own murder, "I can't believe this, man. Mom, I love you. I love you" and "Tell my kids I love them. I'm dead," kept going, even talking back to Floyd.

"I can't breathe or nothing, man. This is cold-blooded, man. Ah-ah! Ah-ah! Ah-ah!" cried Floyd.

"You're doing a lot of talking, man," Chauvin replied.

His fellow responding officers seemed just as unfazed by the presence of Frazier's cell phone:

"I can't breathe," cried Floyd.

"You're fine, you're talking fine," Officer Kueng replied.

"You're talkin', deep breath," Officer Lane added.

"I can't breathe. I can't breathe. Ah! I'll probably just die this way," cried Floyd.

"Relax," Officer Thao replied.

And as bystanders entreated, "He's not even resisting arrest right now, bro," and "He's about to pass out," Chauvin kept his knee on Floyd's neck, unfazed by the crowd, unfazed by Frazier's videoing. Nine minutes and counting.

"I'm through, I'm through. I'm claustrophobic. My stomach hurts. My neck hurts. Everything hurts. I need some water or something, please. Please? I can't breathe, Officer," Floyd said.

"Then stop talking, stop yelling," Chauvin replied.

"You're going to kill me, man," Floyd said.

"Then stop talking, stop yelling, it takes a heck of a lot of oxygen to talk," Chauvin replied.

"Come on, man. Oh, oh. I cannot breathe. I cannot breathe. Ah! They'll kill me. They'll kill me. I can't breathe. I can't breathe. Oh! . . . Ah! Ah! Please. Please. Please," Floyd cried.

And then George Floyd was dead.

Frazier's video emerged the night of Floyd's death. The initial coverage of the death framed it as a medical event, one in which the police interceded on Floyd's behalf. The coverage seemed guided by a news release posted on the police department website: "Man Dies After Medical Incident During Police Interaction." The release painted the police as struggling against a man resisting arrest. "Officers were able to get the suspect into handcuffs and noted he appeared to be suffering medical distress," the release said, noting that "at no time were weapons of any type used by anyone involved in this incident."

Frazier's video shattered that narrative. It went viral first on social media and later on outlets of mainstream news. In the height of isolation, only a month after President Trump suggested injecting disinfectant to treat COVID, people began to march in the streets, the Black Lives Matter movement finding even greater coalition across color lines, the marches ongoing even after Trump threatened, "when the looting starts, the shooting starts," and even globally with massive protests across the world.

On our own pandemic couch island, Quincy and I watched reports of protesters getting tear-gassed first in Minneapolis, then in Cleveland and Seattle and as far as France, where thousands defied a police ban and converged at a courthouse in solidarity with U.S. Black Lives Matter protests.

"This is huge," I said to Quincy.

"This will pass," Quincy said.

"I don't know," I said.

He is a Black man who I worry about daily. I worry about him if we bicker on the street on one of our pandemic walks to stave off the stir-crazy. I worry about him when we plan road trips since I have no desire to be on a plane right now. I worry about him even in our building, where in an elevator a white neighbor who we have met before asked him, "What brings you here?" But I know my worry, even for the man whose spoon I curl up into at night, is nothing compared to what he feels, he has seen, he has experienced.

"It will pass" annoys me now. Maybe it's isolation getting to me. A couple's fight. Maybe I just don't want him to be right. Either way I am ready for some improv with my sister-wives. I just want to play.

We arrive one by one. Usually one of us is missing, but it's a full house. I take a screenshot when we have a full team. And if we are all together now, maybe we'll really get into it, maybe practice an improv form for Zoom shows?

"Wow, ladies, we all made it, I was thinking maybe—"

"We need to talk to our parents."

"We need to educate them."

"I read this post on talking to parents about George Floyd's death."

We usually make a little small talk before we start, and I wait for a lull. I wait and wait.

"We need to educate them."

I'm supposed to jump in, like an improv group game.

"I read this book, have you guys heard of it?"

If this was an improv group game, I would be the "squeaky wheel" who doesn't play along.

"We need to talk to our families, too, you know."

Who is this we? What about those of us who have been trying to talk?

I would be the teammate too "in her head" and not enough "group brain."

"It's like this thing I heard on this podcast . . ."

But it's not an improv group game. And I feel terse as Quincy was with me.

"Nine minutes. We need to tell them that."

....

A few days into the pandemic, my father had called me. I picked up on the fourth or fifth ring. "Nina," he bellowed as loud as the passing Mack truck. He treats the phone like a microphone—a device to amplify rather than communicate. "We have masks from the hospital. I can send you masks . . ." He goes on and on, debriefing me like Cuomo.

"We're okay, Dad," I said.

We were not. We still didn't have access to masks. But I didn't want them from him. I didn't want to jump the line when first responders still didn't have masks. And beyond that, I didn't want the pandemic to be an excuse for him to call me willy-nilly and flex his medical expertise.

We need to talk to our families, too, you know.

"Whatever, 'bye," he said, hanging up.

We need to talk to our families, too, you know, my Biwis said. I could have told them this story. But I didn't want to. As they shared book recommendations and cool things they had seen or heard over the interwebs, I felt myself recede. I wanted to be away from the "trending conversation." What if you had been trying to talk to your family before it was trendy? What if your love life was this conversation entirely?

In 2017, the same year I started improv, I took a picture. It was the fifty-year anniversary of Loving Day, and the story of Richard and

Mildred Loving was in my sight line more than any other year: I began to see social posts wishing people a happy Loving Day, an unofficial holiday made official by the power of likes and hearts. The 2016 Hollywood studio movie *Loving* had made its way to cable and streaming services, and Quincy and I were asked to be part of a project to re-create one of the Lovings' *Life* magazine photos.

It started when Quincy noticed an open call for interracial couples, and he asked me if I wanted him to submit us. I had a year of improv under my belt and I felt more and more comfortable with my desire to be seen, not just my clever mind but my whole physical body. He sent in our names, we were chosen, and I began my prep by studying the photo of their kiss we were meant to be reenacting.

The photos for the Lovings' 1966 *Life* profile, titled "The Crime of Being Married," were taken by Grey Villet, a white photographer of South African descent. By that point, the Lovings' almost decade-long fight for their interracial marriage had made it to the Supreme Court. A white father in Virginia found the profile so reprehensible that he wrote to the magazine saying that if his daughter ever so much as entertained the idea of intermarrying, he "would personally kill her and then myself, thus saving the state the expense of a hanging."

Villet preferred a natural style, no lighting, no staging, "as real as you can get it," he would say. His term for these close-ups was "psychegraphs," and he would use a handheld long lens to capture moments that were expressive of inner emotions.

You can't see much of their faces, planted as they are on each other. You can see more of Richard's, a face that seems weather-beaten from outdoor work, eyes shut as he leans in and wraps his workingman's hand around Mildred's back. Mildred does not lean in in kind. Her back is straight, no embrace, her arms at her sides. Her dress is plain black, her hair is held up by bobby pins—two, angling into each other to keep hair out of her face, more for efficiency than style. It's as if he caught her between things.

I did my hair the same way as Mildred, pins and muss. Our clothes were representative of our day-to-day, as real as we could get it: I wore my "Nasty Woman" shirt, which I hoped would communicate what had cast a shadow on all of us. Quincy wore his teaching blazer and a button-down. In the picture, Quincy's eyes are shut like Richard's. I am smiling, aware of the camera in a way Mildred does not seem or care to be.

When the photo project was released, my picture got tons of likes and loves and comments. I refreshed and checked and refreshed and checked my Facebook. The likes kept growing, more than I ever expected. Interracial love was trending. My favorite grad school professor liked it. I didn't even know she checked her Facebook.

"Mom likes it when people send her photos," my sister Diksha said. In that same year when I started improv and took the Lovings picture, I also began to get calls from Diksha conveying complaints from my parents that I hadn't been calling home that much.

"Don't you know Indian daughters look after their fathers," my father said when I did call. His voice had that same playful lilt as when he was up at the mic at weddings.

I told my mom that my father had given me this dutiful daughter spiel. "Can you all just think of me as your son?"

"No, no," my mother said as if I was mistaken, "we don't want anything of you."

I began to send my mom photos, but not any like our photo of the Lovings' kiss. No psychegraphs, just random cell phone snaps. I closed them off from my inner world.

....

"Even a light conversation doesn't feel light with them," I say to Quincy. "What's wrong with me?"

"In my family, jokes meant things were on the mend. In your family, it seems like jokes were a sign that something bad was going to happen," he says.

The cast of the 2016 *Loving* film also studied the *Life* photos. Discussing the other iconic photo from the spread—the one where they are sitting on the couch, Richard's head in Mildred's lap, Joel Edgerton, the actor playing Richard Loving, said:

> To me, [this portrait is] very indicative of the fact that she really was the spine and strength of the relationship . . . Richard is obviously a very hard-working physically laboring man, but it says something emotionally that she's the sturdier of the two.

When Quincy and I watched the film, it felt more like her "sturdiness" and the vulnerabilities that inform it were less fleshed out. From beginning to end, it seemed more interested in Richard Loving's coming-of-age story. Take the opening sequence. We await his response to her "I'm pregnant," relieved when he says, "Good, that's real good." We see him next at a car drag race giving expert advice to his team where he is but one of two non-Black racers. We see him after the race with his team, getting the stink eye from the boys of the all-white team, one of them flicking a lighter open and shut. We see him seated in the middle of Mildred and her kinfolk at a post-race party. Then we see him laboring—layering cement on concrete. At last we see him put a stick in the ground in the middle of a field—"I bought it, this whole acre"; the sentimental music begins—"I'm going to build you a house . . . our house"; he proposes to her. It's only then that the narrative switches off to Mildred, telling her sister of the good news. Later, after the court wedding and just before they are picked up by the cops, there is a brief convivial dinner scene at Mildred's parents' place where Mildred's brothers ask Richard questions about cars and racing, and when they ask how many races he has won, he says, running out of fingers on his hands, "Too many to count." Everyone laughs and we can see how comfortable he is at an otherwise all-Black gathering. We see his integration. Could it be that the white male director had more confidence, more ease, more comfort grappling with interraciality through him?

Scenes of Mildred are quieter. It's as if we are spying on her more than anything, and yet the actress, Ruth Negga, makes us not want to turn away for one subtle moment. In a scene toward the end of the movie, she stops the car she is driving, just for a moment, and takes a breath.

The thing that always gets to me with the Lovings is that their story is not merely a love story between the two of them, but a story of family and community. As the *Life* profile put it: "Both Lovings were born and raised in the isolated hill country around Caroline County, north of Richmond, where there has always been an easygoing tolerance on the race question." In a televised interview with ABC News from the 1960s, as kids mill about them (both their own and neighborhood kids, the voice-over points out), the Lovings talk about how their rural Virginia community was so far outside the rest of the world that, as Mildred put it, she didn't realize "how bad it was"—the world's outlook on interraciality.

It's a way of talking that goes outside of legalese or the righteous tones of social justice. It makes no nod toward the deep roots of segregation they were challenging: from as far back as pre-Independence America. It makes no nod to the nation's first-ever anti-miscegenation law, passed by the Maryland General Assembly in 1691. It makes no nod to Abraham Lincoln's 1858 vow, "I am not, nor ever have been in favor of making voters or jurors of negroes, nor of qualifying them to hold office, nor to intermarry with white people." It makes no nod to how these laws survived and thrived through post-Reconstruction, when thirty-eight U.S. states had anti-miscegenation statutes. It makes no nod to the twentieth century when, by 1924, the ban on interracial marriage was still active in twenty-nine states. And it makes no nod to extralegal permutations in the 1950s, when a number of white parents sent children to mental health professionals, to conversion therapy, if they dated across the color line.

"I didn't know how bad it was"—simple and spare as the photos.

Five weeks after getting married in D.C., they were hauled off to jail in the middle of the night. The verdict came down: they would be spared a year of jail time if they stayed out of Virginia for twenty-five years.

So they left their hometown, a house newly built by Richard for them to live in, their community, Richard's Sumerduck Dragway weekend race car crew, and Mildred's family.

"But the way I understood, the lawmen said we could come back and visit when we wanted to. So that Easter we came back and they got us again," Mildred continues. She speaks delicately, with a demureness that seems strategically indirect.

"We had come and gone a few times before then," Richard says more clumsily, in a thicker Southern accent.

On June 9, 2020, *The Washington Post* ran an article with the headline, "'A Man Was Unjustly Killed Here.' Interracial Families Face Challenge Explaining George Floyd's Death to Their Children."

The article came out in the wake of Trump decrying peaceful protesters in Washington, D.C., then relishing in a photo op in that very spot where they had been tear-gassed. Twenty-one minutes after police "forcibly cleared" Lafayette Square by pummeling demonstrators with rubber bullets, pepper spray, and tear gas, Trump strode in, flanked by military officials, slouching toward the front of a church. Reports said he made the unscheduled visit to the church because he "wanted the visual." The visual became him holding the Bible first around his midsection area, turning it around as if to check out the phrase "Holy Bible" on the spine; him raising it in his left hand. "Is that your Bible?" a reporter asks. "It's a Bible," he snaps back.

In the article, interracial couples are interviewed to discuss how they experience this moment, how they do or do not discuss it with their children, how and when and why they choose to talk to their relatives. There are no interracial couples without a white partner. Many of them have cop relatives. One story stays with me: a white-white couple tried to discuss Floyd's murder with their multinational adopted kids after visiting a George Floyd memorial. One of the couple's children, an eleven-year-old Haitian boy, stayed mostly quiet during these conversations. His father notes the moment he did not: "We were taking a walk, and he said, 'Dad, I just have to think about the fun stuff. Legos, video games.'" The parents' sincere "we need to talk to our families" was met by the kid's more complex response— the yearning to play, understanding that play, too, is processing, is grieving.

When I Google "how to talk about George Floyd," most of the articles I come across are like this one, some form of "How to Talk to Your Kids" about the murder of George Floyd or anti-Black racism. This reminds me of all the times I have Googled "family estrangement." Most articles, at least when I started Googling the concept in 2017, take pains to center the parents' gaze: how parents can cope, how parents can grieve, how parents can manage and go on.

When Quincy and I went with my mom to get our marriage license, the biggest worry on my mind was the bit of wax still lingering from my lip hair waxing appointment earlier, making a crinkly sound as we walked into the New Jersey courthouse. Even though it wasn't a court marriage like the Lovings'—we were simply going to the health department to get our license—I still did myself up a bit for the occasion, wearing a minidress and blowout from some Jersey salon that teased my hair up big with tons of spray. When we got to the health department office, we looked to the staff member, a white soccer mom, as if she was our officiant.

"Mom," she called to my mom, "is that right? Do they live on 4700 City Avenue?"

"Yes," my mom said. She smiled. She, too, had done herself up for the occasion. She stood tall and proud. She stood still, for once.

The only drama was playacted:

"Are you sure now?" my mom said as we signed the papers, giving us a stern look.

"Listen to her," our soccer-mom officiant said.

Quincy paid the $28 that got us our recognition.

"Oh, honey, I should do that," my mom said.

"You can take care of the other wedding," Quincy said, and we laughed as we exited.

"So that's it?" my mom said as we left.

"We just got the certificate," Quincy explained. "The priest still marries us that day."

"Oh," my mom said, looking a little let down.

I didn't show it, but I was, too—the whole thing, the hot baking wax, Aqua Net, and minidress was all for that?

"Well, why don't you just say congratulations and we'll kiss anyway?" I said to my mom.

And she did, so we did, a kiss as we stood sandwiched between New Brunswick, New Jersey, municipal buildings, with a few moving trucks from Rutgers students passing us by.

That was it. No one slapped us with any lawsuits. No one sent letters saying they were offended by the idea. No one threatened to take this all the way to the Supreme Court. No one threw either of us in jail. And even with everything I went through with my family, there were no discussions of sending me back to the mental institution (at least none of which I'm aware).

Six years after our court wedding, I began to get text messages from my mother that were mistakenly sent to me and meant for Diksha. "At least she called." I would burst into tears at this text I was not supposed to see. I hadn't known how bad it was.

....

November 2018. Bad Bunny singing in the Macy's Thanksgiving Day Parade. Quincy and I are getting ready to go to my parents' for Thanksgiving. Our holidays are a well-oiled machine by this point. We go to my parents' for Thanksgiving and his for Christmas. I am pleased with how systematized things have become. I am pleased that systemic and interpersonal anti-Blackness is no longer at the top of my mind when we visit my family. Since we've married, they haven't said anything negative or racist about Quincy, at least not to me. We are unstoppable. It would take something as far-fetched as a global public health crisis to stop us.

We are getting ready to go while watching the Thanksgiving parade on TV. By this point in the semester, we haven't done something as mindless as watching a giant Garfield flail in the wind in months. November becomes an undertow of student papers, eking out time for our own writing in between grading. Giant stacks of student papers, books, unopened mail, and bent-up packages flail about the apartment, moving from random corner to random corner whenever a new space is needed. It's more mess than I like to see, so when Quincy riffles through it, then brandishes the contents of an Amazon package, a pair of socks dangling from his hand as if he caught a prizeworthy fish, I don't stop my blowout, my requisite going-home look.

"I figured it out."

I work heat protectant into the wet hair strands.

"Going to wear these socks today."

I start to section off the hair in little alligator clips.

"So I can keep up with your mom in the kitchen."

In one hand I cock the blow-dryer like a gun.

"They got these little tire treads."

In another, I wrap the round brush around a section of hair.

"They grip against the floor."

Thick black curls clench back, put up a good fight.

We pull into the driveway. I play Princess Nokia's "Brujas" one more time before we enter. Just as Nokia starts her incantation, "Don't you fuck with my energy, don't you fuck with my energy," I see my nieces and their dogs waving happily up to us.

"Should we go in now?"

"I have to pee," I say.

I zoom through the door. I hear Diksha and my mom coming toward me.

"Why are you hiding in here?" Diksha says as her dog comes in, more friendly behind her.

"I have to pee," I say, trying to ignore the word "hiding."

I come out ignoring my sister's initial accusation, and we settle in. Quincy goes to the kitchen, where my mom is making food. I go to hug my nieces and nephews and the husbands. My father is asleep and when he wakes up and comes through, I hear him say, "Nina, come sit by me."

"Is that a command or a request?" I say. My own candor throws me off, and I can see one of my brothers-in-law looking flummoxed.

"A request," he says. I sit by him until he seems to grow tired and leaves, then I go to check in on Quincy. Relieved, I take in this scene: Quincy in his gripper socks confidently moving from oven to stove with my mother, petting dogs and skirting running children in the process. My mother in her Thanksgiving finest, calling Quincy "beta" and getting ready to go to the supermarket. I always wanted my family to be as comfortable, as real as they can get, with Quincy. Now I got my wish. It was remarkable, to get something this ordinary with Quincy and my family. It could have been our own postracial *Life* magazine photo spread.

As we file in for dinner, my father at the head of the table says, "Who will say the homily?"

I have noticed his recent turn toward Christianity in recent years. But this feels next level, the word hanging there like an awkwardly held Bible.

"We need someone to say the homily," he bellows. I shiver. My nieces and nephew giggle and roll their eyes.

"Do you mean grace?" I say.

"Quincy, you say the homily," my dad says.

Quincy offers a simple speech, giving thanks for this food, sending a prayer out to the world, and as he says this, I feel tense. The world Quincy cares about, the world that enrages him, the world he says he will go down fighting for, is a world my family cannot imagine.

Aria chimes in at the end, "And thank you to our parents for all they have done, we are so grateful," as if Quincy forgot the most crucial thing, as if saying, *Forget the world—get back to the important thing.*

We break bread and the thing happens that I didn't notice until Quincy came into the picture. "Everyone talks at the same time," Quincy pointed out at a family dinner. I see it now. Not one conversation but, between all of us, a twelve-way intersection of a dinner table. I eat.

Around dessert, people peel off from the table one by one: the kids go to their movies and video games; my father announces he must "pass water," then he and my brothers-in-law watch football together until my father retires to his bedroom. My sisters linger, scrolling through their phones. Quincy is next to me. My niece made a home-made pie.

I grab one more slice. Blueberries ooze out of a golden flaky crust, succumbing to an avalanche of Breyers vanilla ice cream. As I take it in, a pain hits me. Must be my nylons against my belly. I take another bite. It feels like period cramps. Must be getting my period. Another bite.

"I don't feel well."

"It's the pie, isn't it? I made it wrong." My niece's face is all distressed tween insecurity.

"No, no." I don't want to set the fork down, but I have to. My stomach is churning as I rush past the kitchen, into the bedroom, into the bedroom's bathroom, where I barely make it in time to lift the toilet bowl lid.

I throw up and throw up. All of it. Every last bit of today.

I come out, sit on the bed next to Quincy—throat burning with stomach acid, eyes bleary from tearing up.

My mom comes in, making other kinds of Thanksgiving meal plans with Quincy—"Give her this nausea medicine."

She sets a pill down onto the desk, a pill so large I can see the imprint code from my bed. For the first time all night, I cannot imagine swallowing anything.

"I don't need it."

"She threw up already." Quincy rubs my back.

She leaves. I slink into Quincy's back rub further.

"Nina." I hear my father before I see him.

"Nina," he bellows as if he is on the home phone intercom system.

The pill is back. It's between my father's thick, clubby fingers. I always imagined my father's hands were the product of growing up at high elevation, in a town "near the Himalayas," as he put it, altitude swelling that never left. They were the mountains to me.

"Take the pill." He lands in the center of the bedroom.

"It's okay, Dad."

"Take it, you'll feel better." There is a table next to him, the one where my mom put the pill down. But he does not put it there, it remains suspended in his hand.

"But I do feel better."

"Take it." He brandishes the pill.

It's not that he wants me to take it. He wants me to take it in front of him. Therein lies the difference. It's no longer about me getting better. It's about him. Take the pill. Laugh at my jokes.

"Okay," I say, but I don't outstretch my hand in return.

"Take it!" His knobby brown fist slams against the desk and he lunges forward.

"Give it to me." Quincy is a few inches taller than my father, but for this split second as he rises he seems to have just met my father's height. "I will give it to her," he says, calm as a hostage negotiator.

And then, for a moment, my father's face goes from blind rage to completely blank. In all my years of knowing him, no one has ever *not* bought what he is selling in the rage store.

I cry then, as Quincy holds the pill, as my father stands there, still hovering over me, his mountain hands empty. I always wanted my family to be as comfortable, as real as they can get, with Quincy. Now I got my wish.

I hear Diksha in the hallway talking to my mom. "Why did you send him in to do your bidding?" When she comes in, my father finally stops; he waves a hand up, turns, and leaves.

She settles into a chair across from me.

"You can go." I nod to Quincy.

For the first time in a long time I am left alone with a member of my family. And it continues to feel like there is a force field around the room. I see Aria around the corner with a bottle of Perrier, but she turns away.

It's never one big bruise, but a thousand paper cuts.

Diksha and I talk about what we share despite our age difference. We piece together what we can of our past, a past it seems we have both willfully put out of mind—a tense household, dinner table scenes. Growing up, our dining area had a swing rather than open-and-shut door, meaning, unlike the other doors in the house, it was hard to slam. Maybe that's why we hurled words more than objects—my mother's "All you care about is food and friends," or "Another drink?" or most simply, "Alcoholic"; to which my father would say, "She spoiled my appetite," or "Your mother is the reason I have heart disease," or most simply, "I should have married another woman."

After a while, especially after my sisters went off to college, we stopped eating together as a family entirely. I ate with a TV tray up in my room. Sometimes my mother sent me down to keep my dad company. She was not always there. And even sitting next to me, he didn't seem always there either.

Diksha and I talk about why they fought. We talk about the time and traumas we shared in the house. We talk about the time and traumas we did not. We talk.

Just eight years after the Supreme Court overturned the miscegenation laws, Richard and Mildred Loving were struck by a drunk driver running a red light. Mildred lost sight in one eye; Richard, who worked with cars his entire life, died.

Every time my Biwis urged, "We need to talk to our families," I wanted to say talking to our families is not as easy as *Here is this infographic* or *I read Audre Lorde and here is all I know about Audre Lorde, Mom and Dad* or *I read Ibram X. Kendi and here is how to be antiracist for you.* Me and my South Asian sister-wives' collective familial trauma, our shared but also distinct immigration and assimilation traumas, is part of that conversation whether we like it or not. The immigrant experience is part of Floyd's murder whether we like it or not. The owner of Cup Foods (outside of which Floyd was murdered), Mahmoud "Mike" Abumayyaleh, is Palestinian American. His immigration was informed by British colonial occupation of Palestine and the consequent U.S.-supported Israeli military and settler colonial occupation of Palestine. Abumayyaleh's presence within this moment also speaks to the complicated relationship between Black and immigrant store owners in low-income neighborhoods, a through line between him and the shooting of Latasha Harlins by store owner Soon Ja Du just before the L.A. riots. And one of the four officers involved in the killing, Officer Tou Thao, who stood between the witnesses and officers as they murdered Floyd, facing and ignoring the pleas of witnesses, is a Hmong American. Thao is from a community who came to the U.S. not as doctors and scientists through the 1965 Hart-Celler Act, but as refugees subject to deportation, whose flight was born out of the U.S.'s illegal war on Vietnam (and the CIA's "secret war" in Laos)—a war in which Black Americans were disproportionately drafted, assigned to combat units, and killed. Minnesota is home to the second-largest Hmong population in the country, and Derek Chauvin's wife is also Hmong American. She has gone on to file for divorce. Officer Thao was sentenced to forty-two months in prison. Cup Foods remained in business, the trial on TV every day.

Anti-Blackness and colonialization, these histories, these present-day realities, are linked. The policing of the movement of Black bodies and the migrations of South Asian American families are linked. Partition and trauma and silence are linked. It's these kinds of hurts my parents carried with them over shores, barely shared, barely dealt with, and more often showing up as pervasive anti-Blackness, the oppressed now emulating the oppressor.

We must go there, I want to say to my Biwis. Past the fantasy of conversation. Past the Instagram infographic. Into something very hard. Without doing that my Biwis and I will just reproduce white supremacy that has for generations tried to pit Black Americans and Asian Americans against one another, we will just be reproducing the not-quite-white life our parents chased. In "The Myths of Coalition" Stokely Carmichael and Charles Hamilton wrote:

> Liberal whites often say that they are tired of being told "you can't understand what it is to be black." They claim to recognize and acknowledge this. Yet the same liberals will often turn around and tell black people that they should ally themselves with those who can't understand, who share a sense of superiority based on whiteness. The fact is that most of these "allies" neither look upon the

blacks as co-equal partners nor do they perceive the goals as any but the adoption of certain Western norms and values.

"We need to talk to our families about George Floyd"—yes, but it is also more than that. To my Biwis, to any person who shares our "our," I want to say that "talking to our parents" is about dealing with something murky in "our" families. It is the assimilation, the desire to have something close to "superiority based on whiteness," that causes "us" to hurt each other.

I have been trying to both talk and not talk to my family about race for the last eleven years, since that Fourth of July weekend when I met Quincy, since before that—since my mom asked me when I was young what the N-word means, since my mother murmured the cruelties she and my father suffered in England, since my birthmark. Talking and not talking, for me that's truly talking to parents about race, existing in that paradox.

We need to talk to our families, one of my Biwis said.

I found this guide on talking points, another said.

The way we were stationed on Zoom, it looked not unlike one of the zillion MSNBC panels. I was a nontalking talking head.

I came back out, to Quincy on our couch.

"How was practice, baby?" he asked.

I shrugged.

"How's the world?"

"America likes to kill us. Americans like to watch," he said.

....

Talking with family feels to me not unlike vomiting, words mixed with stomach acid burning my throat.

I never did talk with my parents about George Floyd.

I wrote a piece of comedy instead.

It was satire. It was my first piece of satire.

I hope it made some people laugh.

WE CAN NEITHER CONFIRM NOR DENY THAT KAMALA HARRIS IS OUR TIME-TRAVELING DAUGHTER

t's November 2020. The announcer says, "Please welcome the Vice President Elect of the United States of America, Kamala Harris," the first strains of Mary J. Blige drop, a chorus equal parts buoyant and purposeful:

> Work your thing out
> Work your thing out

I am watching her strut out, her stride born out of years of working her thing out. I think, *She is really coming out to Mary J. Blige's "Work That."* On Twitter I read, "She is really coming out to Mary J. Blige's 'Work That.'" Even Mary J. Blige mentioned her surprise and delight: "She didn't even pick one of my hits . . . 'Work That' is a song only fans know." I grew up in the 1990s. I have waited for this moment longer than my lifetime. I cannot help but be overwhelmed, even though this isn't necessarily a Mary J. Blige song meant to elicit tears, or at least not on a "No More Drama" level; in spite of the sight of Quincy bopping his head along to its beat; in spite of myself. I don't want to cry. But I do.

It's January 2021. As she stands there, behind her the Capitol that seems to wail no more drama, she places her hand on the Bible with a knowing smile.

A smile that acknowledges this moment is history.

She is our first female, first woman of color, first Black woman, first South Asian woman, first biracial person vice president. All at one time.

I tear up again as I see her getting sworn in.

Harris stands on the shoulders of Fannie Lou Hamer, who in 1964 announced her candidacy for the Mississippi House of Representatives but was barred from the ballot. Hamer co-founded the Mississippi Freedom Democratic Party to challenge Democrats' efforts to block voter participation. And at the 1964 Democratic National Convention, in front of the convention's credentials committee, Hamer called for mandatory integrated state delegations. President Johnson held a press conference so that her speech would not get national airtime. That speech, held with Malcolm X, contains her famous declaration: "I'm sick and tired of being sick and tired!"

Harris stands on the shoulders of Shirley Chisholm, the third African American woman* in the New York State Legislature and the first African American woman in Congress, who entered the U.S. House of Representatives in 1969. Chisholm would become the first Black woman to run for president, attempting to become

---

*Bessie Buchanan was in the New York State Assembly in 1954 and Constance Motley was in the New York State Senate in 1964.

the Democratic Party's challenger to Nixon in 1972. She ran exclusively in a pool of white men, one of them Alabama governor George Wallace, who ran on "Segregation now, segregation tomorrow, and segregation forever."

And Harris stands on the shoulders of Carol Moseley Braun, who in 1992 became the first African American woman to serve in the Senate. After Chisholm and Moseley Braun, Kamala Harris became the third African American woman in Congress.

Harris stands alongside Stacey Abrams, who ran for governor of Georgia against Governor Brian Kemp. The race was tight despite his gerrymandering, voter suppression, and racist campaigning. Abrams came so close in her first run that Kemp admitted (in leaked audio at a supporter event) that he might lose "if everybody uses and exercises their right to vote."

Harris stands alongside Wandrea Shaye Moss and Ruby Freeman—Lady Ruby—Black women, a mother and daughter team of poll workers during the 2020 presidential election, who, after Trump, along with his campaign members and allies, including Rudy Giuliani, falsely accused them of putting in fraudulent ballots, received death threats all the way to the doorstep of their house.

Harris is standing with all that history, in front of the Capitol just ravaged by Trump's coup plot and the mob of insurrectionists he guided and stoked, whose terror included assaulting roughly 140 police officers, causing $1.5 million worth of damage to the Capitol Building, and resulting in five deaths.

And she stands there with her own legacies—the first female and Black American attorney general of California, winning by a margin of less than 1 percent. The third Black woman to run for president under the Democratic Party, after Chisholm and Moseley Braun. A product of the busing system that Biden, after narrowly winning

Senate elections in the 1970s, supported, as she pointed out during a presidential debate. "That little girl was me."

As she stands there, hand on Bible, Biden in a mask just behind her, and alongside him, Douglas Emhoff, white, Jewish, and the first second gentleman, I tear up. I take it personally. I think of Harris, born of a South Asian mother and Jamaican Black father, whose physical presence is a reminder of the possibility of Black and brown solidarity, of all the solidarities that could come. I think of my and Quincy's Afro-Asian solidarity, of what we have made together so far, of what we could create.

I turn to Quincy and say:

"I'm so proud of our child, Kamala Harris."

I am aware of the history of minimizing, infantilizing, and making mammies of Black women. I am aware of how anti-Black racism is present intimately in the lives of Black women in this way. And I hope in the moment I say this, Quincy doesn't see me as making a child out of Harris, minimizing this historic moment. More than that, I hope, if he did, he would say something.

I hope he always calls me out. But I hope he doesn't notice something else.

Saying the word "child," out loud, to Quincy, always fills me with a sadness, a Mary J. Blige "Not Gon' Cry"–level sorrow, even in the most lighthearted of moments. Even now, I feel it.

Please don't notice. Please don't see that I've brought up the possibility of us having kids.

"Yes," Quincy agrees. "We are totally proud of our time-traveling child."

It's May 2021. I'm scrolling through my Instagram. I stop and look at my friend's now nine-year-old child.

"Can you believe it?" I say. "She's nine!"

"Yeah," Quincy says from behind his computer screen. "If we had a kid when we got married, we'd have a ten-year-old."

"Are you disappointed?" I snap. "Is that something you wanted?"

"No, I was just . . . counting." He's right. There was a time when we were planning to have a child just after our wedding in October 2011. If we had, that child would be ten by now.

But I have stormed off.

"Baby . . ."

We go on two honeymoons. In October, still in the midst of our teaching semester, we take a three-day mini-moon right after the wedding to New Orleans. Mostly I sleep, getting up only to eat before sleeping more.

Then, during winter break, in January 2012, we go on a more traditional honeymoon in Jamaica: ocean sunsets, walled-up resorts, vacay like the colonizers do. Between October and January, baby conversations heat up. Not between me and Quincy, but with my mom and Quincy's mom.

"You can give the baby to me and Celia and we will take care of it," my mother says.

I tell Justine this. "Isn't that ridiculous?"

"I don't know. It's a good deal actually."

My mother-in-law says, "Your mom says I will chase after the kids because she is old. Just so you know, I don't do that. You will be doing that."

My mom looks around at Quincy's parents' house during their Christmas party. "Celia will make Christmas fun for the kids," she says.

We briefly call Quincy's parents to tell them we arrived safely in Jamaica. They both have just retired.

"What are you up to?" I ask my mother-in-law.

"I have no grans, so I'm not up to much!"

I am feeling the weight of their retirement already.

"Celia will do things like math books with the kids," my mother says.

In comparison, I only have but one conversation, more like a passing moment, with Quincy about kids. These are the years when I pretend to have far more certainty than I do, the *Mad Men* years when I am all Betty Draper and not much Nina, ready to plan everything out to fit into my vision for our married life.

"Are you ready? Do you think this is the time?"

"Of course!" I say as if he was missing an obvious truth.

By our Jamaica honeymoon, I am not so sure. My feelings about getting pregnant seem as confused, as conflicted as the bat that flies into our hotel room the night I am finally off my period.

It's January 2012. I return from Jamaica carrying not a baby but a secret, a secret it feels like I am keeping from myself. Quincy settles back in Philly, I go to my parents'. In the haze of being barely awake, the sun peeking through the drawn shades, I can feel my mind ready to turn, to tell myself the secret. It's not words in my head. It's a weight, each tear shed like an unburdening of this heavy, heavy weight, more than I am comfortable admitting, coming down more and more steady until I hear my mom come in with a cup of chai and a cookie.

"What is it?"

"Mom. I really don't want to have kids right now," I say, as if I have committed a crime, as if I am finally coming clean.

"Okay. Wait." My mom puts down the tea, shrugs, and goes about the rest of her day.

That's it? After months of her planning, of her and Celia co-conspiring? The weight turning into wait?

It's January 2021. I storm out of the room angry at Quincy's counting. Ten years married with nothing but a fictitious ten-year-old child, our time-traveling Kamala. Everything feels like work.

It's July 2022. I type in "Kamala Harris mother" into Google Images. I cannot stop scrolling. There is a photo of an elderly South Asian woman in a salwar between two shoulder-padded mixed-race daughters. There is a photo like the type my parents have from their youth, black-and-white, Indian woman in salwar with hair braided, but instead of a Western suit-and-tie mustachioed Indian man there is a suit-and-tie Black man with a cropped afro, the pose just as aspirational and full of promise. There is the requisite grandparent photo, generations marked from unsmiling elders to more carefree kids. All these scenes are so familiar to me. All these scenes are something I wouldn't mind seeing more of. And so, when I get up, to a house that's just me and Quincy, I feel it again, this weight.

It's May 4, 2022. I received a text from my mom. Our time-traveling daughter Kamala has been VP for a year now. It's a wild time. When pressed on border security, our daughter tells undocumented migrants, "Do not come." I'm, like, *What in the give me your tired, huddled masses?* On the eve of Putin invading Ukraine, our daughter says, "There's about to be a war in Europe" and I'm, like, *What in the day of infamy?* Her delivery in both cases unflinching, direct, and . . . surreal.

My mother texts me: "I have been meaning to write to you to let you know that I am here for you to support you physically, financially should you decide to have baby IVF or surrogate . . ."

I don't respond. I don't tell her that for the past few months, I have been in a three-way argument between Cigna and Cornell Reproductive Medicine over a $1,200 bill to store my eggs, a bill Cigna has covered for the past five years, a bill that I will now have to pay annually, a bill I hope to fight to not to pay. I wanted all the egg-freezing stuff to come out of my and Quincy's financial planning. I hadn't factored in surprise billing.

"I am here for you to support you physically, financially."

I wonder if Justine would say, "Good deal actually."

I think of what Quincy's mother once said: "I hear grandparents do things like pack the car full of stuff for the kids."

She was right. Whenever my sisters prepared to leave my parents', a good hour seemed to be spent on Tetrising into the trunk the bags they originally came with plus a supercluster of leftovers and home goods from my mother. "But your daughter *needs* this soft blanket." This all seemed to be part of the hubbub of having grandkids. I want to give them this hubbub. The event planner in me wanted to give both sets of parents not grandchildren but the event of grandchildren, the party atmosphere that "grans" can bring.

I wonder if I am horrible for not texting my mother back. I wonder if I am getting too old for "not yet," for still wanting to wait. A momentary glance at my mother's text pulls apart the timeline of my day. Quincy walks through the room and I try to play things off.

I am on our couch. The TV is on in the background, our afternoon MSNBC loop. A variety of talking heads switch out, but the chyron doesn't change: "Developing Story: Roe v Wade Leaked."

Two days before, May 2, the website *Politico* published what appeared to be an initial draft majority opinion, an unprecedented leak, suggesting that the U.S. Supreme Court intended to strike down *Roe*, ending a fifty-year federal protection for abortion rights.

"What are you up to?" Quincy says.

"Oh, nothing, just watching the nation-state take over our bodies," I say.

"That sounds about right."

As women cross state lines, risking paychecks or a job, hoping to find an appointment at clinics that once saw five to eight out-of-state patients a day and now see over twenty; as women make multiple appointments in other states so if one state's abortion clinics close down they will still have some options; as doctors, such as those in Texas, worry about getting sued and delay treating pregnancy complications until patients' lives are in danger, my fight to refuse support, "physically, financially," from my mother feels like the worst of my worst activism.

It's 2012. I am signing petitions to get canceled TV shows back on the air. Long live *Awake*!

It's 2017. I'm looking through a stack of paperwork—Quincy's health insurance plan from his teaching job at the fancy high school where they pay him a grown-up, nonadjunct salary. We can afford to entertain the option of freezing eggs. My mother doesn't know about this yet. No one knows I'm doing this besides Quincy. I don't want to get anyone's hopes up. I just know that that "not right now" feeling won't go away. I'm not thinking of our time-traveling daughter Kamala. I'm just thinking of myself. The AAWW program planner in me fancies a plan and here's as good a plan as any.

At our first doctor appointment, they stick an ultrasound wand in me. As they swish it around, Quincy sits on a chair facing me and the TV screen. The doctor explains the procedure as my empty uterus flickers in black-and-white on the screen. Afterward, as we walk out, I ask, "What was it like to see my uterus on the TV screen?"

"That was amazing." I realize he had been wanting to say that for a while.

It feels like the most grown-up thing I have ever done. Not telling my mother, not telling anyone besides Quincy that I am freezing my eggs. Just doing it and going about my day. I feel proud, I feel righteous, I feel like, if I am not a good woman who wants to have a baby, I am second to that, an okay woman who might have a baby.

This year our time-traveling daughter Kamala Harris is sworn into the U.S. Senate. I don't know who she is. I don't even know many Afro-Asian people yet. It will be just a few years until I start teaching at Barnard, where Afro-Asian first-years start to trickle into my classes, seeming to seek me out. (Maybe it's young Kamala, time-traveling under a different name.) But right now, in 2017, I just know the cringeworthy comments—"You'd make such beautiful children"—I just know the comments that piss me off, about whose skin color, whose features the kid might get, I just know the heartbreaking comments. "Nina Masi, when are you going to have a baby? I want to hold that baby," my nephew said.

It's 1958. Kamala Harris's mother comes to America just shortly before my parents and for the same reasons—opportunities to live more freely and pursue scientific dreams. But whereas my parents come together, an Indian family unit, Kamala's mom, Shyamala, comes alone. Studying at Berkeley in the 1960s becomes a totally different experiment in freedom for Shyamala than my parents undertook. In four years she will attend a lecture by Donald Harris: a young Jamaican PhD student and a fellow immigrant who shares in her desire to find something better than the colonial imprint left on his nation and its psyche. She will come up to him following his lecture on race on campus. Donald will later describe her as "a standout in appearance relative to everybody else in the group of both men and women."

Shyamala actively seeks out a life outside of the "home science" degree her British Indian ladies' college limited her to, leaving India to pursue biochemistry at Berkeley. And she actively seeks out a life outside of her supposed field of study—immersing herself in the radical politics on campus. She actively seeks out a life both of and bigger than the sum of her and Donald's parts, them together joining a fledgling study group that will go on to be the Afro-American Association, an integral force in the Black Power movement, and whose membership will be limited to people of African descent—aside from Shyamala, that is. When she and Donald break up, Shyamala actively makes the choice to remain in their Berkeley revolutionary cauldron, choosing to raise their two young daughters amid her Black community, leaning on her study group colleagues, Black women, like-minded thinkers, consciousness-raisers, activists who see in these kids what she sees—a legacy.

It's 2009—no, it's 2010. We are in bed, one of our beds, still doing long distance, and our flirty late-night pillow talk seems to be turning into something deeper and more abiding. I must have asked for his thoughts on having children. Did I dare? Back then, more foggy-headed about the future and in the habit of conflating flirtation with provocation, I'm sure I did.

He says he has had an image in his mind, an image that he is afraid of sharing.

"It's okay, I'll only judge you for it."

He laughs and shares the vision: "I'm at my computer, typing with one hand, holding a baby on my shoulder with the other—" His sentence stops abruptly. He sets his face into a pillow, and when he raises it, I see a single wet tear track.

Instead of kids, we make a reading series to bring our respective NYC and Philly communities together. We call it Nor'easter Exchange: Black women, consciousness-raisers, like-minded thinkers.

It's 2014. Another Christmas party with Quincy's family. They have settled into retired life a bit more, going on world travels, coming home with pictures and stories. We often watch a slideshow of an African safari on the plasma screen, sometimes mixing the trips up. This year someone has brought a baby, a Christmas baby. Someone has put the baby in Quincy's arms. Maybe it's the perspective of a tall person holding something so small, but it seems like Quincy grows an inch with that small, soft thing in his arms. He stands, he sways, he seems calm and in control, if not at peace. No one cares about the safari photos.

Instead of kids, we make our way through our respective MFA programs. And beyond our programs something is forming. A writer friend tells me that another writer friend once asked them, "Are your friends Nina and Quincy of 'Nina and Quincy'?"

It's 2017. I broach the subject of egg freezing to Quincy.

"What if I don't want to use the eggs? How would you feel?"

"I think everyone wants to leave a legacy. Some people's legacy is their children. Some people's legacy is their work. Ours could be our students. Ours could be our writing. Ours could be many things."

Surely, it can't be that easy.

"But you once shared a vision of holding a baby . . ."

"I think it was just that you were the first person I ever had that feeling for. I just want to have a future with you."

Instead of kids, we make our way through an uncertain postgrad future, snagging jobs as much for passion as for health care and pretax Metrocards. And we make our way through the Trump era, marching and making protest art (also known as art).

It's 2019. I write "Shithole Country Clubs" and it gets me so thoroughly trolled by MAGA people that we begin to plan all types of future scenarios together: *If I'm getting kidnapped as a political dissident, you'll know I'm trouble when I call and say "Feed Swisspers."*

It's 2000. But time as I know it has broken down. I look out the window, its plastic "human impact"–resistant pane a reminder of where I am, Payne Whitney Psychiatric Clinic. I don't need its barricade. I have already gone so far inward. I'm a collapsed star, consumed by a gravity that feels inescapable, that's swallowing me up, all the light in me.

Maybe this was the window Marilyn looked out of, too. Marilyn Monroe was admitted here for forty-eight hours before asking for a transfer. "I'd have to be nuts if I like it here," she said. But if there is no time, maybe she is still here, alongside me, the two of us constantly flowing toward nowhere, melting and solidifying, folding and crystallizing, becoming glass, becoming sand, becoming diamonds, a girl's best friend.

It's 2017. I am in the waiting room of Cornell Reproductive Medicine, where I will go every day for fourteen days before the egg retrieval. CRM is right across the street from Payne Whitney, where seventeen years ago I was a nineteen-year-old girl, at the start of her first of several mental hospital stays. If time travel means all time states may occur at once, there is a chance she sees me, as she looks out the window.

She might catch me in my athleisure finest striding into the CRM building, newer and fancier than any other on the block, she might wonder if she will ever be as put-together as that woman, she might wonder what that woman has survived to get to this point . . . or she might not notice me at all. I get to CRM before most of the city has woken up.

Rising out of bed at 3:45 a.m., I hit the train in my fancy tech-spandex, while everyone else, mostly Latinx, is wearing a hard hat or a uniform and heading toward jobs no one else wants while this country and its racist "take back our jobs" president seems to want them to go away. At five a.m., I arrive for the gothically named "blood hours," where every day they will draw several vials of blood and do an ultrasound to chart the amount and size of my ovarian follicles. Follicles are the name of the game in egg freezing—each having the potential to release an egg during ovulation. I go home afterward. At five p.m., I pay a nurse to come over and help me with my hormone injections, which induce follicle growth.

After my evening shot, I head over to improv, where I either take a class or practice with friends or do a jam. I go there even as the egg retrieval procedure is underway. In thirty-six hours, I will be on the operating table. I have just taken the "trigger shot," the last one, which preps your body to release the eggs—timed so that they drop just at the time of the retrieval surgery. In that thirty-six-hour window, I perform in an improv show and get interviewed for an improv scholarship—I debate canceling it, but Justine gives me the nudge I need. I shift around in my chair as me and my interviewer, who will go on to be a teammate, chat. As I ask him what "diversity" means to the theater, I imagine my uterus crowded up with follicles.

I get the scholarship. They get six eggs.

A few months later, I do it all again, even doing the exact same show before my egg-freezing procedure. I tell an improv buddy, if

Quincy and I have a kid this way, they will probably arrive silly and giggling.

My favorite part of the whole thing is the pre-op meeting, when I and several other women and their partners are debriefed on what to expect day of and sign a stack of papers waiving all liability. We are all told to have someone pick us up. We are asked to raise our hands to affirm. "I don't need anybody," insists one woman, holding up the rest of the orientation. I whisper to Quincy, "Love her."

It's June 2022. On TV, the chyron reads: "Roe versus Wade has been overturned." A couple of hours later I hear our time-traveling daughter at the mic, talking about *Roe*:

> This is the first time that a constitutional right has been taken from the people of America. "And what is that right?" some might ask. It is the right to privacy. Think about it. The right for each person to make intimate decisions about heart and home . . .

She goes on in heartbreaking detail and then says, ". . . decisions about whether to have a child including as Senator Durbin mentioned through in vitro fertilization . . ."

"What?" I say to Quincy.

"You okay?" he simply says.

Social media is ablaze with mourning and fury. I read a friend's post where she wrote that she has spent the morning calling friends and crying with them. There is no one I want to call, no one I want to cry with. I feel like that "I don't need anybody" woman.

Except I do. I need Quincy. I need to know that whatever decision

I make, we are okay. I wonder if he secretly wants me to have a kid. "There is no 'secretly,'" he has said over and over again. I wonder even if we create a great legacy, am I disqualified on the grounds of being a dent in the legacy itself? For I am a defective woman with no desire to fix her broken, so far nonticking biological clock.

It's 1978. Five years after *Roe* passes, the same year the first baby conceived via IVF is born, Richard Cohen publishes his article, "The Clock Is Ticking for the Career Woman." Cohen narrates a day in the life of "Composite Woman," a mash-up of the women he interviewed. With each mention of Composite Woman I can only picture a person with a blurry face, one to match his vague descriptors: "Sometimes, the Composite Woman is married and sometimes she is not. Sometimes, horribly, there is no man in the horizon." The article reads as if the desire to have children is innate, as if Ms. Composite or "the pretty one," the one with a "nice figure," during her twenty-seventh– to–thirty-fifth year, puts her blurry face in her hands as she realizes this deep and abiding "want" to have a child. Cohen notes that some of his interviewees did not want children, but then says, "Anyway, most of them did not say that. Most of them said that they could hear the clock ticking."

It's 2022. And even while listening to the experts react on MSNBC, I hear no ticking, I have never "heard" any ticking, and for that I have felt some sense of biological defectiveness, even though I know Richard Cohen is an op-ed writer and not a scientist, even though studies show the desire to have kids is more a product of culture than biology, even though Cohen himself reveals the article is more about him than Ms. Composite. "I recognized that I had been something other than a dispassionate reporter when I was going around asking women about the biological clock. I was getting aid and comfort from their answers," he writes, ending on a note of personal relief that he is on the "'right side' of it—the side of Charlie Chaplin and Pablo Picasso and all other senior citizen fathers, the side that heeds no clock." All ends well for him and these two men whose legacies remain largely un-marred despite charges of sexual misconduct.

I still often feel like my soul is a seashell, a hollow roar where that clock noise should be.

I feel this way not only in the midst of all the Great Legacy–building things that Quincy and I may do together.

I also feel this way amid all our idle, non-legacy-building things: I feel this way on a trip to Miami where I see an elegant woman in a gorgeous white kaftan three beach chairs over not lounging but on her feet, the kaftan flailing with her as she cleans up ketchup stains her toddlers have left all over their cabana chairs. "Look at the mess my children made," she says to her group, and it's not "mess" but "my children"—the possessive—that possesses me. I feel this way during a spur-of-the-moment midweek brunch with Quincy where I glance across the patio and see a friend at another table not sitting but hovering over her kids, waving not to me as I first thought but flagging her husband over to hurry up down the street. And I feel this way most of all every period I get. Every time the blood pours out of me. "What a waste of fertility," Ms. Composite might moan out of her blurry face.

It's January 2021. Kamala Harris puts her hand down on the Bible of her childhood caretaker, Mrs. Shelton, one of the Black women with whom Shyamala chose to surround her children. The kids spent time in Mrs. Shelton's home when Shyamala had to work. She spent so much time at Mrs. Shelton's that Harris referred to it as "the house" and wrote an op-ed entitled "Without This Woman, I Wouldn't Be the Leader I Am Today." Kamala Harris is a very real, noncomposite woman, a product of intersectional mothering, who grew up to not have biological children of her own. "Mamala" is the nickname given to her by her stepchildren, coming from Yiddish meaning "little mama." But to me Mamala feels like a mix between Shyamala and Kamala, a type of motherhood that is born out of the efforts of her mother and the community of Black women that surrounded her and helped her. It's her very Mamala-ness, a mash-up of maternal legacies, that frightens white America. Her ancestors were immigrants and her ancestors were slaves, an inscrutable, blurry contradiction.

Maybe for Kamala Harris the best term isn't a mom or little mama or any derivation, but instead another compound word: "funt," as in Maya Rudolph's *Saturday Night Live* impersonation of Kamala Harris:

> I'm also America's cool aunt. A fun aunt. I call that a "funt"—the kind of funt that will give you weed but then arrest you for having weed. Can I win the presidency, probably not, I dunno. Can I successfully seduce a much younger man? You better funting believe it.

This, the least maternal term, the one that is not in line with mom, mamala, mammy but a cognate of cunt—this is the one that resonates most with me.

It's 2011. Quincy notices my mom's habit of saying a woman is "clever"—her own C-word. "It doesn't seem to be a good thing," he says.

"You are too ambitious," my father once said to me as I pulled further and further away from him into adulthood.

"What is it that you do?" he also said. I was ambitious but in a vague, Composite Woman, blurry way.

At the same time—Quincy never seems to take issue with my ambitions.

At the same time—whenever a friend of mine says she is pregnant, I say congrats hoping I sound sincere, hoping she doesn't see that her pregnancy feels like my shame.

At the same time—

Every year since 2011, I can't stop seeing Quincy's face buried in the pillow, the tear stain as he lifts his face.

"Are you crying?" I said.

"No," he said.

I have never cried like that over children. I have only cried like a child, to my mom, until she said simply, "Okay. Wait."

I feel so guilty I have not given Quincy this thing that he probably wants. I am the kind of person in the habit of anticipating wants and one of his wants *must* be a child.

"I feel like I'm disappointing him," I say to Justine, "being this unusual woman"—"unusual" being a euphemism for defective. I know she would not stand for "defective."

"But he's never wanted a usual woman," she says. It's the only time the ghost of his dating past has comforted me.

It's 2018. I finally wake up from my second egg-extracting procedure. The nurse whispers that they retrieved five good eggs. I do the math—six from the last one makes eleven total. I try not to feel upset; I had heard stories of twenty and thirty. Quincy comes in and I don't share the number with him. "How long was it?" I ask. "Two hours," he says, gripping a wrinkled cookie packet. "Really? It felt like two seconds. I imagine that's what traveling through a wormhole is like."

It's 2020. Quincy and I make a video piece out of one of his poems. I say lines of Quincy's poems, while he stands behind me with cue cards flipping the words. It was my idea—to "Subterranean Homesick Blues" it. I like being Dylan, not Sara (nor any of the other women in his songs). We practice the video more times than we thought we would—practicing the timing of flipping the cards to my saying the words. The thought crosses my mind, we have the luxury of time to practice flipping these cards because I have not made children. The video gets love, gets likes. It competes with baby pictures, at least that's how it feels to me.

It's 2022. At our college teaching gig, where we both teach first-years, Quincy and I both get promotions. We are a Nina and Quincy of Nina-and-Quincy there. It hurts to know we are so good at teaching in a way that makes me feel like we might actually be great at parenting. Our students say, "He talks about you." Our students take his class one semester and my class another. A student says, "We have 'heart eyes' for you." "What are heart eyes?" I ask, showing my age, or, as my ob-gyn calls it, my "advanced maternal age"—the accepted term for women thirty-five and older. Quincy keeps teaching. I leave the job. I wake up in a cold sweat sometimes from dreams where I'm still teaching and feel guilty, another set of kids I have turned away from.

It's May 2022, just at the end of my last semester of teaching.

The school year is over, I'm getting something from campus. There is a bench on campus that says "Stupid people shouldn't breed"— etched there in stone like some Greek quote should be. In all my years of walking to and from campus I have not seen it, but I see it today. I realize I often live the reverse of the phrase—I did not have kids, so I am a stupid person.

As I exit campus, I see a T-shirt, "What will be your legacy?"

Maybe it's easy to see things when they are at the top of your mind.

All day, I have been on the phone with either Cigna or Cornell. Cigna says since the procedure was medically unnecessary they will not pay for my egg storage. I call my doctor's office:

"Please say it's necessary."

"We can't say it is necessary unless you use them this year."

I think of the nineteen children shot in Texas today.

I think of *Roe* at risk.

I think of my mom's bribe.

I count:

Every Afro-Asian student that has come to my class.

Every year of marriage as a child's age.

Every day I feel relieved I didn't have one.

How much is that worth?

"It looks like they are charging you for more than storing the eggs. But you are just storing—let's see if we can appeal on that."

It's June 2022.

Late on the Friday afternoon of a long weekend, as we get ready to go to the beach, Cornell calls me again, tells me I have to pay up. I put the phone on speaker and Quincy hears the whole exchange. I ask to speak to the manager. I am the "speak to the manager" person now, at my advanced maternal age. I want Quincy to hear. I don't need to have it on speaker. But this call contains all the emotions I cannot bring myself to otherwise say.

Am I crying?

No.

At the end of the beach weekend, I get another call. My appeal was not accepted. I say that I've never had to pay any other year. "That is a mistake. You probably should have paid every year." I am worried. Would they ever charge me retroactively? I think about paying up right then and there. I think about destroying the eggs entirely. "Thanks for letting me know."

In his book *Black Holes and Baby Universes*, Stephen Hawking says, "The best evidence we have that time travel is not possible, and never will be, is that we have not been invaded by hordes of tourists from the future."

In our home office space, I tell this to Quincy.

"Maybe this isn't the time they want to visit. Would you want to come here from the future? First of all, there is a virus around, second of all, dictatorships seem to be hot, oh! and the environment is kind of falling apart. Maybe this isn't the best vacation. I really feel like we are the Florida of timelines right now. Dictators and giant brain slugs." He is on some kick with Florida slugs.

He says this while rolling up a page of the family wall calendar, a calendar that is sometimes two or three months behind, until July gives me a blank stare. I stare back. We have a family calendar. We are already a family. It's hard for me to see that.

I think of bad reasons to have a kid: to make a "family,"

> to fill up space on a family calendar,
> to fill up an empty feeling,
> to feel good enough relative to others.

It's 1907 and Einstein's special relativity posits that time is an illusion in that it moves relative to the observer.

....

It's 400 BC and the Mahabharata states, "O King! The princes that you thought would become the bridegroom of your daughter all died; their sons and grandsons and their friends even have all passed away." Time, Brahma goes on to explain, runs differently on different planes of existence.

It's 2014 and in "Rejecting the Biological Clock," Jenna Healey writes, "If female fertility is a clock, then it can be unwound, repaired, or even stopped." She is writing in response to companies like Apple and Facebook offering to cover egg freezing for their employees. "This fascination with technological solutions has distracted us from addressing the real reasons why women feel compelled to postpone pregnancy later and later in life." She writes that corporate culture should be remade in a way where reproduction is valued and supported, not to the detriment of career advancement.

Something Justine says always sticks with me: "Why does everyone say 'All I want is the child to be healthy'? You can't count on that."

I think there is only one good reason to have a kid: you want to raise it.

It's 2018. I visit a friend after she has survived a terrible car accident without a scratch on her, her husband, or their child. She asks me about my desire to have children. I tell her about the eggs. She bursts into tears. "Anyone who can have children should have them," she says.

It's July 2022 and Quincy is watching a pro-lifer talk about her mother's abortion on TV. "I could have had more family."

"More family is not always a good thing," Quincy taunts back.

....

The Afro-Asian American family is a complication of parallel if not opposing histories—Du Bois's "How does it feel to be a problem?" and Prashad's "How does it feel to be a solution?" Not everyone is a Shyamala. And not even Shyamala could control what Kamala would become or what would become of Kamala—neither the actual arc of her political career nor the fantasy projected on her as a poster child for interraciality: the fantasy that interraciality has a kind of end point or proof, that end point or proof being a child, a child who can go on to be VP, who can even be president of a country (as Kamala Harris was briefly while Biden was getting a colonoscopy).

It's 2018 and *National Geographic* publishes a special issue, "The Race Issue," picturing on the cover twin tween half-Black, half-white girls, one white-passing and the other not. The caption underneath states that the twins will "make us rethink everything we know about race." Such a cover stokes the fantasy that if the multiracial child is an interrogation of race, revealing race to be a social construct, then that same multiracial child (especially the white-passing one) *is* the construct overcome. Racism over. No need to acknowledge how even if race is a construct, that does not mean it is not real in one's lived experiences of race-based discrimination and inequity. No need to acknowledge that with the repeal of *Roe*, Black and Indigenous women, long marginalized, used and abused by the American medical system, are in the most danger. No, in adorableness of the mixed-race child, love and postraciality simply win. Barack Obama can go back to being America's smoothest politician. Meghan Markle can go back to being an ex-monarch in L.A. White women can go back to dressing up as handmaids at repeal of *Roe* protests even as Atwood admits to the ways that the text erased race while basing its violence on American slavery.

It's 2019. I snuggle up on the couch with Quincy as we watch *Contact*. Whenever I think of time travel, I think of this movie, where Jodie Foster travels through a wormhole and meets an alien in the shape of her father, who tells her about time pathways (even that movie cannot escape the allure of procreation). At one point, asked what she would say to the aliens that have sent Earth a message, a set of instructions for a spaceship, she says, "Well, I suppose it would be, how did you do it? How did you evolve, how did you survive this technological adolescence without destroying yourself?" It's the thing I wonder all the time. Two things I realize I should have asked Quincy when we started dating:

Where do you stand on having kids?

Where do you think we are on the timeline of the world destroying itself?

"We won't go down without a fight," Quincy often says.

He would be such a good dad. I would be such a good mom. People notice that about me. That I have a maternal nature. But what people don't realize is that it comes less from a child-bearing desire and more from growing up in a home where being nurturing, self-annihilating, meant you were spared the destruction of others.

I am sorry still, every period I get; those hundreds of children that I don't have a maternal feeling for . . . at least not yet. I am sorry that I don't have a biological clock but can only listen to my feelings of hesitation, honoring them. All while hoping Quincy does the same—tells me if his mind ever changes.

It's July 2022.

I get a letter from Cigna that there is a new appeal opened up on my behalf. It's like I'm getting a letter from the past, present, and future all at once.

On TV, I see a GOP senator ask if women can give birth to turtles and tacos. On the street, I see a T-shirt that reads "Proud Dog-Mom and Aunt." In the park, I see myself in midworkout, feeling this weight again, the immense guilt for the ability to attend to my hip flexors in the middle of a Tuesday, the luxury of not having a child.

It's May, just after the beach weekend, before I got the new appeal letter. I go to the CRM website to pay, using the money Quincy and I made from writing an article together on Afro-futurism. I pay the $1,200 in full, close my computer, and there, on the edge of the bed, ten years after our wedding, one month from losing *Roe*, finally I cry.

It's 2011. We are on our way from Philly to Cape May where Q will propose to me. The car radio is a foggy jumble, our distance mapped in the resounding shush of snowy feedback, that is, except for WDAS, famous for its long-range signal. It is unavoidable, and so, as the evening light begins to cast its glow, we catch the tail end of Michael Baisden, a Philly radio personality who is best described as what would happen if Steve Harvey and Charlamagne Tha God had a baby.

"Hey, fam, our topic today is being Blasian."

"Blasian?" I said.

"Black and Asian both," Baisden said, nearly at me.

"Friends don't let friends listen to Michael Baisden," Quincy said.

"But it's Baisden on Blasian—that's us or, um, could be," I said.

I quickly switch off Baisden and hunt around for a CD. I find two choices in the center console—a romantically inclined mix made by Aisha and one marked "new shit" that Quincy had made pre-me.

I debate the two CDs as we edge closer to our end point—the exit to Cape May, the last exit in New Jersey, 0.

> 0—the number that holds our future
> 0—Steven Wright once said, "Black holes are where God divided by . . ."
> 0—the amount of eggs I have stored as we drive to Cape May

When zero is divided by zero the answer is undefined, it's a singularity. We don't really know what that looks like, just as we don't really know what it looks like on the other side of a black hole. All we see is the event horizon.

I slip a CD in. A remix of Biggie's "Hypnotize" comes on, featuring Shabba Ranks. I've made my choice. I pick "new shit."

ACKNOWLEDGMENTS

A teacher of mine once said, writers don't need just a community to thrive, we need an ecosystem. Here is mine:

Thank you to my agent, Maggie Cooper—the blank page is less daunting with you by my side. Thank you, Todd Shuster, for this excellent matchmaking. Thank you to my editor, Juliana Kiyan, for helping me find not only my Harry and Sally but Nina and Quincy on the page.

I am grateful likewise to Victoria Lopez for her thoughtful eye and support at every step. Thank you also Yuki Hirose, Tanvi Valsangikar, Lavina Lee, Heather Lewis, Elisabeth Calamari, and Jessie Stratton Zhou for your insight and guidance. Thank you, Vi-An Nguyen, for this beautiful cover. Thank you Ann Godoff, Scott Moyers, Matt Boyd, and Sarah Hutson and my entire Penguin Press family.

Thank you to my fact-checker, Caryl Espinoza Jaen. What luck to find you. May our conversations over research and reportage be lifelong.

This book is about allyship from the margins. There are three people who have read drafts of this entire manuscript and whose friendship feels like a lifelong practice of allyship. I am grateful for their trust, consistency, and accountability in life and on the page. I am especially grateful for their crucial critical feedback in the last stages of working on this book:

Thank you, Erica David, for reading these stories from day one, wedding mehndi still on my hands. Thank you for helping me find and trust in their rhythm.

Thank you, Jyothi Natarajan, for first editing "Not Dead" and "Shithole Country Clubs" for AAWW's *The Margins*. Thank you for so deeply "listening to the piece" then and now.

Thank you, Mecca Jamilah Sullivan. The way we bear witness to each other, our intimacy of scrutiny as Audre Lorde says, is one of the greatest pleasures and honors of my life. Knowing you is being at the right party.

To my earliest teachers from grade through high school who encouraged my writing life, for all their nudges that I only see now as a teacher myself, I am so grateful. Thank you to my professors at Barnard College, especially Timea Széll. *The Way You Make Me Feel* would not be were it not the way you made me and many other young writers feel about writing.

Thank you, Wen Jin and Shinhee Han. I first began to write into Afro-Asian allyship, personal and collective grief, in your classes during my American Studies grad program.

Thank you to the Asian American Writers' Workshop for all that you gave me at the very start of my writing life and all that you continue to give. Thank you, Ken Chen, Anjali Goyal, and Jeannie Wong. Thank you to the community I came into through AAWW. Thank you, Kundiman, Cathy Linh Che, Sarah Gambito, and Joseph O. Legaspi, and thank you, Cave Canem. Thank you to the writers whose workshops in these places I was lucky enough to take. Thank you especially to Bushra Rehman and her Two Truths and a Lie workshop, which I first took at AAWW and then many times after. You created a radical, tender space of welcome for me and my work and I know I'm far from alone and I'm lucky to call you a friend.

Thank you, Thaddeus Rutkowski, for your workshops in NYC, where I began to experiment with creative nonfiction, and the one in Philly through which I found more writing family. Thank you to Minter Krotzer whose Life Writing workshop is where I began to work on this collection. Thank you, Minter and Hal Sirowitz, for your mentorship and friendship. Thank you, Rahul Mehta, who read an early version of this collection, for your invaluable guidance.

Thank you to my teachers in the Columbia University MFA writing program. Phillip Lopate, thank you for sharing your love of the essay so generously. Thank you, Margo Jefferson, in whose class I wrote the title story to this collection. Thank you for helping me reach back into the past with less judgment and stigma and more accuracy and depth. Thank you also to Hilton Als, Alana Newhouse, and Meghan Daum.

Thank you, Elizabeth Walters, for your precise eye in our postgrad years on an early draft of this book.

Thank you to the Asian Women Giving Circle for funding "No Name Mind: Stories of Mental Health from Asian America" and the Asian American Writers' Workshop for giving it physical space. Thank you to t. tran le, Katie Mahabir, and every NNM writer "always trying to get things straight, always trying to name the unspeakable"—your work emboldened me here. Thank you, Maxine Hong Kingston.

Thank you to my entire writing community, we chip away together.

Thank you to my comedy and performance community; so many of these stories either began onstage or became better the more I found my feet and my people.

ACKNOWLEDGMENTS

Thank you to my team Not Your Biwi improv: Kavita Patel, Ramya Ramaswamy, and my Brown Swan sister Sarita Ekya. Our collective joy is in the sinews of these pages.

Thank you to the places where a few of these pieces were initially published: AAWW's *The Margins, The Blueshift Journal*, especially Jeffery Renard Allen and Tyler Tsay, and Hematopoiesis Press. Thank you, Sari Botton, for publishing "Pee and Fury" in *Longreads* and for being a longtime friend in the personal essay.

Thank you, Maryam Mir and Ani Otiv, who dreamed cover dreams with me, for your crucial insights and visions. Thank you, Ani, for joining the book team and nudging me into my light; may we continue to share pages and stages.

Thank you to places that gave me writing space and community, including: New York State Summer Writers Institute, Vermont Studio Center, and St. Nell's Humor Writing Residency. Thank you, Lee K. Abbott, Emily Flake, Amy Hempel, Sandeep Jauhar, Judith Claire Mitchell, Darryl Pinckney, and Julia Slavin.

Thank you to all my writing students past and present and thank you to Aynika Nelson, preceptor to a number of my classes. I learn so much from you all.

Thank you, Jessi Davidson, Eddie DeLaRosa, Chris Hunt, Samantha Jacobsen, and Nathaniel Oliver for the sport of writing. Thank you, Deganit Love Nuur, Crystal Luther and Tim Murphy, and Harriet Lotus Hawk Mandeville for the spirit of it.

Thank you to Laura Kent; space I hold is because of the space you hold.

Thank you to all the people who make up my chosen family, a root system as vast as it is deep.

Thank you, Ritika Dutta. Our friendship is one of the things I'm most proud of in the world.

308

Thank you, Kamilah Aisha Moon.

Thank you to my Rockes and Joneses, Mom and Aero-Dad.

And thank you to my family. It's not easy to have a writer in the family, let alone a nonfiction writer. Thank you for loving me still (I hope). Thank you to my sisters, my brothers-in-law, and my nieces and nephews. Thank you to my parents. The most creative act in the world I can imagine is to immigrate. I can only hope to be as visionary as you are.

To Quincy, you don't want me to say how every day is a great day because you are in it, you don't want me to say thank you for loving and supporting me both through the process of working on this book and in every part of our life, you don't want me to say my muse, my beloved, thank you for the way you make me feel, so I will just say, feed Swisspers.

SOURCES

Kissable

ABC News, "Analysis of Confessions in '89 NYC Rape," September 26, 2002.

Allen Jr., Phil, "Dramatizing Blackness: Black Filmmakers Retelling the Narrative," *The Prophetic Lens: The Camera and Black Moral Agency from MLK to Darnella Frazier*, Minneapolis: Fortress Press, 2022, pp. 189–212.

Brown, George F., "San Juan Entertainment," *Virgin Islands Daily News*, December 14, 1966, p. 14.

"Central Park Exonerated Five," PSYCH 424 blog, October 14, 2022.

"Central Park Five—Korey Wise (Full Coerced Video Confession)," YouTube, uploaded by djvlad, June 15, 2019.

Davis, Angela, "Rape, Racism and the Myth of the Black Rapist," *Women, Race and Class*, New York: Random House, 1983, pp. 172–201.

Eisen, Lauren-Brooke, "The 1994 Crime Bill and Beyond: How Federal Funding Shapes the Criminal Justice System," The Brennan Center for Justice, September 9, 2019.

Gore, Tipper, "HATE, RAPE AND RAP," *Washington Post*, January 8, 1990.

James, Caryn, "The Nation; When a Kiss Isn't Just a Kiss," *New York Times*, August 20, 2000.

"Jimi Hendrix on Performing the National Anthem at Woodstock | The Dick Cavett Show," YouTube, uploaded by The Dick Cavett Show, April 22, 2019. Originally aired September 9, 1969.

"Jimi Hendrix Talks Life as a Young Musician | The Dick Cavett Show," YouTube, uploaded by The Dick Cavett Show, February 17, 2019. Originally aired September 9, 1969.

Lorde, Audre, "The Uses of the Erotic: The Erotic as Power," Kore Press, January 1, 2000. Originally published December 1, 1978.

Mauer, Marc, "Bill Clinton, 'Black Lives' and the Myths of the 1994 Crime Bill," The Marshall Project, April 11, 2016.

Meares, Hadley Hall, "The Burden of Brilliance: Nina Simone's Tortured Talent," Vanity Fair, April 6, 2022.

"1996: Hillary Clinton on 'Superpredators' (C-SPAN)," YouTube, uploaded by C-SPAN, February 25, 2016. Originally aired January 28, 1996.

Reesman, Bryan, "25 Years After Tipper Gore's PMRC Hearings, the Opposing Sides Aren't So Far Apart," Vulture, September 20, 2010.

Robinson, Major, "On the Line in New York: Nina Simone," Pittsburgh Courier, September 17, 1966, p. 11.

Schonfeld, Zach, "Parental Advisory Forever: An Oral History of the PMRC's War on Dirty Lyrics," Newsweek, September 19, 2015.

Simels, Steve, "Tipper Gore's Secret," Entertainment Weekly, July 24, 1992.

Smith, Michael, "Pucker Up, Science of Kissing Yields Us Some Tangled Truths," The Pilot, June 21, 2022.

Trewn, Pranav, "Eastern Imagery and Rock Ideals: Thoughts on Axis: Bold as Love at 50," Stereogum, December 1, 2017.

After Hours, a Postscript

Pennsylvania General Assembly, Act No. 21 of 1951, Liquor Code, Section 104, enacted April 12, 1951.

Staff Writer, "Booze on Sunday: Pa. Bastion Takes Long Time to Fall," Pocono Record, November 30, 2002. Updated January 7, 2011.

Animal Strip Club

Cheng, Anne Anlin, "The Melancholy of Race," Kenyon Review, vol. 19, no. 1, 1997, pp. 49–61.

Crowley, James, "INCIDENT REPORT #9005127," Cambridge Police Department, July 16, 2009. Accessed via Wayback Machine, https://web.archive.org/web/2019 0106235659/http://www.samefacts.com/archives/Police%20report%20on %20Gates%20arrest.PDF.

Dirks, Sandhya, "It Started with Oscar Grant: A Police Shooting in Oakland, and the Making of a Movement," KQED, June 5, 2020.

Younger, Jamar, ed. "Henry Louis Gates Jr. Gives Behind-the-Scenes Look at Popular PBS Show During Q&A," Walter Cronkite School of Journalism and Mass Communication News, Arizona State University, May 9, 2022.

Kane, Ashleigh, "The Story of SAMO©, Basquiat's First Art Project," Dazed, September 6, 2017.

Kappeler, Victor E., "A Brief History of Slavery and the Origins of American Policing," Eastern Kentucky University Online, January 7, 2014.

Lee, Henry K., "Firing of BART Cop in Oscar Grant Case Upheld," SFGATE, December 8, 2014.

Lewis, Sukey, et al., "'On Our Watch' Litigation Reveals New Details in Police Shooting of Oscar Grant," NPR, July 8, 2021.

"List of Unarmed African Americans Killed by Law Enforcement Officers in the United States," Wikipedia, Wikimedia Foundation, last edited February 15, 2023.

Pilkington, Ed, "Harvard Scholar Henry Louis Gates Outraged at Arrest at His Home," *Guardian*, July 21, 2009.

"Richard Pryor 1977 40th President," YouTube, uploaded by Zeke62 Nostalgia, January 31, 2016. Originally aired September 13, 1977, on *The Richard Pryor Show*, ep. 1.

"The Shooting of Oscar Grant," The Oscar Grant Foundation. Accessed February 15, 2023.

Stanley, Alessandra, "Genealogy for a Nation of Immigrants," *New York Times*, February 9, 2010.

Sweet, Lynn, "In 'A Promised Land,' Obama Reflects on the 'Issue of Black Folks and the Police,'" *Chicago Sun Times*, November 16, 2020.

Taylor, Otis R., "Oscar Grant's Legacy: A Viral Video and a Movement That Continues Today," *San Francisco Chronicle*, December 26, 2018.

Tinonga, Alessandro, "Oscar Grant's Killer Goes Free," *Socialist Worker*, June 14, 2011.

"TRANSCRIPT: 911 Call and Police Radio Dispatches in the Arrest of Henry Louis Gates Jr.," ABC News, July 27, 2009.

"TRANSCRIPT: Obama's Fifth News Conference," *New York Times*, July 22, 2009.

Wilkes, Donald E., "The Arrest of Henry Louis Gates, Jr.," *Flagpole*, December 1, 2010, p. 8. Accessed via Digital Commons at University of Georgia School of Law.

Zwick-Maitreyi, M., et al., "Caste in the United States. A Survey of Caste Among South Asian Americans," Equality Labs, 2018.

Thin Love

Center for Drug Evaluation and Research, "FDA Drug Safety Communication: FDA Revises Description of Mental Health Side Effects of the Stop-Smoking Medicines Chantix (Varenicline) and Zyban (Bupropion) to Reflect Clinical Trial Findings," U.S. Food & Drug Administration, March 9, 2015.

"Early Communication About an Ongoing Safety Review of Varenicline (Marketed as Chantix)," U.S. Food & Drug Administration, November 20, 2007. Accessed via Wayback Machine, http://wayback.archive-it.org/7993/20161022204619/http://www.fda.gov/Drugs/DrugSafety/PostmarketDrugSafetyInformationforPatientsand Providers/DrugSafetyInformationforHeathcareProfessionals/ucm070765.htm.

Fisher, M. F. K., "Once a Tramp, Always . . ." *The New Yorker*, September 7, 1968.

Kelley, Kristin J., "FDA Removes Black Box Warning from Varenicline's Label." *New England Journal of Medicine*, December 19, 2016.

"Public Health Advisory: Important Information on Chantix (Varenicline)," U.S. Food & Drug Administration, February 1, 2008. Accessed via Wayback Machine, http://wayback.archive-it.org/7993/20161022204614/http://www.fda.gov/Drugs/DrugSafety/PostmarketDrugSafetyInformationforPatientsandProviders/ucm051136.htm.

Rodgers, Kaleigh, "The Best Drug for Quitting Smoking Can't Shake Its Suicide Stigma," *Vice*, November 24, 2015.

"Running with Scissors," *Sex and the City*, directed by Dennis Erdman, season 3, episode 11, Darren Star Productions, 2000.

Don't Even Tell Him

King, Stephen, "Why We Crave Horror Movies," *Playboy*, January 1981.

Jersey Jahru

Deak, Mike, "50 Years in Plainfield's History: From Devastating Riots to Long-Awaited Rebirth," *My Central Jersey*, July 16, 2017.

Fang, Marina, "Mira Nair and Sarita Choudhury Look Back at 'Mississippi Masala.'" *HuffPost*, April 20, 2022. Updated July 20, 2022.

Garrity, Megan, "50 Years Ago, Uganda Ordered Its Entire Asian Population to Leave," *Washington Post*, August 4, 2022.

"How Does Ventura County Differ from Los Angeles County? (Thousand Oaks: Home, Sales Tax)," City-Data Forum, City-Data.com. Accessed February 17, 2023, https://www.city-data.com/forum/ventura-county/1465590-how-does-ventura -county-differ-los.html.

"Immigration and Nationality Act of 1965," History, Art & Archives, U.S. House of Representatives.

"The Legacy of the 1965 Immigration Act: Three Decades of Mass Immigration," Center for Immigration Studies, September 1, 1995.

Linder, Douglas O., "The Holliday Videotape," famous-trials.com/lapd/586-videotape.

Muir, John Kenneth, *Mercy in Her Eyes: The Films of Mira Nair*, New York: Applause, 2006.

"Overturning Exclusion, Limiting Immigration," History, Art & Archives, U.S. House of Representatives.

Qiu, Linda, "What Is 'Chain Migration'? Here's the Controversy Behind It," *New York Times*, January 26, 2018.

Risen, Clay, "George Holliday, Who Taped Police Beating of Rodney King, Dies at 61," *New York Times*, September 22, 2021. Updated November 1, 2021.

Sastry Krbechek, Anjuli, and Karen Grigsby Bates, "When LA Erupted in Anger: A Look Back at the Rodney King Riots," NPR, April 26, 2017.

Solomon, William L., "Images of Rebellion: News Coverage of Rodney King," *Race, Gender & Class*, vol. 11, no. 1, 2004, pp. 23–38.

United States Congress, House. "AN ACT to Amend the Immigration and Nationality Act, and for Other Purposes." HR 2580, 89th Congress, 1st Sess., October 3, 1965.

Ximénez de Sandoval, Pablo, "Meet the Man Who Recorded the World's First Viral Video," *El País*, May 25, 2017.

Sacrifice

Abraham, Amelia, "A Brief History of the Good, the Bad, and the Ugly Side of Hair Extensions," *Dazed*, April 28, 2020.

Bhadra, Rupsha, "What Sadhus and Sadhvis at Kumbh Told Me About Their Long and Important Dreadlocks," News18.com, February 3, 2019.

Byrd, Ayana D., and Lori L. Tharps, *Hair Story: Untangling the Roots of Black Hair in America*, New York: St. Martin's Griffin, 2014.

Chin, Ku-Sup, et al., "Immigrant Small Business and International Economic Linkage: A Case of the Korean Wig Business in Los Angeles, 1968–1977," *International Migration Review*, vol. 30, no. 2, 1996, pp. 485–510.

Cobb, Jasmine Nichole, *New Growth: The Art and Texture of Black Hair*, Durham, NC: Duke University Press, 2023.

"The CROWN Act," The CROWN Coalition, thecrownact.com. Accessed February 17, 2023.

Edison, Thomas A., "Hindoo Fakir," Edison Manufacturing Company, 1902. Accessed via *Smithsonian Magazine*, February 28, 2023.

"8 Nations Accept Curb on Wig Export," *New York Times*, March 24, 1966.

Griffin, Chanté, "How Natural Black Hair at Work Became a Civil Rights Issue," *JSTOR Daily*, July 3, 2019.

"The History of Hair Extensions," Milkandblush.com. Accessed February 17, 2023.

"A History of Hair Weaving: Christina Jenkins Inventor of the 'Hairweeve,'" Prestige-hairextensions.co.uk. Accessed February 17, 2023.

"Killing of Latasha Harlins," Wikipedia, Wikimedia Foundation, last edited February 9, 2023.

Kobalia, Vera, "South Korea: From the Poorest to the Most Developed in 30 Years," *Forbes Woman Georgia*, November 12, 2019.

"The Legacy," Memory Bank, The Korean War Legacy Foundation. Accessed February 17, 2023.

Lorenzen, David N., "Who Invented Hinduism?" *Comparative Studies in Society and History*, vol. 41, no. 4, 1999, pp. 630–59.

Masters, Kim, "Paris Hilton's Jail Time Cut After Three Days," NPR, June 7, 2007.

Oddie, Geoffrey A., "Book Review: *Was Hinduism Invented? Britons, Indians, and Colonial Construction of Religion*, by Brian K. Pennington," *Journal of Asian Studies*, vol. 66, no. 3, 2007, pp. 863–66.

Prashad, Vijay, *The Karma of Brown Folk*, Minneapolis: University of Minnesota Press, 2000.

Rogers, John, "Freed Paris Gets Back to Being Paris," Boston.com, June 26, 2007.

"Rogers v. American Airlines (1981)," Wikipedia, Wikimedia Foundation, last edited May 11, 2022.

Smith, Erica D., "The Killing of Latasha Harlins Was 30 Years Ago. Not Enough Has Changed," *Los Angeles Times*, March 17, 2021.

Toppa, Sabrina, "Black Women, Indian Hair," Adesiwoman.com, May 12, 2021.

Wei, Wendy, "How Women—and Their Hair—Transformed South Korea," *Atlas Obscura*, March 30, 2022.

"Who Invented the Weave," Thirstyroots.com. Accessed February 17, 2023.

Wood, Tony, "Summer of 2011, Another Hot One," *Philadelphia Inquirer*, August 31, 2011.

Shithole Country Clubs

Associated Press, "Donald Trump, PGA Agree to Move Grand Slam Event to New Venue," *Hartford Courant*, July 7, 2015.

Aizenman, Nurith, "Trump Wishes We Had More Immigrants from Norway. Turns Out We Once Did," NPR, January 12, 2018.

Bearak, Max, "At Hindu-American Rally, Trump Pitches India and U.S. as 'Best Friends,'" *Washington Post*, October 15, 2016.

Burke, Monte, "How Indo-Americans Created the Ultimate Neighborhood Bank," *Forbes*, June 6, 2012.

Cohn, D'Vera, "How U.S. Immigration Laws and Rules Have Changed Through History," Pew Research Center, September 30, 2015.

Davis, Julie Hirschfeld, et al., "Trump Alarms Lawmakers with Disparaging Words for Haiti and Africa," *New York Times*, January 11, 2018.

Dawsey, Josh, "Trump Derides Protections for Immigrants from 'Shithole' Countries," *Washington Post*, January 12, 2018.

"Donald Trump Remarks on President Obama's Birth Certificate," C-SPAN, April 27, 2011.

"Dotbusters," Wikipedia, Wikimedia Foundation, last edited February 17, 2023.

Foderaro, Lisa W., "Angered by Attack, Trump Urges Return of the Death Penalty," *New York Times*, May 1, 1989.

"Former Undocumented Worker for Trump Golf Club Sandra Diaz: When Stephen Miller Goes to Sleep at Bedminster, We Make His Bed," *InsiderNJ*, April 22, 2019.

Gabbatt, Adam, "Golden Escalator Ride: The Surreal Day Trump Kicked Off His Bid for President," *Guardian*, June 14, 2019.

Germain, Sophie, "TRUMP GOLF COUNT," Trumpgolfcount.com. Accessed February 18, 2023.

Hingston, Sandy, "20 Local Native American Place Names and What They Mean," *Philadelphia*, October 12, 2015.

History.com Editors, "U.S. Immigration Timeline," History.com, December 21, 2018. Updated August 23, 2022.

"Immigration Act of 1924," Wikipedia, Wikimedia Foundation, last edited February 16, 2023.

Jordan, Miriam, "Making President Trump's Bed: A Housekeeper Without Papers," *New York Times*, December 6, 2018.

Jordan, Miriam, "Trump Administration Says That Nearly 200,000 Salvadorans Must Leave," *New York Times*, January 8, 2018.

Kent, Spencer, "Trump Energizes Hindu Community at Charity Event in Edison," NJ.com, October 16, 2016.

Kolhatkar, Sheelah, "The Foreign Workers of Mar-a-Lago," *The New Yorker*, March 13, 2017.

Lyon, Cherstin M., "Immigration Act of 1917," Densho Encyclopedia, last updated July 17, 2015.

"National Origins Formula," Wikipedia, Wikimedia Foundation, last edited January 30, 2023.

"NY Official: Trump Golf Workers Object to Wages, Conditions," AP News, May 1, 2019.

Parker, Ashley, and Steve Eder, "Inside the Six Weeks Donald Trump Was a Nonstop 'Birther,'" *New York Times*, July 2, 2016.

Partlow, Joshua, and David A. Fahrenthold, "At Trump Golf Course, Undocumented Employees Said They Were Sometimes Told to Work Extra Hours Without Pay," *Washington Post*, April 30, 2019.

"Patel Brothers," Wikipedia, Wikimedia Foundation, last edited January 17, 2023.

Prashad, Vijay, *The Karma of Brown Folk*, Minneapolis: University of Minnesota Press, 2000.

Reilley, Steve, "Hundreds Allege Donald Trump Doesn't Pay His Bills," *USA Today*, June 9, 2016. Updated April 25, 2018.

Russo, Amy, "Trump Takes Off to Mar-A-Lago After National Emergency Declaration," *HuffPost*, February 16, 2019.

Shear, Michael D., "With Document, Obama Seeks to End 'Birther' Issue," *New York Times*, April 27, 2011.

Shear, Michael D., and Julie Hirschfeld Davis, "Stoking Fears, Trump Defied Bureaucracy to Advance Immigration Agenda," *New York Times*, December 23, 2017.

Sirohi, Seema, "Meet Shalabh Kumar, Donald Trump's Favourite 'Hindu,'" *Economic Times*, February 12, 2017.

Star-Ledger Staff, "Heavy Rain Drenches, Cancels One of Two India Day Parades," NJ.com, August 14, 2011.

Stochel Jr., Walter, et al., "Who Was John P. Stevens Jr, & Why Is the High School Named for Him?" The Metuchen-Edison Historical Society.

"'This Week' Transcript: Donald Trump and Ben Carson," ABC News, November 22, 2015.

Time Staff, "Here's Donald Trump's Presidential Announcement Speech," *Time*, June 16, 2015.

"Treaty of Shackamaxon," Wikipedia, Wikimedia Foundation, last edited February 18, 2023.

Mad Marriage

Disparte, Dante, and Tomicah Tillemann, "A Pandemic of Racism," *The Great Correction*, Washington, DC: New America, 2020, pp. 15–17.

Hanna, Beth, "Matthew Weiner Talks Writing Women and Race in 'Mad Men,' Criticisms of Don's Storyline and More," *IndieWire*, March 27, 2014.

"Mansion at Bala," Mansionatbala.com. Accessed February 18, 2023.

Miller, Martin, "Matthew Weiner Is the Warden of 'Mad Men.'" *Los Angeles Times*, June 7, 2012.

Moynihan, Daniel Patrick, "The Moynihan Report: The Negro Family, the Case for National Action," 1965. Accessed on Blackpast.org.

Pettersen [i.e., Petersen], William, "Success Story, Japanese-American Style," *New York Times*, January 9, 1966.

Stokes, Wendy, "Where Are the Black Folks on 'Mad Men'? Matt Weiner Explains," *The Frisky*, September 3, 2018.

Zlotnick, Sarah, "Why Women Traditionally Took Their Husband's Last Names," Brides.com, November 18, 2022.

The Joke Limit

Ephron, Nora, "Moving On, a Love Story," *The New Yorker*, May 29, 2006.

Ephron, Nora, and Delia Ephron, "You've Got Mail," Dailyscript.com. Accessed February 18, 2023.

Not Dead

Bishop, Bryan, and Nick Statt, "The Walking Dead Quitter's Club: Goodbye for Real," *The Verge*, October 24, 2016.

Chew, Ron, "Federal Grand Jury Convicts Vincent Chin's Killer," *International Examiner*, July 4, 1984.

Cummings, Judith, "Detroit Asian-Americans Protest Lenient Penalties for Murder," *New York Times*, April 26, 1983.

Darden, Joe T., and Richard W. Thomas, *Detroit: Race Riots, Racial Conflicts, and Efforts to Bridge the Racial Divide*, East Lansing: Michigan State University Press, 2013.

Franklin, Vincent, "A Victim's Relatives Hope for Justice on 3rd Try," *Chicago Tribune*, April 19, 1987.

Guillermo, Emil, "Ronald Ebens, the Man Who Killed Vincent Chin, Apologizes 30 Years Later," The Asian American Legal Defense and Education Fund, June 22, 2012.

Guillermo, Emil, and Frances Kai-Hwa Wang, "Man Charged with Vincent Chin's Death Seeks Lien Removed, Still Owes Millions," NBC News, December 11, 2015.

"Immigrant Filmmaker Christine Choy Identified with Vincent Chin," *AsianWeek*, June 2, 1989.

"Japan Bashing," *Detroit Free Press*, October 27, 1986.

Johnson, Jason, "'T-Dogging' Through the Walking Dead Season 5 Finale," *The Root*, March 27, 2015.

Kogan, Rick, "Death and Cultural Wreckage in Auto City," *Chicago Tribune*, July 21, 1989.

"No Asians on Chin Jury," *AsianWeek*, vol. 5, issue 42, June 15, 1984.

"Reenacting the Vincent Chin Trial," *Harvard Law Today*, March 21, 2017.

"The Silence of Anti-Asian Violence Is Broken," *AsianWeek*, vol. 8, issue 47, July 10, 1987.

Stanley, John, "Oscar-Nominated Documentary / The Night Vincent Chin Was Brutally Killed / System Frees Killer After Racial Murder," *San Francisco Chronicle*, February 1989.

Tambio, Megan, "The Weary Dead: Brutality, Slipping Ratings and The Walking Dead," CBR.com, December 4, 2016.

Tseng-Putterman, Mark, "On Vincent Chin and the Kind of Men You Send to Jail," Asian American Writers' Workshop, June 23, 2017.

United States Court of Appeals, Sixth Circuit, *United States of America v. Ronald Ebens*, No. 84-1757, Law.resource.org.

Vincent Who?, directed by Tony Lam, Tony Lam Productions, 2009.

Wang, Frances K., "From a Whisper to a Rallying Cry: Commemorating the Vincent Chin Case," *Asian American Policy Review*, vol. 19, 2010, pp. 23–26.

"Who Killed Vincent Chin Excerpt 2 MPEG 4," YouTube, uploaded by Smithsonian-APAC, February 23, 2013.

Wu, Frank H., "The Case Against Vincent Chin," *HuffPost*, April 30, 2014. Updated September 24, 2014.

Wu, Jean Yu-Wen Shen, and Thomas C. Chen, eds., *Asian American Studies Now: A Critical Reader*, New Brunswick, NJ: Rutgers University Press, 2010.

Yip, Alethea, "Remembering Vincent Chin: Fifteen Years Later, a Murder in Detroit Remains a Turning Point in the APA Movement," *AsianWeek*, vol. 18, issue 43, July 19, 1997.

The Days That Have Come (Or, How Is This Not a Hate Crime?)

"Atlanta Spa Shootings: Who Are the Victims?" BBC News, March 22, 2021.

Billet, Alexander, "The Ending of The Walking Dead Season 1 Explained," *Looper*, May 18, 2022.

Davies, Peter Ho, "Tell It Slant," *The Fortunes*, Boston: Houghton Mifflin Harcourt, 2016.

Gómez-Gardeñes, J., et al., "Explosive Contagion in Networks," *Scientific Reports*, January 28, 2016.

Gray, Gabran, "The Entire Walking Dead Timeline Finally Explained," *Looper*, December 8, 2022.

Hswen, Yulin, et al., "Association of '#covid19' Versus '#chinesevirus' with Anti-Asian Sentiments on Twitter: March 9–23, 2020," *American Journal of Public Health*, vol. 111, issue 5, May 2021. Published online April 7, 2021.

"Over 3,000 cases in the U.S.; Airport Chaos Due to New Screenings," NBC News, March 16, 2020.

Park, Hanna, "He Shot at 'Everyone He Saw': Atlanta Spa Workers Recount Horrors of Shooting," NBC News, April 2, 2021.

Regan, Helen, et al., "March 8 Coronavirus News," What We're Covering Here, CNN, March 8, 2020.

Trump, Donald [@realdonaldtrump], "The United States will be powerfully supporting those industries, like Airlines and others, that are particularly affected by the Chinese Virus. We will be stronger than ever before!" Twitter, March 16, 2020.

Yam, Kimmy, "Trump Tweets About Coronavirus Using Term 'Chinese Virus.'" NBC News, March 16, 2020.

How Can We Talk About Interracial Love Without Talking About the Lovings?

"Anti-miscegenation Laws," Wikipedia, Wikimedia Foundation, last edited February 14, 2023.

Barker, Kim, and Richard A. Oppel Jr., "New Transcripts Detail Last Moments for George Floyd," New York Times, April 1, 2021.

Broaddus, Adrienne, "A Walk to the Store: Youngest Witness in Derek Chauvin Trial Writes Book to Help Children Cope with Trauma," CNN, October 15, 2022.

Carmichael, Stokely, and Charles V. Hamilton, "'The Myths of Coalition' from 'Black Power: The Politics of Liberation in America,'" Race/Ethnicity: Multidisciplinary Global Contexts, vol. 1, no. 2, 2008, pp. 171–88.

"The Crime of Being Married," Life, March 18, 1966. Accessed via Document Bank of Virginia.

Ebbs, Stephanie, and Benjamin Siegel, "Police Did Not Clear Lafayette Square So Trump Could Hold 'Bible' Photo Op: Watchdog," ABC News, June 10, 2021.

"France: Police Use Tear Gas Against Racial Injustice Protesters as Floyd Outrage Goes Global," Euronews, June 3, 2020.

Goodwin, Gerald F., "Black and White in Vietnam," Opinion, New York Times, July 18, 2017.

Graham, Ruth, "The Inconceivable Strangeness of Trump's Bible Photo-Op," Slate, June 2, 2020.

Hatewatch Staff, "Trump Tweets, 'When the Looting Starts, the Shooting Starts', Extremists Will Respond," Southern Poverty Law Center, May 29, 2020.

Jefferson, Lauren, "Mark Loving on the Film 'Loving' and a Supreme Court case That Changed the Nation," EMU News, November 3, 2016.

Klemko, Robert, "'A Man Was Unjustly Killed Here:' Interracial Families Face Challenge Explaining George Floyd's Death to Their Children," Washington Post, June 9, 2020.

Levenson, Eric, "How Minneapolis Police First Described the Murder of George Floyd, and What We Know Now," CNN, April 21, 2021.

Mandell, Andrea, "These 'Loving' Re-creations Will Move You," USA Today, November 1, 2016.

"NBC News' Jo Ling Kent Hit by Firework as Seattle Protest Gets Chaotic," YouTube, uploaded by MSNBC [@MSNBC], June 2, 2020.

Nguyen, Viet Thanh, "Asian Americans Are Still Caught in the Trap of the 'Model Minority' Stereotype. And It Creates Inequality for All," Vietnguyen.info, June 25, 2020.

"President Trump on 'Injecting' Disinfectants," C-SPAN, April 23, 2020.

"Richard and Mildred Loving Interview (1967)," Historyvshollywood.com. Accessed February 19, 2023.

Shabad, Rebecca, et al., "'The Bible Is Not a Prop': Religious Leaders, Lawmakers Outraged over Trump Church Visit," NBC News, June 2, 2020.

Shaffer, Cory, and Staff, "Cleveland's George Floyd Protests Went from an Afternoon of Peace to Volatile in Minutes: See the Timeline," Cleveland.com, June 2, 2020.

Sidner, Sara, "Inside Cup Foods, Where It Seems George Floyd Never Left," CNN, April 10, 2021.

Tavernise, Sabrina, "They Fled Asia as Refugees. Now They Are Caught in the Middle of Minneapolis," *New York Times*, June 1, 2020.

Villet, Barbara, "The Heart of the Matter: Love," *New York Times*, January 18, 2012.

West, Ella-Marie, "Before 'Loving,'" Washington University College of Arts and Sciences.

We Can Neither Confirm Nor Deny That Kamala Harris Is Our Time-Traveling Daughter

Aderoju, Darlene, "Mary J. Blige 'Surprised' Vice President Kamala Harris Used Her Song 'Work That' for Election Victory Speech," *People*, February 23, 2021.

Associated Press, "Richard P. Loving: In Land Mark Suit, Figure in High Court Ruling on Miscegenation Dies," *New York Times*, July 1, 1975.

Barry, Ellen, "How Kamala Harris's Immigrant Parents Found a Home, and Each Other, in a Black Study Group," *New York Times*, September 13, 2020. Updated October 6, 2020.

Berlatsky, Noah, "Both Versions of The Handmaid's Tale Have a Problem with Racial Erasure," *The Verge*, June 15, 2017.

Bollinger, Alex, "GOP Congressman Asks If Women Can Give Birth to Turtles or 'a Breakfast Taco.'" *LGBTQ Nation*, July 13, 2022.

Breuninger, Kevin, "Biden Briefly Transfers Power to Vice President Harris While He Undergoes Routine Colonoscopy," CNBC, November 19, 2021.

Brotherton, Mike, "Dividing Space by Zero," *Lightspeed Magazine*, issue 13, June 2011.

Bruggeman, Lucien, "Attacks on Mother-Daughter Election Workers Continue as They Prepare to Receive White House Honor," ABC News, July 6, 2023.

Brumback, Kate, "Judge Won't Dismiss Election Workers' Suit Against Giuliani," Associated Press, October 31, 2022.

Center for American Women and Politics. "Women Elected Officials," Rutgers Eagleton Institute of Politics, accessed May 2023.

"Charlie Chaplin, the Sexual Predator?" Familylawguys.com, The Blog.

Cohen, Richard, "The Clock Is Ticking for the Career Woman," *Washington Post*, March 16, 1978.

"DNC Town Hall—SNL," YouTube, uploaded by Saturday Night Live [@Saturday-NightLive], September 29, 2019.

"Fact check: Kamala Harris Was in the Second Class of Berkeley Public Schools Busing," Reuters, August 21, 2020.

"Fannie Lou Hamer—'Im Sick and Tired of Being Sick and Tired,'" YouTube, uploaded by Fannie Lou Hamer [@FannieLouHamerInstitute], December 16, 2013.

Faus, Joan, "Museum Protesters Denounce Picasso's Treatment of Women," Reuters, June 4, 2021.

Gerstein, Josh, and Alexander Ward, "Supreme Court Has Voted to Overturn Abortion Rights, Draft Opinion Shows," Politico, May 2, 2022. Updated May 3, 2022.

Goldsberry, Jenny, "10-Year-Old Denied Abortion in Ohio, Forced to Travel to Indiana," *Washington Examiner*, July 2, 2022.

Harris, Kamala, "Without This Woman, I Wouldn't Be the Leader I Am Today," *Bustle*, February 4, 2019.

Hawking, Stephen, *Black Holes and Baby Universes and Other Essays*, New York: Random House, 2011.

Healey, Jenna, "Rejecting the Biological Clock," Yale Institution for Social and Policy Studies, October 2014.

Hendry, Erica R., "Who is Wandrea ArShaye 'Shaye' Moss and Why Is She Testifying Before the Jan. 6 Committee?" PBS NewsHour, June 21, 2022.

"History of In Vitro Fertilisation," Wikipedia, Wikimedia Foundation, last edited February 1, 2023.

"Jenny Holzer Sculpture Arrives on Barnard's Campus," Barnard College, Columbia University, June 2, 2011.

"Jodie Foster: Eleanor Arroway," IMDb.com. Accessed February 19, 2023. Images from *Contact* (1997).

"Kamala Harris Tells Guatemala Migrants: 'Do Not Come to US,'" BBC, June 8, 2021.

Little, Becky, "'Unbought and Unbossed': Why Shirley Chisholm Ran for President," History.com, December 4, 2018. Updated January 12, 2021.

"LIVE: VP Kamala Harris Speaks About Roe v. Wade Abortion Ruling in Chicago Area," YouTube, uploaded by ABC 7 Chicago [@ABC7Chicago], June 24, 2022.

Lockhart, P.R., "Joe Biden's Record on School Desegregation Busing, Explained," *Vox*, July 16, 2019.

"MAMALEH," Jewish English Lexicon, jel.jewish-languages.org. Accessed February 19, 2023.

Michals, Debra, "Fannie Lou Hamer," National Women's History Museum, 2017.

"One Year Since the Jan. 6 Attack on the Capitol," United States Attorney's Office District of Columbia, U.S. Department of Justice, justice.gov. Updated December 30, 2021.

"On This Day: Marilyn at Payne Whitney," The Marilyn Report, February 11, 2022.

"Progress to Power: The Legacy of New York's Black Legislators," empirestateplaza.ny.gov, November 7, 2014.

"The Race Issue," *National Geographic*, April 2018.

Smith, Jamil, "Exclusive: In Leaked Audio, Brian Kemp Expresses Concern over Georgians Exercising Their Right to Vote," *Rolling Stone*, October 23, 2018.

"Time Travel Mythology: Mahabharata," Sreevidyatantram.blogspot.com, May 12, 2017.

"Vice President-Elect Kamala Harris | Election Speech Entrance (Mary J Blige)," YouTube, uploaded by Christina [@wrighcd], November 8, 2020.